ON SALAFISM

Stanford Studies in Middle Eastern *and* Islamic Societies *and* Cultures

ON SALAFISM

Concepts and Contexts

Azmi Bishara

STANFORD UNIVERSITY PRESS
Stanford, California

STANFORD UNIVERSITY PRESS
Stanford, California

A previous version of this work was published in Arabic in 2018 under the title *Fil Ijābati ʿan Suʾāl: Mā as-Salafīa* (On the question: What is Salafism?) ©2018, Arab Center for Research and Policy Studies.

Printed in the United States of America on acid-free, archival-quality paper

Library of Congress Cataloging-in-Publication Data

Names: Bishārah, ʻAzmī, author.
Title: On Salafism : concepts and contexts / Azmi Bishara.
Other titles: Fī al-ijābah ʻan su'āl, mā al-Salafīyah? English | Stanford studies in Middle Eastern and Islamic societies and cultures.
Description: Stanford, California : Stanford University Press, 2022. | Series: Stanford studies in Middle Eastern and Islamic societies and cultures | "A previous version of this work was published in Arabic in 2018." | Includes bibliographical references and index. | Translated from Arabic.
Identifiers: LCCN 2021061200 (print) | LCCN 2021061201 (ebook) | ISBN 9781503630352 (cloth) | ISBN 9781503631786 (paperback) | ISBN 9781503631793 (ebook)
Subjects: LCSH: Salafīyah. | Islam and politics. | Religious fanaticism.
Classification: LCC BP195.S18 B5613 2022 (print) | LCC BP195.S18 (ebook) | DDC 297.8/3--dc23/eng/20220202
LC record available at https://lccn.loc.gov/2021061200
LC ebook record available at https://lccn.loc.gov/2021061201

Cover design: Angela Moody
Cover art: Anna R | Adobe Stock
Typeset by Newgen North America in 10.4/14.4 Brill

Contents

Preface vii

1 What Is Salafism? 1

2 On Apostasy 48

3 Religious Associations and Political Movements 63

4 Wahhabism in Context 95

Conclusion 134

Key People and Religious Associations 151

Glossary 157

Notes 161

Bibliography 197

Index 211

Preface

THE 2018 RELEASE OF THIS BOOK IN ARABIC TOOK PLACE IN A rather roundabout fashion. During the same period, I published a book on the Islamic State of Iraq and the Levant (ISIL),[1] and in the course of writing its introduction, I became concerned that I might create the impression that an entity like ISIL is a natural outcome of Salafism (which it is not). Consequently, I decided to develop what had begun as a mere introduction to a book on ISIL into a separate work on Salafism, the English translation of which is now in the reader's hands. In addition to making the book available to interested readers who do not speak Arabic, this English translation gave me the opportunity to revise the book and incorporate additional secondary literature.

As will become apparent in the next four chapters, this book problematizes the term *Salafism* (*Salafiyya*), whose current widespread use appears at first glance unproblematic. This problematization is not an end in itself, of course. Rather, it is intended to facilitate a better understanding of the phenomenon to which the term *Salafism* is meant to refer and, in so doing, to transform a widely used, but poorly defined, term into a conceptualization of a particular phenomenon, and then to explore its interactions with other phenomena.

Chapter 1 provides an overview of the many phenomena to which the term *Salafism* applies. I identify the similarities and differences among the various types of Salafis and describe the juristic traditions with which modern Salafis associate themselves. I distinguish between two types of Salafism; modern and premodern (like Wahhabism). The modern Salafism can be categorized in types of return (or appeal) to the *Salaf* (righteous ancestors) and the sacred text and discussed in terms of how these appeals relate to the fundamental principles of Islam. Reformists advocate for the first type of return: bringing about renewal through *ijtihād* and the removal of impediments (such as misguided religious traditions) to Muslim societies' advancement and evolution within the context of modernity while still affirming these societies' identification with the Islamic civilization.[2] In fact, the "purification" of religion advocated by Islamic reformists (*Iṣlāḥiyyūn*) like Jamal al-Din al-Afghani (1838–1897 CE), Muhammad Abduh (1849–1905 CE), and Abd al-Rahman al-Kawakibi (1849–1902 CE) is comparable to that of religious and secular reformers who advocate returning to the pristine fundamentals as a "new" point of departure to progress. The second type of return is promoted by both puritan and jihadi Salafis who aim to reshape the modern and contemporary era of Muslim history by turning Islamic teaching into a regressive ideology of political movements, jihadi or otherwise, and by proselytizing puritan groups that claim not to involve themselves in politics.

While chapter 1 seeks to clear up the confusion that often surrounds these two "returns," it also justifies the initial application of the term *Salafi* to both types of returns despite the fact that they differ substantially with respect to aim, method, and their understanding of Islamic fundamentals and the Salaf. As such, the need to differentiate between these returns is a sine qua non if we want to understand these different phenomena, and the concept of Salafi is ultimately only applied to one of them. This book maintains that it is valid to apply the term *Salafi* to the reformists initially, in the same way that Protestant Reformation try to return to biblical text and uphold the right of individual believers to read and understand it for themselves. The term *Salafi* can also be applied to other contemporary Salafis (be they politicized, jihadi, or otherwise) because they have adopted a particular type of juristic theorization and a literal understanding of both the prophetic Hadith and the Qur'anic text.[3] They promote a return to the past, not for the purpose of renewal and adaptation to modernity but instead for confrontation with and resistance to what they consider decadent modernity from which they cannot otherwise free themselves. They also entertain a utopia modeled on an imagined past either through preaching and evangelization or through political activism and/or by force. It is not a coincidence that the term *Salafism* became linked to the second type of return.

Chapter 2 examines an important issue that has marked antireformist types of modern Salafism and even fundamentalist political Islamist movements. This issue is the practice of *takfīr*—the branding of an individual or a group as infidel. Specifically, I highlight how contemporary discussions overlook the distinction between abstract takfīr (*al-takfīr al-muṭlaq*),[4] which is the categorization of positions, ideas, and actions as being un-Islamic, and specific takfīr (*takfīr al-muʿayyan*), which is the branding of particular individuals and even entire groups of Muslims as being unbelievers. This issue is relevant to the ongoing discussion of the takfīr of rulers as opposed to unconditional allegiance regardless of whether these rulers are upright or corrupt.

This leads us to chapter 3, which discusses how Salafi political transformation interacts with the contemporary political religiosity of Islamist movements (as opposed to the unfortunate but widely used term *political Islam*). I discuss how the interaction between the Muslim Brotherhood and the Salafism of the Arabian Peninsula led Salafi currents to shift away from obedience to the Muslim ruler and toward an explosive mix of Salafism and jihadism, describing how sociopolitical conditions in regions marked by sectarianism and weak state control facilitated its spread.

Chapter 4 examines Wahhabism and its evolution. In its early days, Wahhabism was a religious movement that allied itself with a powerful and politically ambitious tribal chieftainship in order to more effectively impose its oversimplified conception of *tawḥīd* (monotheism) and strict practicing of religious commandments on communities that had embraced "innovations" of popular religiosity and religious permissiveness. This involved the takfīr of those who rejected the Wahhabi message, which justified waging jihad against them. Over time, Wahhabism transformed into a religious institution, state madhab (religious legal doctrine),[5] and state ideology in Saudi Arabia; put differently, it transformed into a Salafism of obedience to ruling authority. Wahhabism gradually evolved from using political power in the service of spreading its madhab and rejecting everything "strange" and new as a *bidʿa* (innovation) to serving the logic and interests of the state. The state has subjugated the Wahhabi religious establishment to the extent that the latter has to justify the marginalization of the doctrine itself. In reaction to this shift, other Salafi movements began to appeal to the original teachings of Muhammad Ibn Abd al-Wahhab

(1703–1792 CE / 1115–1206 AH) and others against the official Wahhabism, including meetings of the minds with Saudi religious and political opposition movements.

Throughout the book, I refute any sort of natural intellectual progression from the jurists who were retroactively labeled Salafis (having also been called Ahl al-Hadith, then Ahl al-Sunna wa al-Jamāʿa) to Taqi al-Din Abu al-Abbas Ahmad Ibn Abd al-Halim Ibn Taymiyya al-Harrani (1263–1328 CE / 661–728 AH), then from him to Ibn Abd al-Wahhab, and then to the jihadi Salafi movements of the present day.

Political movements are not ideas or texts but, rather, social phenomena. And from the perspective of the history of ideas itself, Ibn Taymiyya was not the Ahmad Ibn Hanbal (780–855 CE / 164–241 AH) of his day, nor was Ibn Abd al-Wahhab the Ibn Taymiyya of his day.[6] Apart from differences in the level and scope of knowledge and intellectual production, each of these figures produced thoughts in the context of his own era; as such, they were inspired by the thoughts of their predecessors, but when they appealed to specific juristic traditions for support or justification, they tailored the traditions to their goals and the age in which they were living, interpreting the ideas and presumed attitudes of the Prophet and his companions from their own perspective—and as a consequence, changing them.

For the original Arabic edition of this book, I would like to thank all the researchers at the Arab Center for Research and Policy Studies (ACRPS) who provided valuable feedback, especially Raed al-Samhouri, who assisted me with identifying sources. Similarly, I thank Jamal Barout, who managed the review process and with whom I discussed ideas and sources, and the Editorial and Publication Department at the ACRPS for their indispensable work.

I also wish to thank everyone who contributed to the publication of the English edition of this book: Raphael Cohen, who carried out the initial translation of the book into English; Nancy Roberts, Chris Hitchcock, and Melissa Carlson, who edited the translation; the anonymous reviewers and Kate Wahl of Stanford University Press; and my friend and colleague Abdelwahab el-Affendi, who read the text. Thanks also to my academic assistant, Israa Batayneh, and to Yara Nassar.

ON SALAFISM

Chapter 1

WHAT IS SALAFISM?

THE TERM *SALAFISM* (*SALAFIYYA*) RAISES MORE CRITICAL QUESTIONS than common usage suggests. It is this issue that I am interested in when I repose the question, What is Salafism? This question might appear simple, but it is nonetheless useful to deconstruct it and consider it in depth due to the widespread careless, simplistic, and reductionist use of the term. This book explores and answers this question critically.

The simplest and most succinct definition of Salafism is the return to original sources—the Qur'an and the Sunna (accounts of the Prophet Muhammad's daily life and practice)—and the rejection of "innovation" (*bid'a* and *muḥdathāt*). However, Salafism is not a single or singular phenomenon. If we dig deeper, we discover that the term *Salafism* is a purely historical designation that refers to a variety of Sunni and Shi'i "Salafisms." Within each of these threads, one can identify several "sub-Salafisms" or even distinct schools of thought. Although the dominant usage today, whether in Middle Eastern studies or in Islamists' own texts, refers to a homogeneous and coherent body of ideas, historically the return to the righteous Salaf was not always a part of the production of a specific ideology.

Just as there was a surge of interest in Islamism following the rise of al-Qaeda and its various offshoots in the wake of 9/11, Salafism has become topical again with the rise of ISIL. While politicians and the media across the West have attempted to understand Salafism and "political Islam," or "Islam" as a whole (!), they have done so by arbitrarily projecting their preconceptions onto the diverse range of ideas, facts, institutions, and histories that make up Islamic heritage. The monolithic conception of Islam and religious doctrine has led not only to simplistic generalizations and stereotypes but also to the ignoring of important sociocultural and political factors that shaped the formation and rise of such movements.

Indeed, it is impossible to understand groups like ISIL without examining the context in which they emerged, including their struggle with Arab and Muslim cultures and societies, Arab regimes and states, and what they consider the West. This struggle takes place against a complex backdrop of issues in the Arab and Muslim worlds, including different patterns of modernization and the advent of new sociocultural phenomena, the emergence of the modern state and its crisis under authoritarian regimes, the emergence of sectarianism, the complex relationship between memory and history, the national question, issues of integration, and the Palestine question.

What is currently considered a Salafi tradition in Islamic heritage has not always been known by this name. In the writings of the early generations of Hanbalis in the tenth and eleventh centuries CE,[1] they commonly referred to themselves as Ahl al-Athar (People of Narration).[2] The close association of this term with the Hanbali school meant that the Hanbalis themselves came to be known as Aṣḥāb al-Āthār or Athariyyūn (Narrativists).[3] The Athariyyūn followed the example of *al-salaf al-ṣāliḥ* (the righteous ancestors), namely the companions of the Prophet and the following generations of ("sincere" or "faithful") successors immortalized in the formulaic conclusion to all Sunni prayers and sermons: "O God, bless the Prophet Muhammad, his family, his companions, their successors, and their sincere followers, until the Day of Judgment."

We should be wary of moving from mechanical projection of class analysis to a history-of-ideas approach that treats contemporary political Islamic movements as a natural continuation of a stream of ideas and traditions with its own autonomous history. The Islamists themselves claim that they represent no more and no less than the protracted history of an idea, the tradition of Ahl al-Sunna wa al-Jamāʿa. Different parties do not form part of the Sunna or the Jamāʿa, which are both inimical to partisanship. The term *Ahl al-Sunna wa al-Jamāʿa* itself was only adopted by the Ahl al-Hadith stream of jurists at a later stage when the Isma'ilis and Mu'tazilas also claimed the title which was, until the 420s AH, used only rarely in theological contexts, but not as a concept that designates a specific school of thought.

The term initially referred to Ahl al-Hadith jurists who accepted more dubious hadiths (not transmitted by a chain of credible narrators), preferring such hadiths to reasoned opinion as a guide for making juristic judgments and rejecting the primacy of rational inference in interpreting the Qur'an. Later it became associated with a cluster of specific juristic positions. Abd al-Qahir al-Baghdadi (d. 1037 CE / 429 AH) was the first Sunni theologian to use the term *Ahl al-Sunna wa al-Jamā'a* in a way that framed his understanding of the other Islamic confessions. He defines *Ahl al-Sunna wa al-Jamā'a* as those who "hold that the blessings of paradise are eternal for its residents and hellfire eternal for the infidels; accept Abu Bakr, Umar, Uthman, and 'Ali as imams; give high praise to the righteous ancestors (*al-salaf al-ṣāliḥ*) of the religious community; rule that it is obligatory to pray the Friday prayer behind any Imam who has renounced those who do not keep the basic tenets of the religion (*ahl al-ahwā' al-ḍālla*); rule that it is obligatory to derive legal rulings from the Qur'an, the Sunna and the consensus of the Prophet's companions . . . and say that it is obligatory to obey the Sultan in everything that is not a sin."[4] Is this a sufficient foundation from which to understand the historical specificity of Islamist movements? If it were, then it would be impossible to imagine that a contemporary Islamist extremist group calling itself Ahl al-Sunna would distinguish itself from the Muslim Brotherhood and the Jamā'at al-Tablīgh wa al-Da'wa. And yet we find the Yemeni Salafi Muqbil Ibn Hadi al-Wadi'i (1933–2001 CE) explaining his group's choice of name: "We were only called Ahl al-Sunna because we thought that the Muslim Brotherhood and the Jamā'at al-Tablīgh wa al-Da'wa espoused innovation. . . . Ahl al-Sunna are those who follow the Prophet's words, choices, and actions."[5]

"Archeological" investigations of history often produce findings at odds with prevalent conceptions of Salafism. A good example is the discrepancy between the historical development of the concept and terminology of Salafism and the way Salafism is reproduced and consumed even in academic circles. I single out contemporary Middle Eastern studies, which has abandoned the historical archeology of classical Islamic texts that underpinned the work of classical Orientalists. Under the influence of radical epistemological critiques of traditional Orientalism, some post-Orientalist academics have disavowed Orientalism in its entirety, including its conclusions regardless of their soundness and accuracy. Doing so has led to an enduring ignorance of historical texts and the origins of some of the concepts under investigation in contemporary research. The general shift toward "area studies" directed at Western readers and decision-makers tends to ignore both classical and contemporary Arabic texts (except in studies of modern ideologies, such as "Islamism"). The works of classical Orientalists produced valuable knowledge even when they were intended to provide expertise both to decision-makers and more broadly. By contrast, recent works (with a few excellent exceptions) rely mainly on preexisting schemas or selectively adopted textual fragments.

Although classical Orientalism was epistemologically constrained by an East-West dichotomy often tinged with an overt or covert sense of superiority, we can learn a lot from the studies that it produced. To be sure, the paradigmatic approach criticized by Anouar Abdel-Malek (1924–2012 CE), Bryan Turner (b. 1945 CE), and Edward Said (1935–2003 CE) permeated historiography, the social sciences, linguistics, and (in particular) anthropology.[6] Orientalists think of Muslims as "religious beings" and Islam as an autonomous and monolithic entity that, while complex, is incompatible with modernity and enlightenment and that has "essential traits" that are permanent and fixed. This stereotypical view—tied to the West's monopoly on knowledge and power and based largely on anecdotal evidence that confirms its existing prejudices—was characteristic of a larger field that encompassed the writings of travelers, diplomats, and academics as well as Western literary impressions of and fascination with an imagined Orient. Nonetheless, some Oriental scholars have understood Arabic better than many critics of Orientalism. Many Orientalists have respected Arabic and other indigenous languages and have edited and published classical manuscripts. By doing so, they have benefited Arabophone culture more than many critics of Orientalism, who often fail to quote a single classical Arabic writer, let alone a modern Arab scholar, in their work. While all scholarship should be critiqued from epistemological, factual, and methodological perspectives, select Orientalist scholarship needs to be distinguished from the rest for its valuable contributions.

All this leads us to question another concept connected to Salafism and used in contemporary literature on the Middle East: fundamentalism. Many contemporary scholars consider *fundamentalism* synonymous with *Salafism* in its precise terminological sense, and they believe that *fundamentalist* is an appropriate designation for all of today's Islamist movements on the basis that they are revivalist trends both in terms of religious awakening and of commitment to fundaments of Islamic doctrine.

However, fundamentalism is not unique to Islam, structurally or historically, as counterparts and parallels can be found in Judaism, Christianity, and other religions. The English term originates in the US. In the beginning of the twentieth century CE, American Protestant churches in Southern California began to advocate for a return to religious "fundamentals" in response to burgeoning modernization and secularism.[7] Indeed, a growing oil industry, Hollywood, and extreme forms of consumerism have made Protestants increasingly concerned about the threats that communism, liberalism, and Darwinism posed to their religion. A series of free volumes entitled *The Fundamentals: A Testimony to the Truth* provides intellectual grounding for the term.[8] Funded by the ultrareligious Stewart brothers, these volumes present an intellectual defense of Christianity, ranging from the story of the creation and the Trinity to the miracles of Jesus. As this religious revivalism became increasingly popular, it spread from Southern California to strongholds of religiosity in the South and the center of the US. It is no wonder that American academic research on fundamentalism, which proliferated during the 1980s and 1990s CE, defines it as "a strategy or set of strategies, by which beleaguered believers attempt to preserve their distinctive identity as a people or group."[9]

If it is appropriate to speak of Christianities rather than Christianity and Islams rather than Islam, then it is even more appropriate to recognize that multiple fundamentalisms also exist, even within a single religion. Fundamentalism is a way of thinking, a perspective, and an approach. It is not a self-contained social or even religious phenomenon, unless it is tied to a particular mode of religiosity, for example that of a religious establishment,[10] a folk religiosity (in today's terms I would prefer *mass religiosity*,[11] which is more vulnerable to ideological formulations of religion), or an activist political mode. Different forms of fundamentalism tend to arise from the desire to preserve or strengthen an existing identity against newer identities produced by major social transformation. Indeed, these movements may seek to adapt by reaffirming fundamentals in a "purer" form. Within a single religion, there are various sources of consciousness that inform the "return" to what are deemed the fundamentals, leading to interaction with and modification of multiple modes of religiosity.

This contemporary concept of fundamentalism, typically translated into Arabic using the word *uṣūlī*, is completely at odds with the traditional Islamic usage of that word. *Uṣūlī* in classical usage is not taken from social science scholarship. Rather, it is an adjective referring to the fundamentals of jurisprudence (*uṣūl al-fiqh*), namely the method or "science" guiding the development of practical legal rulings on matters of worship or daily conduct based on the fundamental principles of the Shariʿa. It may also refer to the principles/fundamentals of the faith (as in *uṣūl al-dīn*), which might be termed *theology*. In classical Islamic discourse, the term *uṣūlī* connotes independent thought, reasoned opinion, and the use of intellectual reasoning to derive rules or judgments from the basic principles of religion and religious text (*ijtihād*). In Shiʿi terminology of the eighteenth century CE, the term *uṣūlī* was used to describe the school of religious jurisprudence that defended scholars who advocated the use of rational reasoning to derive judgments from religious fundamentals against the *akhbārīs* (those who rely on *akhbār*, i.e., reported traditions), who asserted that the Qur'an and the Hadith (and sayings of Shiʿi imams) were the only sources of religious judgments. The classical term thus refers to a process and conceptualization far removed from the prevalent contemporary understanding of fundamentalism, which tends toward strict religiosity and submission to the fundaments of the faith against religious laxity, a pluralist interpretation of these fundaments and their distortion by modern society and state. It is equally far removed from the use of the term in contemporary Islamic studies, where fundamentalism and Salafism are treated as identical. Using the Arabic word *uṣūlī* as a synonym of the English term *fundamentalist* causes unnecessary confusion in the Arab cultural context unless preceded by an extensive explanation of its origins.

SALAFISMS, NOT SALAFISM

The history of Salafism is complex. Academic objectivity still demands that we speak of multiple and varied Salafisms up to the contemporary period. An inventory of Salafisms would include reformist, proselytizing, jihadist, learned, Sunni, Shiʿi, etc. Does the term *Salafiyya* (Salafism) refer to a "blessed" period, as Muhammad Sa'id Ramadan al-Bouti described it in the title of a book,[12] rather than an "Islamic school of thought"? Is it simultaneously a doctrine of jurisprudence and a theological stance? Is it only the latter? Or is it a tendency found in all Islamic madhabs (schools of jurisprudence), Hanbali or otherwise?

These questions provide a key entry point to understanding the relationship between Wahhabism and Salafism. Wahhabism—also known as Najdi Salafism—is distinguished by its total identification of Salafism with Hanbalism, setting it apart from the Salafism of the classical Ahl al-Athar among the Ahl al-Hadith (followers of the Prophet's sayings and deeds) or Ahl al-Sunna wa al-Jamā'a (followers of prophetic tradition and the consensus among Ahl al-Hadith) in the ninth century CE and after, and likewise from the Salafism of Ibn Taymiyya between the late thirteenth century and the mid-fourteenth century CE. This post–Ibn Hanbal[13] Hanbalism reimagined him as a "Hanbali" in the same way that post–al-Ash'ari Ash'arism reimagined al-Ash'ari himself as an Ash'ari,[14] as did Imami Shi'ism with Imam Ja'far Ibn Muhammad Ibn 'Ali Ibn Abi Talib (82–147 AH / 702–765 CE), known as Ja'far al-Sadiq, and his successors.[15] The process of reimagining usually includes reinventing the deeds and sayings of a figure who is retroactively considered the renowned founder. Specifically, followers integrate and construct this figure's ideas into coherent teachings of a school of thought, a confession, or an ideology. Doing so generates a constellation of meanings that, while novel, are inspired by and rooted in what came before, as is generally the case in the history of ideas, where ideas and concepts extend roots into the past in search of authenticity. Modernist secular ideologies are not exempted from this discursive practice. Communists, for example, deal with Karl Marx (1818–1883 CE) as if he was a Marxist and the arguments and counter arguments in the discussions among the dogmatic adherers to Marxism as an ideology must be justified by quotations and interpretations of his writings.

Before it came to be relatively narrowly defined as a specific doctrinal and religious creed, the term *Salafism* was even vaguer than that of *fundamentalism*.[16] However, the recent and divergent phenomena known as Salafism have proliferated and multiplied to the point that the concept has almost burst open at the seams. Modern scholars often assert that these modern trends emerged from a single "original" current, thus justifying the practice of lumping them together under a single label of *Salafism*.

In its original sense, the term *Salafism* meant exclusively adhering to the Qur'an and Sunna. Scholars would draw on the sayings and actions of the Prophet, the generation of the Prophet's companions (particularly the first four "rightly guided" caliphs), and the generation of "successors" (*tābiʿūn*) who followed them as a model of how to apply the provisions of the Qur'an and the Sunna in practice. This is naturally a diffuse definition; according to the principle of "consensus" (*ijmāʿ*), for a point to qualify as "guidance" it had to be the subject of universal agreement among the Salaf themselves. Determining what points enjoyed such a consensus is controversial, as the question of who is included in the consensus always produces different answers. Does it refer to the companions alone, excluding the second and third generations of successors? Or does it refer to all those described in the famous Hadith as "the finest of generations"?

Contemporary Salafism, however, does not engage with these subtleties, and might even see them as superfluous. It prefers general formulas like "the Salaf said," "the Salaf did," and "this is the way of the Salaf." Salafism typically gives text and narration precedence over reason or opinion based on rational evidence whenever there is a conflict,[17] hence the sharp polarization between Ahl al-Hadith and Ahl al-Ra'y (proponents of opinion) from the third century AH onward. In addition to relying on the literal meaning of texts and narrations, the Salafi approach emphasizes emulation of the personal conduct of the Prophet Muhammad in his daily life as described in the narration and biography books (*Kutub as-Siyar*)[18] as well as that of the rightly guided caliphs and leading companions, or the imams in the case of the Shiʿa.

Relying on the Qur'an, the Sunna, and the recorded statements of the companions and the successors means that anything else is heretical innovation (*bidʿa*), "all heretical innovation is a deviation from the right path, and all such deviations lead to hell." Shiʿi and Sunni authorities concur on this point. The claim that Shiʿism differs from Sunnism because it has maintained the tradition of reasoning in matters of religious law (*ijtihād*) does not detract from this structural alignment, or more accurately, epistemological unity. They too make a distinction between those who looked to prophetic narrations (*akhbārīs*) and those who looked to the fundaments (*uṣūlī*), who as we have noted were willing to accept ijtihād. The two currents have been in intense conflict since the eighteenth century CE. The Shiʿi proponents of narration are directly parallel to the Sunni Hanbalis. In any case, it is debatable whether the uṣūlīs have a substantial body of religious law, and it is also debatable to claim that the Shiʿa maintained this practice while Sunnis abandoned it. This is another oversimplification akin to the simplistic accounts of Salafism and fundamentalism discussed earlier. The original Shiʿi authorities (*mujtahidūn*) are closer to what Hadith "sciences" call "a mujtahid within the madhab."[19] Specifically, they innovate within the limits set by their particular jurisprudential tradition rather than really "independent" authority, except in radical cases. They are distinct from the Sunni Ahl al-Hadith inasmuch as they accept rational discretion (*raʾy*) as one of the basic elements of religious law; while discretion was central to the broad Sunni current represented by Abu Hanifa al-Nuʿman Ibn Thabit (699–767 CE / 80–150 AH), Uthman al-Batti (d. 760–761 CE / 143 AH), and Rabia al-Raʾi (d. 753 CE / 136 AH), this current was ultimately eclipsed by the *atharīs*. Shiʿi authorities went further than their Sunni counterparts in recognizing a greater role for independent reasoning in religious law, thus splitting into akhbārīs and uṣūlīs, whose religious law involves ijtihād and little more than contextualizing the sayings of their imams and drawing analogies.

The widely accepted simplistic identification of Salafism with Wahhabism ignores the problematic relationship between the two. Wahhabism represents, in fact, a specific reimagined version of Salafism, that is, *atharī* or Hanbali Salafism. This is a post–Ibn Hanbal Hanbalism that reimagines Ibn Hanbal by reconstructing his sayings (actual or ascribed) and narratives, which are not without contradiction and variations. As a consequence, Hanbalism became simultaneously a juristic and theological school.[20] Hanbali Salafism, like Shiʿi Imami Salafism, emerged as a simultaneously juristic and theological doctrine. Most other Islamic schools of law took much longer to evolve an affinity with a specific theological doctrine, with a gestation period lasting more than 150 years. This applies to the association of Ashʿari theology with the Shafiʿi and Maliki schools of jurisprudence, Māturīdi theology with Hanafism, and so on. Sunni Hanbali Salafism's and Shiʿi Imami Salafism's early and intimate connection of legal doctrine and theology makes these schools into a "confessional doctrine," distinguishing them from other forms of Salafism. All juristic-theological confessionalisms have deeply rooted Salafi aspects. However, Hanbali Salafism is unique in viewing itself as pure Salafism, in both legal (*uṣūl al-fiqh*) and theological (*uṣūl al-dīn*) terms.[21]

The term *Salafism* as currently popular in Middle Eastern studies is understood as referring to a puritanical model of religiosity, an early form found in the Arabian Peninsula in the eighteenth century CE. But this form is neither specific to the Peninsula nor to Sunni Islam because it encompasses the Shiʿi world as well. That is, it is not just Sunni but also Shiʿi.

The term remains a source of confusion because of its multiple uses: at certain times it signifies conservatism and return to the Salaf, and at others it signifies the defense of Muslim identity and culture while still accepting the values of progress and freedom. This is especially true of modern religious reformism in the Muslim world, where Salafism was reclaimed or reconstructed as the return to an imagined foundation, or "origin," free from "heretical innovations," "impurities," and "innovations" (*bidʿa*). Every reformation demands a return to the fundamentals of religion and the emulation of pious predecessors in a quest to rid religion of foreign impurities. These impurities, according to this version of modernist reformist Salafism, distort the fundaments of religion and impede progress and adaptation to modernity. Impurities and innovations include superstition and practices widespread in folk religiosity, such as miracles, expectations, and the intercession of saints. The modernist littérateur Taha Husayn (1889–1973 CE) gives an amusing account of an argument he had with his father when he returned to his small Egyptian village after a year studying at al-Azhar, where he had become a disciple of the reformer Abduh. Hearing his father recite supplications to saints and holy men from a popular book, the young Taha Husayn condemned the prayers as heretical nonsense. "Is this what they teach you at al-Azhar?" his father responded angrily. "Yes," the young man said, "and I also learned at al-Azhar that much of what you read in this book is prohibited according to religion (*ḥarām*), damaging, and of no benefit. People should not pray to prophets and saints. There should be no intermediary between God and man, for that is a kind of idolatry."[22] In the case of young Taha Husayn, the same aversion to received customs and superstitions and the same education to return to the uncorrupted fundaments spurred the onset of an evolution that led to philosophical rationalism and liberalism after studying in France. In the case of other disciples of Abduh, this was a consistent track of reformist Salafism.

Allal al-Fassi (1910–1974 CE) is a good example of the functional relationship between reformist Salafism and modernity. Al-Fassi combined advocacy of democracy and nationalism with a reformist perspective that advised adherence to "the best of the authentic Islamic legacy from the Salaf." Abduh pioneered this modern reformist stance. Abduh had many disciples, including modernists, who split in the 1920s CE into liberal Egyptian nationalists and Salafi followers of his disciple Rashid Rida (1865–1935 CE), who further developed Abduh's reformist stance but placed greater emphasis on Salafism and less emphasis on commitment to the imperative of reform. They asserted that Rida was Abduh's closest and most faithful disciple and was often tasked by Abduh with answering questions on his behalf. He collected and published the biography and writings of Abduh in three volumes (under the title *Tārīkh al-Ustādh al-Imam Muhammad Abduh,* 1931). Rida "emphasized the purely religious legacy of Abduh . . . and presented the Salafi as an Islamic intellectual committed to political and social activism, hostile to Sufi practices, radically divergent from the class of the *ʿulamaʾ* [Muslim religious scholars who have specialized knowledge of Islamic law and doctrine], and finally as representative of an urban petty-bourgeoisie far removed from the governing classes."[23] This was the Salafism of an Arab urban life dramatically transformed by modernization. It advocated orthodox religious practices and an end to heretical innovations and "magical" elements that were alien to the spirit of Islam and responsible for entrenching backwardness. It defended Islam's ability to reroot itself by returning to its origins in the face of the modernist waves buffeting the ship of Islamic tradition. It also emphasized Islam's capacity to incorporate many aspects of modernity by linking them either to the spirit or intentions of Islam's teachings.

As founder and publisher of the reformist journal *Al-Manār*—and against a political backdrop that included the French occupation of Syria, the Anglo-French partition of the Levant, the failure of the Hashemite project of a united Arab kingdom[24]—Rida began an intellectual shift away from Abduh's intellectual and educational Salafi reformism toward the militant Salafi reformism of al-Afghani.[25] The Islamist element gradually eclipsed the reformist element in his thought. Rida felt that the separation of the caliphate from political power (sultanate) in 1922 CE was simply a prelude to the abolition of the caliphate entirely in 1924.[26] After these events, Rida began to advocate for the restoration of the caliphate. Rida's beliefs stood in contrast to Abduh's teachings. Indeed, Abduh believed that the idea of Islamic unity in one state was madness: "As for the endeavor to unify the Muslims, as they are in their current situation—it has not crossed anyone's mind, and if someone were to advocate it, he would best be committed to an asylum. The true aim of advocating for the religious bond . . . should be understood as simply the desire of the Muslims to help each other to reform what is corrupt in their beliefs or unsound in their actions, and mutual defense against the famines, oppression, and misfortune befalling them."[27]

Echoing al-Afghani with some modifications, Rida advocated for a return to text and tradition as well as an intense political activism. While al-Afghani believed that politics was limited to petitioning and advising rulers, Rida engaged with political associations regardless of whether they were popular or secular in character. His politics focused on writing, thereby giving expression to the modern public-associational political activism of the last two decades of the Ottoman state. Rida helped establish the Ottoman Party for Administrative Decentralization in February 1913 and was involved in developing its manifesto.[28] He was also deputy chairman of the Syrian Congress (1919–1920 CE), which drafted a constitution that was secular except in matters of personal status law. At this point, the Muslim Brotherhood had not yet emerged; matters of personal status and Shariʿa had yet to become the focus of a mass party politics and used as a tool to mobilize the urban masses and in particular the middle classes.

In the latter part of his career, Rida began to admire the Islamic awakening in the Arabian Peninsula led by the third Saudi dynasty under ʿAbd al-ʿAziz Al Saʿud (Ibn Saʿud) (1875–1953 CE) and the Wahhabis, who promoted a return to the Qur'an and Sunna and reliance on some writings of Ibn Taymiyya and his close disciple, Shams al-Din Abu Abdullah Muhammad Ibn Abi Bakr Ibn Qayyim al-Jawziyya (1292–1350 CE / 691–751 AH). They fought against heretical innovations and social phenomena that had "infiltrated" Islam from other traditions and religions. Rida praised Ibn Abd al-Wahhab's rejection of unthinking obedience to tradition and saw religious reform as a matter of rooting out "blind imitation" of a particular school of jurisprudence (madhab) and jurisprudential partisanship.

Other turn-of-the-century intellectuals in the Levant and Egypt also praised the "simplicity" and "authenticity" of the Wahhabi movement and Ibn Saʿud, whom people addressed by his first name, ʿAbd al-ʿAziz, without ceremony. Even the liberal Taha Husayn characterized Wahhabism along these lines. For him, it was "no more than a powerful call for the sincere and pure Islam cleansed of all taint of polytheism (*shirk*) and idolatry. . . . It is a revival of Arab Islam and a rejection of the products of ignorance and mixing with non-Arabs."[29] Taha Husayn was particularly interested in the revival brought about by Wahhabism in the printing of classical juristic texts and the competition between Wahhabis and Zaydis of Yemen to print them in Cairo and elsewhere. He thought that, if the Turks and the Egyptians had not joined forces against the Wahhabis and had used weapons the Wahhabis were unfamiliar with, "it is probable that this doctrine would have united the Arabs in the twelfth and thirteenth centuries AH as the appearance of Islam had united them in the first century AH. However, what is of interest to us about this doctrine is its impact on the intellectual and literary life of the Arabs. . . . It awakened the Arab soul and gave it an ideal it loved and fought for with sword, pen, and tongue."[30]

Despite Rida's admiration for Ibn Abd al-Wahhab, he criticized the Wahhabis' extremism, particularly their animosity to other Muslims and their tendency to alienate others.[31] Similarly, Jamal al-Din al-Qasimi (1866–1914 CE)—a pioneer of the modern scientific and religious renaissance in the Levant in the late nineteenth century CE who considered Salafism a theological term—wrote that, unlike the moderate Salafis in Iraq, the Hijaz, Greater Syria, and Egypt, the Wahhabi followers in historical Saudi Arabia were "Salafiyya in creed" but were "dominated by harshness (*al-jafā'*) and extremism (*al-ghulū*)."[32]

Rida was thus a critical admirer of Ibn Abd al-Wahhab as a man whose project had a clear Islamic identity and was rooted in the "pristine" teachings of Islam. He may also have taken too seriously Ibn Abd al-Wahhab's rejection of partisan "madhabism." In fact, Ibn Abd al-Wahhab fused a Salafi understanding of Islam with a juristic-theological amalgam of imagined Hanbalism.

Here we can distinguish the Salafism of Ibn Abd al-Wahhab from reformist Salafism, which believed firmly in the capacity of Islam to engage with issues of the modern Muslim individual, state, and society and thus formed an intellectual base for a model of political-activist religiosity with roots in both Salafism and reformism.

Rida, like other Reformers, advocated religious law (*Shariʿa*) because he believed that Islam, correctly interpreted, suited every age. By contrast, Wahhabi and other regressive nonreformist Salafisms—which have emerged in both premodern contexts (like Wahhabism itself) and in modern contexts (like jihadi Salafi movements)—believe that every age should be tailored to their idiosyncratic understandings of Islam. Many Salafi reformist schools were impressed by

Wahhabism's ability to mobilize communities en masse and inspire an Islamic revival. In particular, Salafi reformists admired Wahhabism's rejection of heretical innovations and its propagation of Islam in a tribal desert community where religious influence was weak and religiosity low. However, Salafi reformism was not aware of, nor did it follow, Wahhabism's shift from attempting to move past madhabs to becoming a distinct madhab in its own right. Wahhabism's rejection of imitation was based not on advocacy of the original and independent interpretation of the Qur'an and renewal against blind emulation but rather on zeal for the imagined past, rejection of all innovation as heresy, and what it believed to be the original simple religion. Wahhabi Salafis claimed that they were not against derivation of religious rulings through ijtihād, which they viewed as valid until Judgment Day. Ibn Abd al-Wahhab scorned the extensive list of qualifications for those seeking to exercise ijtihād, commenting that they "may not have been fulfilled even by Abu Bakr and Umar" (the first two caliphs).[33] But this was only in theory. Wahhabism was strongly opposed to any ijtihād that did not conform to its specific methodology. Ibn Abd al-Wahhab made a few exceptions, including that "there is nothing unacceptable about ijtihād concerning prayers seeking the Prophet's intercession."[34] This is unquestionably a contradiction, as it advocates ijtihād against ijtihād.

Conversely, modern Salafi reformism advocated a vision that shifted dialectically between defending Islam within the tide of modernity and accommodating progress and development, with the goal of helping people "change themselves so that God would change them," as the Qur'an puts it. Modern Salafi reformism was protestant in a certain sense, in that it called for action and reform so that God and Islam might help those who help themselves, and so that God's law would be implemented by achieving justice and equity.

In the classical reformist definition, Salafism is an appeal to the Salaf not just in terms of a return to the texts in order to discover their judgments in specific issues but also in terms of their spirit and their openness and readiness to adapt to change and engage in disciplined reasoning concerning issues that the ancestors and their texts did not face. Returning to the ways of the Prophet and his immediate disciples and descendants meant eradicating degeneracy, superstition, and myth, thereby opening the doors of ijtihād to achieve progress. In this sense, the Prophet and his righteous successors (*al-salaf al-ṣāliḥ*) mark an authoritative starting point for progress. In reformist Salafism, the return to the teachings and statements of the Prophet and his successors is advocated for the sake of progress, which is derived from their spirit and the overall objectives or aims (*maqāṣid*) of the Shariʿa. By contrast, Wahhabism aimed to reproduce an imagined "correct, original Islam" and sought to return to the teachings of the Prophet and his successors. In this sense, Salafi thought in the Wahhabi mold offers an ideology of regressive consciousness based on an inevitable decline of history in which each age is worse than what came before.

This emphasis on the underlying orientation of Shariʿa objectives over established rulings is what distinguishes modern religious reformism from Wahhabism, which did not emerge in the context of encounters with the modernity nor the "West" through colonialism or otherwise. Reformist figures like al-Fassi offer independent reasoned judgments in the context of the overall objectives of the Shariʿa. For example, al-Fassi believed that democracy is the modern form of consultation (*shūrā*), a concept in the Qur'an that encourages Muslims to decide their affairs in consultation with each other. He wrote, "I do not need to remind you that humanity's first experience of government limited by consultation of the masses—and not just a particular class—came from the pure spring of Islam, when [the Prophet] Muhammad Ibn Abdullah laid down the Constitution of Medina, which was the first constitutional declaration guaranteeing the rights and duties of all citizens without discriminating according to color, language, or race." For al-Fassi, who in the process of adapting his understanding of early Islam to democracy projected modern concepts on the first Muslim community of the first century AH, "shūrā is obligatory; equality in rights and duties is law; and individual responsibility before the law is a legitimate right upheld by the people."[35] Al-Kawakibi—a Syrian reformist and author of the second half of the nineteenth century CE who explored issues of Pan-Arabism, Islamic identity, and despotism—similarly read democracy into sacred texts and early Islam. Meanwhile, Rida displayed greater historical awareness by recognizing how contemporary democracy influenced scholars' interpretation of shūrā as democracy:

> O Muslim, do not say that this kind of governance is one of the fundamentals of our religion derived from the Qur'an and the biographies of the rightly guided caliphs, rather than from interaction with the Europeans or reflections on the condition of the Westerners. Were it not for awareness of the experience of those

> people, neither you nor those like you would have thought it part of Islam. Were it really the case (that the principles of democracy were derived directly from Islamic teachings), then the earliest proponents of democracy should have been in Istanbul, Egypt, and Marrakesh. However, it is they who, for the most part, are the greatest supporters of tyrannical personal government, while most advocates of limited government by consultation (*shūrā*) are those familiar with Europe and the Europeans, and they have been preceded in this by the idolaters.[36]

But what does al-Kawakibi, Rida, and al-Fassi's modern reformist Salafism have in common with regressive Salafis like al-Wadiʿi?[37] What does it have in common with that of Abu Qatada al-Filastini (b. 1959 CE), a key figure in al-Qaeda, or Abu Bakr al-Baghdadi (1971–2019 CE), the leader of ISIL? Not much. To understand these divergent Salafisms and how they are connected, we must examine the historical, sociopolitical, and cultural context in which they emerged and the interaction of ideas that drove their development. It is a matter of understanding the dialectic between the epistemological and the historical.

ON THE RETURN TO AN IMAGINED PURE SPIRIT OF ISLAM

Historically, Abu Hamid al-Ghazali (1058–1111 CE / 450–505 AH) is the representative of moderate Sunni Islam. Despite his fierce criticisms of the Ashʿarites' doctrinal rigidity and their readiness to declare individuals as infidels, al-Ghazali is the best representative of the Ashʿari creed of Ahl al-Sunna wa al-Jamāʿa in many respects. Similarly, Ibn Taymiyya authored many famous treatises while Fakhr al-Din al-Razi (1149–1210 CE / 544–605 AH), a Persian Islamic scholar and pioneer of inductive logic, wrote several seminal works of rational theology and a major work of exegesis *Mafātīh al-Ghayb* (Keys to the unknown). Can disagreements between religious intellectuals explain the conflict between ISIL and Anṣār al-Sunna in Iraq (a group that relies on more or less the same texts but rejects the caliphate of al-Abu Bakr al-Baghdadi) or the conflict between al-Qaeda and the Muslim Brotherhood? Of course not. The writings of jurisprudents cannot account for these complex intellectual and sociopolitical phenomena.

Social and political explanations—the intellectual, psychological, and social backgrounds of sociopolitical actors and the political role of conflict—are indispensable when explaining differences in interpretation between different theorists and texts. Otherwise, we are left with presumed links and continuities that make no distinction between phenomena. Al-Ghazali's responses to philosophers that predate Abu al-Walid Muhammad Ibn Ahmad Ibn Muhammad Ibn Rushd (1126–1198 CE / 520–595 AH) would never have been promoted as if they were responses to Ibn Rushd himself and would not have been widely circulated if not for the need to justify Seljuk rule against Fatimid and Nizārī Isma'ilis rule and the need to confront Ibn Rushd's rationalist understanding of theology and doctrine. In addition, al-Ghazali's books were promoted because many believed that the Sunna needed defending against internal and external political and intellectual challenges. But as soon as this dissemination took place, there was no longer a Sunna per se and al-Ghazali was no longer a simple continuation of it. An additional process of articulation took place within this political and social culture: differentiation of the religious and the political, the native and the foreign (in the form of the translation movement, among others), and the influence of Greek philosophical thought and Persian political thought.

Al-Ghazali has absolutely nothing in common with eighteenth century CE Wahhabis or with contemporary Salafists. He wrote from the perspective of a civilization that had been, until very recently, diverse, pluralistic, full of vitality, and accepting of countless cultures, translations, sciences, arts, literatures, and poetry. Scholars of the traditions of the Prophet Muhammad coexisted with speculative theologians and poets, Greek and Syriac translators, philosophers, women singers, slave dancers, and other mundane occupations unbound by the restrictions of Shari'a. Even al-Ghazali himself celebrated and made open use of Greek formal logic in the religious sciences, belittling those who disapproved. Conversely, Ibn Abd al-Wahhab spread his ideas in alliance with Ibn Sa'ud in a remote desert region of the Ottoman Empire centuries later but socially much closer to the advent of Islam. What could possibly connect them?

As such, this study contends that Ibn Abd al-Wahhab's movement seemed to resemble the foundation of a new religion allegedly identical to Islam as it had first appeared not only in terms of content and texts but also in terms of method, mode of propagation, and social environment. This observation was also made by his contemporaries. Note that Ibn Abd al-Wahhab denied that he had created a new school of thought, asserting that he had no issue with the existing four. In an important text, he restates the accusations of his opponents:

> They say that I invalidate the books of the four schools of Islamic jurisprudence. They allege that I say that for six hundred years, people lacked true beliefs, and that I claim to be an original authority of Islamic law. According to them, I am outside the tradition, and I say that disagreement between Muslim scholars is a curse. They say that I deem those who seek the intercession of the righteous with God to be infidels. . . . They say that I condemn ritual visits to the Prophet's tomb and the graves of parents, etc., and that I call infidel anyone who makes an oath other than by God. To these twelve issues, my reply is, "Glory be to You! This is a mighty calumny." Before them was one who slandered the Prophet Muhammad by saying that he insulted 'Isa Ibn Maryam and the righteous whose "hearts are much alike" and slandered him for claiming that the angels, 'Isa, and 'Azira are in Hell.[38]

It may be useful to recall that Ibn Abd al-Wahhab's mission was opposed by his own father, Abd al-Wahhab Ibn Sulayman, who was a Hanbali judge and jurisprudent, and that "there were arguments between him and his father, and between him and the people in the village of [Huraymila]. He continued along these lines until his father's death. . . . Then he declared his mission and repudiated [his father's position]."[39]

Ibn Abd al-Wahhab grew up in a traditional Hanbali scholarly family from Uyayna, an established mud-brick village not inhabited by nomadic Bedouins of the desert. They descended from the Banu Tamim, a historically settled tribe in Basra, Najd, and both sides of the Gulf. Several family members were judges in Huraymila, Uyayna, and other villages. Ibn Abd al-Wahhab's brother Sulayman—also a Hanbali jurist—accused his brother of ignorance and failure to meet the conditions needed to undertake *ijtihād* (independent or original interpretation needed to address problems not covered by fundamental religious texts).[40] Sulayman considered matters that Ibn Abd al-Wahhab deemed as disbelief or faithlessness not necessarily to be the major sin of polytheism that placed one outside the community. Sulayman accused his brother of defying consensus and declaring Muslims as infidels for matters that did not constitute faithlessness, even if they were uncontestably reprehensible. It is notable that, in Ibn Abd al-Wahhab's arguments with his brother, he cited statements from Ibn Taymiyya and Ibn Qayyim and accused his brother of not understanding either scholar. Ibn Abd al-Wahhab was even accused of branding contemporary

Hanbali scholars like Ibn Fayruz al-Ahsa'i (1694–1762 CE / 1105–1175 AH) as infidels and declaring it permissible to kill them.[41] Uthman Ibn Mansur al-Najdi (d. 1865 CE / 1282 AH), a Hanbali scholar, wrote a rebuttal of Wahhabism entitled *Manhaj al-Maʿārij li-Akhbār al-Khawārij*. Remarkably, his book is endorsed in some Hanbali juristic circles to this day. More striking is that, despite the fact that its author had written it as a refutation of early Wahhabism, the foreword of this recently republished book in Saudi Arabia was written by an extremist Salafi precisely to refute the arguments of jihadist movements he deemed unfaithful to the teachings of the pious predecessors.[42]

Prior to contemporary Orientalist thought that emphasizes Islamist movements' interaction with the West, classical or essentialist Orientalist scholars viewed these movements as merely a continuation of a preexisting Sunni or Shiʿi tradition unrelated to modernity, social conditions, or the nature of the regime under which they emerged. Unlike contemporary Salafism and like other Islamist awakenings in the eighteenth century CE, early Wahhabism is not a product of the interaction with the West.[43] However, this does not mean that Wahhabism was an incarnation of an eternal substance of Islam.

This kind of Orientalism holds that few new phenomena have emerged in Islam and that its substance has remained the same and thus closely resembles Islamism's own self-perception and its account of its origins. These Orientalists treat a whole civilization as if it were a manifestation of religion and furthermore a religion that has a fixed essence.[44] Essentialist Orientalists would draw on the work of jihadi Salafi ideologues like Abu Abdullah al-Muhajir to trace a straight line connecting parts of the Qur'an and the Sunna (such as Sura al-Tawba and reports of the killing of prisoners from Banu Qurayza) to the practices of ISIL, just as al-Muhajir and ISIL itself do. However, this view neglects the fact that hundreds of millions of other Muslims have read these same parts of the Qur'an and the Sunna without understanding them as a guide for action or anything more than religious texts from a sacred time. Only a shrinking minority of Muslims have interpreted them as a handbook for political action. So, are the religious texts really the problem?

An understanding of ISIL neither begins nor ends with analysis of religious texts or juristic works. ISIL literature is ideological in the Marxist sense of false consciousness that takes the extreme form of inverted consciousness. It only believes in restoring history as reimagined in a way accounted for by its present rather than from the perspective of the first generation, "the generation of the good," or "the best of generations" in Islamic historiography. The Islamic messianic, eschatological, and Christological consciousness is closely linked to the consciousness of a decline from a virtuous origin that has been corrupted over time.

With respect to how these ideas are structured and have become established, both modern reformist Salafism and Wahhabi Salafism hearken back to a hypothetical or imagined pure Islam. But these two returns have little in common. Modern reformist Salafism seeks to capture the pure spirit of Islam as represented in texts and biographies by drawing on the overall objectives (*maqāṣid*) of Shariʿa, reinterpreting it for the modern age, and constructing a new imagined system transcending elements of backwardness and irrationality that, according to modern reformers, prevent Muslim societies from catching up with Western civilization. This Salafism turns its gaze back to the maqāṣid of the Shariʿa. It should be noted here that because its structure is based on analogy with precedent, the traditional jurisprudential model of uṣūl al-fiqh does not incorporate the maqāṣid nor does it consider them to be an independent source of authority in the absence of the proper conditions for ijtihād. The approach to maqāṣid found in classical writers like al-Ghazali, Imam al-Haramayn Abu al-Maʿali Abd al-Malik Ibn Abdullah al-Juwayni (1028–1085 CE / 419–478 AH), and above all Abu Ishaq Ibrahim Ibn Musa al-Shatibi (1320–1388 CE / 720–790 AH) has been reclaimed as part of reformism's reconstruction of Salafism.[45]

Meanwhile, regressive contemporary Salafism (which includes Wahhabism) emphasizes a return to the literal meaning of the text and believes that the text has only one meaning. Despite this approach, regressive Salafis select meanings and parts of the text that suit their purposes. Unlike modern reformist Salafism, which seeks to build a dynamic conception of Islam that interacts with the issues of modern times, regressive Salafism does not go back to a "spirit" of the text and its maqāṣid. Instead, it allegedly interprets the text from an atavistic perspective, selectively adopting citations that demonstrate its preconceived notions of past Islam. It takes citations out of context and interprets them in isolation from that context, whether the goal is the legitimization of efforts stymieing development and modernization or the justification of bloody campaigns of retribution against actually existing Muslim cultures, societies, and governance, as in the case of jihadi Salafism.

Western intellectuals have often conflated Modern Salafi reformism and regressive Salafism, inevitably generating confusion over the origin and development of these movements. This approach can be traced back to observations of the famous French Orientalist Louis Massignon (1883–1962 CE).[46] Massignon argued that Salafism was an intellectual movement pioneered by Sayyid Ahmad Barelvi (1786–1831 CE / 1201–1246 AH)[47] and his disciple Siddiq Hasan Khan (d. 1890 CE / 1307 AH)[48] during the early nineteenth century CE in India. According to Massignon, al-Afghani and Abduh then spread Salafism to Baghdad, Damascus, Cairo, and even the Maghreb. However, between 1920–1925 CE, Massignon changed his views on Salafism's origins, instead arguing that it was a modernist reform movement led by al-Afghani and Abduh.[49] Henri Laoust (1905–1983 CE), a French Orientalist scholar who had studied the Hanbali school of thought in Morocco, spread Massignon's theories despite their obvious inconsistencies. In 1932 CE, Laoust developed a conceptual framework of Salafism based on Massignon's assumption that al-Afghani, Abduh, and other Islamic modernists who aimed to establish a multifaceted reformist program used Salafism as a slogan. Hamilton Gibb (1895–1971 CE), a Scottish orientalist, based his theories on the same ideas, which helped spread this assumption in English-language scholarship.

In 2010 CE, Henri Lauzière, a professor of history at Northwestern University, challenged this widespread assumption about the origins of Salafism. He argued that, while modernist Reformers like al-Afghani, Abduh, and Rida were Salafis, they were only so in the sense that the term was understood at that time. Lauzière contends that Muhibb al-Din al-Khatib (1886–1969 CE), a prominent Syrian Salafi writer, and Abd al-Fattah Qatlan (d. 1931 CE), a Sunni Hanafi Muslim scholar who became a Syrian Muslim Brotherhood leader, were the first to use Salafism as a slogan for "commercial purposes" in the early twentieth century CE. In 1910 CE, both al-Khatib and Qatlan began speaking of Islam's forefathers—but they used the term not in its narrow religious sense but to refer to Muslim heritage in general. Indeed, they named their bookstore and publishing house the Salafi Bookstore (Al-Maktaba al-Salafiyya) where they sold a wide variety of books, all under the Salafi label. They included works of the Egyptian historian and polymath Jalal al-Din al-Suyuti (1445–1505 CE / 849–911 AH), the linguist and grammarian Ahmad Ibn Faris al-Qazwini (941–1004 CE / 329–395 AH), the pedagogue and linguist Tahir al-Jaza'iri (1852–1920 CE), and the classical philosophers Abu Nasr al-Farabi (874–950 CE / 260–339 AH) and Abu ʿAli al-Husayn Ibn Abdullah Ibn Sina (980–1037 CE / 370–428 AH). Al-Khatib and Qatlan sought to emphasize Muslim medieval scholars' contributions to the Western renaissance of their time and the rise of modernity and "to bridge the gap between the Muslim world and the West by arguing that the former was on a par with the latter."[50] Despite the reference to Salafism in the name, this was not a conceptual application of the term. The bookstore did not promote a single Salafi theology and instead emphasized the rationality and dynamism of Islam. Neither of the owners consciously attempted to redefine Salafism in relation to Islamic modernism. Their use of *Salafiyya* in the bookstore's name led the label to spread elsewhere in the Muslim world. The bookstore itself received praise and publicity from journals that represented different intellectual orientations and world views in the framework of the Arab renaissance in Egypt, such as *Al-Manār*, *Al-Hilāl*, and *Al-Muqtaṭaf*, as well as the Syrian journal *Al-Muqtabas*.[51]

In 2015 CE, Frank Griffel (b. 1965 CE), a professor of religious studies at Yale University, argued that the term *Salafism* could be retroactively applied to modernist reformers, even though they did not describe themselves as Salafis at the time.[52] He points to the fact that many call Baruch Spinoza (1632–1677 CE) an enlightenment philosopher even though the term *enlightenment* was not used during his lifetime; similarly, Henri de Saint-Simon is considered a socialist although he did not use the word to describe himself.[53]

Griffel argues that Orientalist scholars of the 1920s and 1930s were confused regarding modernist and Wahhabi Salafis because there was a "real similarity of approaches to Muslim reform in the late nineteenth and twentieth centuries." He notes that it was only after the period of polarization between the 1930s and 1970s CE ("after the end of Hourani's 'liberal age,'" as Griffel puts it) that the two became clearly distinct. "Neither the Muslim protagonists of this era nor contemporary observers from the West could perceive these lines of division as clearly as we see them today."[54] A good illustration of the blurred lines between modern reformism and Wahhabism is the fact that Muhammad Hamid al-Fiqqi (1890–1959 CE), a prominent Egyptian Salafi scholar who established the purist Islamist fundamentalist association Anṣār al-Sunna al-Muḥammadiyya in 1926 CE, was Rida's student and follower. While al-Fiqqi and other traditionalist Salafis recognize Rida's "credentials as a member of—or at least a sympathizer with—the Salafiyya," other contemporary Salafis refuse to acknowledge any link between Abduh, Rida, and their own school of thought. For them, Abduh is the main inspiration of the different groups that make up their doctrinal enemies, namely traditionalist Ashʿaris, modernists, and secular political actors. However, Griffel notes that Albert Hourani—a Lebanese British historian—still argued that there was a strong link between Abduh and Salafism.[55] It is important to note that Hourani, in fact, did not literally use the word *Salafism* in this context. He referred to Abduh's revival of the legacy of the Salaf, among whom he included many scholars from the ages of the flourishing Muslim civilization, some of whom no Salafi would have included among the "righteous Salaf": "for when Abduh talks of the salaf, he does not use the term in a technical sense to mean the first generation of friends and disciples of the Prophet; he uses it more generally to refer to the central tradition of Sunni Islam in its period of development: the great theologians of the third and fourth Islamic centuries, Ashʿari, Baqillani, Māturīdi, are also salaf."[56]

Does this example justify using the same concept to designate these apparently divergent movements? Or does it instead highlight the need for conceptual differentiation? While I agree with Griffel's interpretive conceptual logic, another researcher can use this framework to reach a different conclusion than the one he drew. Even the return to the "pure" Islam of the "Salaf" and the rejection of madhabism served different purposes for regressive and reformist Salafis; neither of these trends were understood or employed in the same way.

Ultimately, the dispute on which this scholarly debate focuses is illusive because it revolves around the categorization of two different phenomena that share certain traits yet are conceptually distinct. Indeed, both historical development and theoretical inference set these two varieties of Salafism apart. In what follows, I distinguish between modernist reformist Salafism and regressive Salafism, and then divide the latter into subcategories. Importantly, while the concept of regressive Salafism includes older phenomena not mentioned in this debate, like the premodern Wahhabi movement of the eighteenth century CE, the concept does not include the reformers of the nineteenth and twentieth centuries CE.

Reformist modernist Salafism and regressive Salafism are two examples from the same historical period that seek to embody the adage that "Islam is suitable for all times and places." This can mean that Islam is suitable for every age because it is a civilization that evolves alongside historical developments—i.e.,

Islam is suitable because of its adaptability as a religion and culture and its capacity to evolve and preserve its original principles. Conversely, however, it can also be understood to mean that that Islam contains detailed instructions for individual, state, and society that are valid for people in all times and places and can/must be imposed on them; every age can be made to fit the Salafi concept of one true Islam, which is derived from the apparent meaning of the text and which serves as an authoritative and valid reference for every age.[57] The same position that dismisses innovations and rejects the bindingness of tradition manifests itself in two contradictory views: while regressive contemporary Salafism advocates returning to the practice of the original Salaf and remaining frozen in one literal (and selective) interpretation of the text and an imagined retroactive utopia of an early Muslim community, reformist Modernist Salafism calls for a purge of traditions and worn-out innovations—which, according to the Reformers, originate from the long "decline" of "decadent Islamic civilization," and are "alien to the spirit of Islam"—in order to renew religion, starting from its foundations and original teachings.

The process of takfīr based on rejection of intellectual tradition can sometimes produce frivolous exegetical practices. Across all disciplines, scholars can draw implausible and far-fetched interpretations from texts to conform with their scientific theory of choice. For example, Islamic scholars have interpreted texts so as to miraculously foretell scientific discoveries and laud the so-called scientific inimitability (*al-iʿjāz al-ʿilmī*) of the Qur'an.[58] These interpretations frequently arrive at a dead end and cannot compete with purist Salafism in their fidelity to the text. The process of interpreting and applying the text to contemporary problems is more likely to generate real religious reform when it avoids forced interpretations of individual words and instead draws inferences from reason, the overall purposes of religion, and higher goals like virtue, justice, and the general good.

As stated previously, the primary difference between reformism and contemporary regressive Salafism—notwithstanding the Salafi element in the former—is that reformism focuses on humanity's progress and contemporary regressive Salafism focuses on humanity's inevitable decline from a historical golden age. Fahmi Jadaan (b. 1940 CE) argues that the Islamic thinkers of the Arab renaissance (al-Nahda) that flourished in modern-day Egypt, Lebanon, and Syria during the latter half of the nineteenth century and beginning of the twentieth century CE, typically proceeded from the premise that Muslims could change their political, economic, and social conditions, thereby progressing toward a better future.[59] The early pure Islam is not used as a retrospective utopia by the Reformers but as an ideal that is used to defy its distortion by backwardness.

Salafism employs various and distinct modes of religiosity, such as seeking guidance in the conduct of the Salaf as an authority, a source of legitimacy, and/or as a generation with a higher religious status. First, the modernist reformist mode views Salafism as a return to the pure sources of religion in order to adapt to modernity and to remove all hindrances to development. Excluding the aforementioned researchers and other academics, reformist streams of thought are no longer referred to as *Salafi* in the prevalent usage of the term in contemporary Muslim societies.

Instead, the designation *Salafism* is monopolized by preachers, movements, and organizations associated with regressive ideology. First, there is regressive Salafism, which is often defined by its focus on teaching people the fundaments of Islam, enforcing strict adherence to its provisions, and promoting the "right" practice of religious obligations and by its public manifestation of religiosity (religious appearance). In practice, regressive Salafism is usually segregationist and conservative, requiring obedience to the ruling regimes and preservation of the status quo to varying degrees. Second, there is political Salafism, which focuses on criticizing the status quo, using religious ideology as a mode of intervention in public affairs, and claiming to represent the religion per se. Third, there is a mode of jihadi Salafism that justifies (from a Salafi perspective) violent rebellion against actual existing Islam as embodied in societies and states. The borders between these sorts of Salafism are not always clear or impervious, and certain scholars subscribe to more than one.

While reformist Salafism did attempt to influence political Islamic movements, these efforts produced outcomes antithetical to the reformists' intentions. Conversely, regressive Salafism's interaction with politics led to increased activism, as in the case of the Islamic awakening in Saudi Arabia in the 1990s CE on the one hand and the global jihadi Salafi movements on the other.

To summarize, reformist and regressive Salafis appeal to the Qur'an and Sunna. However, even if they cite the same texts when speaking to their followers, they do not in fact "return" to the same place but rather to different imagined versions of the early Muslim community, different understanding of the text and its objectives, and opposite intentions concerning their application.

ISLAMIC SCHOLARS AND FOLK RELIGION

Across folk, official, or politicized forms of religiosity, Salafisms are represented by an advocacy of return to the Qur'an and Sunna as understood by the first generation of Muslims. The interactions between this return and these modes of religiosity produce unique and self-contained outcomes. Indeed, Salafi folk religiosity differs from the official institutionalized Salafisms that are either linked to a religious legal establishment or to a secular political authority. Both differ significantly from the outcome of Salafisms' interactions with religious political activism. The nexus between these different forms of religiosity is an important focus of this study and is the specific topic we will deal with now.

In the case of folk religiosity, for example, cultural interaction involves veneration of the Salaf to the point of treating them as holy. Here, folk Salafism relinquishes one of the most important characteristics of ideological Salafism: the absolute refusal to assign divine characteristics to anything or anyone but God. Ascribing sanctity to "pious" ancestors can be considered a vestige of ancestor worship found in nonmonotheistic and pagan religions and is even a part of many definitions of the term *religion* itself. Although at first glance Salafism is hostile to folk religiosity, in practice Salafism and folk religiosity have come to coexist, which in turn has led to sanctification of the Salaf, just without the rites and rituals of folk religion that Salafis detest so much. The aura of sainthood attributed to the Prophet's companions is a feature of Sunni religiosity, and attributing it to the imams of the Prophet's household (particularly Husayn Ibn Ali) is a constituent feature of Shi'i religiosity; like all other religions, Islam is influenced by a certain veneration of ancestors.

This trend also appears in the various forms of Salafism that recast bygone eras as golden ages and a regressive understanding of history seen as inevitable decline from an imagined, perfect, foundational origin.[60] This obsession with the "corruption of time" also impacts other identity groups who evince a regressive consciousness fixated on imagined genealogies. Contemporary social hierarchies are thus imbued with a historical dimension, as religious scholars and worshippers project an imagined history of illustrious ancestors onto the present in the hope of creating symbolic capital that can be used to obtain a higher social status. This projection of present aspirations and frustrations onto an imagined past is a feature of a Salafi mindset common to the religious and the secular alike, a mindset that regards the past as superior to the present. In its folk manifestations, this tendency takes the form of a belief in the sanctity of the Salaf. Unlike "idolatrous" folk religiosity, Salafism does not seek these religious authorities' blessings by visiting shrines vilified by Salafis as idol worshipping, but instead treats their words and deeds as holy.

To illustrate the extent to which the sanctification of the Prophet and his companions has influenced even staunch monotheists that are considered as authorities by contemporary Salafis, I present the following lengthy quote from Abu Yaʿla al-Farra''s (990–1066 CE / 380–458 AH) *History of the Hanbalis*:

> The best of this religious community (*umma*), after its Prophet, is Abu Bakr al-Siddiq, then Umar Ibn al-Khattab, then Uthman Ibn Affan. We put those three first, as did the companions of the Prophet, who did not disagree over this. After these three come the five members of the shūrā council (*Aṣḥāb al-Shūrā*),[61] ʿAli Ibn Abi Talib, Zubayr (Ibn al-Awwam), Talha (Ibn al-Zubayr), Abd al-Rahman Ibn Awf, and Saʿd Ibn Abi Waqqāṣ, all of whom were fit to be caliph and all of whom were imams. Proof of this may be found in the Hadith of Ibn Umar: "When the Prophet was alive and his companions were many, we would count Abu Bakr, then Umar then Uthman, then be silent." After the members of the Aṣḥāb al-Shūrā came those of the emigrants from Mecca (the *Muhājirūn*) who fought at Badr, then the helpers, or residents of Medina (*Anṣār*), then the companions of the Prophet who fought at Badr based on when they made the journey from Mecca to Medina (*hijra*) and embraced Islam, then the best of those companions of the Prophet, the generation to whom he was sent.

Al-Farra', a prominent Hanbali scholar, thus established the hierarchy among the Prophet, his companions, and his descendants. Importantly, al-Farra''s ranking of the Prophet's companions and descendants moves beyond presumed superiority and ascribes a magical quality to the period itself. Regardless of the virtue of individuals who lived at the same time as the Prophet, the mere fact of having lived at the time, having accompanied the Prophet, or having set eyes on him is in itself a value that elevates them above all those who come afterward. Individuals who are considered lowest in rank among those who accompanied the Prophet are superior to the generation who did not see him, even if they are righteous believers that fulfill their religious duties.[62]

This is representative of Ibn Hanbal, the founder of the Hanbali school of Sunni jurisprudence, during his transitional period in which he began to recognize ʿAli Ibn Abi Talib as one of the four rightly guided caliphs. Ibn Hanbal's initial reluctance to recognize ʿAli Ibn Abi Talib as a rightly guided caliph alongside Abu Bakr, Umar, and Uthman is a position referred to as *tathlīth* (trinitarianism). Ibn Hanbal eventually revised his position on this point, embracing *tarbīʿ* (quaternitarianism, i.e., acceptance of four caliphs). Nonetheless, he continued to distinguish between virtue (*faḍl*) and the caliphal office: "We say that Abu Bakr, Umar, and Uthman are more virtuous than ʿAli, may God have mercy on them. . . . We say Abu Bakr, Umar, and Uthman, then we are silent: this is with respect to virtue. With respect to the caliphate, [we say] Abu Bakr, Umar, Uthman, and ʿAli, [that is] with respect to the caliphs. The companions of the Prophet did the same."[63]

What is of interest here is the conceptualization of the companions as an imagined "best generation."[64] It is interesting that this appears in al-Farra''s book because it was written in the fifth century and transmitted the narratives of third- and fourth-century AH Hanbalis after Hanbalism was finalized as a theological doctrine. He wrote this text as both a dogmatic and emotional response to the Muʿtazilas, who rated the Prophet's companions according to moral criteria and not according to seniority. Al-Farra' also meant to send a message to the schools of Islamic jurisprudence (*fiqh*) that were deeply suspicious of "single-narrator" reports of sayings and deeds of the Prophet (*ahādīth al-āḥād*). This was a defining feature of Hanifa's school of Sunni jurisprudence. The Hanbalis of the third to fifth centuries AH treated Hanifa as a heretical innovator, an infidel, an apostate, and a Murj'ite. A Murj'ite is an individual who believes in the deferment (*irjāʾ*) of judgment on those who commit serious sins until Judgment Day. Later Salafi Hanbalis (Wahhabis for example) made their condemnation of Hanifa less extreme by describing him as a juristic but not a theological Murj'ite, meaning that Hanafis could not be accused of being infidels. Nonetheless, Abdullah Ibn Ahmad Ibn Hanbal (828-903 CE / 213-290 AH) and others in the Hanbali tradition did not completely refrain from labeling Hanifa an infidel or an apostate who had been repeatedly called on to repent.[65]

In al-Farra''s *History of the Hanbalis*, the passage highlighting the "best" of the religious community succeeding the Prophet is followed by a section justifying obedience to a ruler whether he is righteous or sinful. Still prominent in Hanbali writings today, this section outlines the duty of obedience, which argues that, because the ruler is the legitimate leader of collective prayers, rebellion against him amounts to infidelity (*kufr*). In this section, al-Farra' theoretically frames the duty of obedience within the paradigm of obedience:

> Obedience is due to the imams and the commander of the faithful (*amir al-mu'minīn*), whether righteous or sinful; whether they took the caliphate with the agreement and consent of the people or fought them with the sword until they became caliph and were called commander of the faithful. The struggle against the enemies of Islam (*jihad*) is valid under the ruler, whether righteous or sinful, until Judgment Day, and should not be abandoned; the distribution of spoils and enforcement of Qur'anically prescribed legal sanctions (*ḥudūd*) by the imams continues; no one can fault them or dispute their authority. Payment of alms to them is permissible and effective. Those who pay alms to them will have discharged this religious obligation, be they righteous or sinful. Performing Friday prayer under their leadership or that of their designated deputies is permitted, two *raka'āt* [i.e., half the normal number],[66] and fulfils the religious obligation. Anyone who repeats them is a heretical innovator and has abandoned the *āthār*, contravened the Sunna, and forfeited the rewards of his Friday prayers for rejecting the privilege of the commander, virtuous or not, to lead the prayers. The Sunna is to pray two prayers with them and regard them as a fulfillment of this religious obligations, harboring no reservation in his heart as to their validity. Those who rebel against one of the imams of the Muslims, upon whom the people have agreed and who has been declared caliph—whether voluntarily or under coercion—have spread division among the Muslims and disobeyed the command attributed to the Prophet.[67]

Contemporary "conservative" Salafism, which attributes this legitimacy to existing regimes, is defined by these two notions—emulating the Prophet and his companions and acting in complete obedience and allegiance to the imam (i.e., the ruler who rules according to the Shari'a). Conversely, "revolutionary" jihadi Salafism appeals to the Prophet and his companions to oppose and delegitimize existing regimes. In some cases, jihadi Salafism brands Muslim rulers as infidels, even if they pay lip service to Islam and assume religious titles.

Of course, the Hanbalis were not solely religious beings. They were social actors, operating in the practical world as extreme pietists under the banner of "commanding virtue and forbidding vice" (*al-amr bi al-maʿrūf wa al-nahī ʿan al-munkar*). During the era of Ahmad Ibn Hanbal (to which we can add the fourth and fifth centuries AH), Hanbalis adopted a stance of passive obedience and forbearance toward the rule of tyrannical imams, reconciling a rejection of rebellion against the imam with an unwillingness to obey him and sin against the Creator.[68] Meanwhile, their theological-juristic system provided the widest possible scope for declaring certain beliefs and deeds as characteristic of infidels (*al-takfīr al-muṭlaq*) and accusing individuals of being infidels themselves (*takfīr al-muʿayyan*). This distinction was often ignored, and conflating the two allowed Najdi (Wahhabi) Hanbalis to conduct violent campaigns against Muslims accused of being "heretical innovators" or "polytheists" during the late eighteenth and early nineteenth centuries CE. Using classical rulings on jihad and conquest against infidels that permitted the taking of spoils and prisoners. Saudi Wahhabis thus massacred and plundered communities in Iraq and the Levant in general and also in the Arabian Peninsula itself during the Saudi conquests.

Ibn Hanbal was not a Hanbali as conceived and depicted by the Hanbalis; rather, they made him a member of their school retroactively. This was one example of creating the imagined companions and descendants of the Prophet.[69] Salafis, in general, believe that the Qur'an is eternal (uncreated)[70] and adopt parts of the Sunna as a higher authority, which indisputably sets an authoritative will above any tyrannical or arbitrary ruler. This is not the position of the Wahhabi Salafi establishment, which is ostensibly Hanbali. From the Hanbali perspective, as long as the ruler does not openly declare that he is an infidel, followers must be obedient to him and assume that his actions are justified, no matter how sinful the ruler may be. This provokes the ire of other Salafi currents from outside the establishment that claim to be the guardians of religion and defend it against those who do not adhere to its precepts.

In contrast, the Muʿtazilas, who believe that the Qur'an was created by God, set limits even for a ruler governing in the name of God and according to the Qur'an and Sunna. Specifically, the Muʿtazilite method prevents the interpretation of the religion and law in a way that contradicts reason and justice. Thus, they moved toward similar conclusions reached by Hugo Grotius (1583–1645 CE) and other social contract theorists of modern Europe who argued that God Himself could not make two times two equal anything other than four.[71] This is a Platonist tradition that, rather than casting doubt on the Creator, ensures He is congruent with universal reason and refutes any attribution of irrationalism or injustice to His acts or word. This issue begs several significant questions: Which argument most effectively confronts a ruler's arbitrariness? Is it the argument based on fixed principles of religion? Or is it the argument that binds even those who confront the ruler using the fixed principles of religion to the fixed principles and axioms of reason and justice? What is the better protection against a ruler's evil doings in the context of a religious culture? Is it interpreting the religious text according to reason and virtue or subduing both reason and virtue to the literal reading of the text?[72]

Puritanism has its own social and political constituencies. Opponents of the proposition that the Qur'an was created—such as Ahmad Ibn Nasr al-Khuzaʿi (d. 864 CE / 231 AH) and Ibn Hanbal—are portrayed as heroes and martyrs because ordinary people often perceive the most intransigent as the most puritanical. Conversely, those killed for their thoughts who were not Hanbalis—including Ghaylan al-Dimashqi (d. 724 CE / 106 AH), al-Jaʿd Ibn Dirham (715–724 CE / 46–105 AH), and al-Jahm Ibn Safwan (696–745 CE / 78–128 AH)—are not considered martyrs or heroes, even though they were subjected to worse torture and deaths. Herein lie the roots of puritanism as heroism and a principled stance against the oppression and tyranny of the ruler. They are taken to represent courage in exhorting the ruler to perform good deeds and warning him against evil deeds. However, they were no more active in this field than the likes of Amr Ibn Ubayd (677–761 CE / 79/80–143/144 AH) or Wasil Ibn Aʿta' (700–749 CE / 80–131 AH), Muʿtazilas who were close to the Abbasid caliphs al-Ma'mun (786–833 CE / 170–218 AH), al-Wathiq (816–847 CE / 200–232 AH), and al-Muʿtasim (796–842 CE / 179–227 AH). Nor were they any more defiant than Ibn Dirham, Ibn Safwan, and al-Dimashqi, who were killed by the Umayyad authorities, some even by religious ruling (fatwa).

There are many legends about the wonders of the puritan dissident Islamic jurists (*fuqahā'*), including their miraculous acts and their endurance and dignity under torture. For example, Ibn Hanbal's belt is said to have miraculously snapped while he was being whipped, before retying itself to cover his nakedness after he murmured prayers to God.[73] Likewise, it is claimed that after al-Khuzaʿi's beheading, his severed head continued to recite the Qur'an and turned toward *qibla*, the direction of the Kaʿba in the Sacred Mosque in Mecca.[74] In folk imagination, charisma is often linked to the ability to perform miracles not even attributed to the Prophet himself. Miracles have also been ascribed to Sufi saints, caliphs, and religious scholars. Abu al-Faraj Abd al-Rahman Ibn ʿAli Ibn al-Jawzi's (1116–1201 CE / 510–597 AH) collection of stories about Ibn Hanbal includes stories that the Wahhabi Hanbalis would find very objectionable indeed. In the chapters entitled "On how Ilyas sent him his greetings"[75] and "How al-Khadir[76] praised him,"[77] Ibn al-Jawzi recounts several imagined miracles, including the prophets al-Khadir and Ilyas appearing before strangers and asking them to bear greetings to Ibn Hanbal. Ibn al-Jawzi also describes how Ibn Hanbal cured the chronically sick with incantations and prayer.[78]

While the religious establishment distinguishes itself from folk religiosity by producing scholars and orthodox theology, the establishment itself is made up of men of their time, who often share the mass's belief in prevalent ideas and forms of faith. It is hard to determine when they genuinely believe in widespread superstitions and when they exploit them due to close connection to commoners' religiosity.

More importantly, folk imagination disregards the heroism and endurance under torture displayed by more open-minded Islamic jurists in opposition to authorities. For example, Hanifa endured prison and torture under the Abbasids because he refused to cooperate with them. To this day, less conservative Muslim 'ulama' continue to show great fortitude in the face of persecution and accusations of being an infidel (*takfīr*). In fact, both puritanical and open-minded "rationalist" Muslim 'ulama' (Ahl al-Ra'y) were typically the most tenacious in the face of tyrannical government, except for a few cases when the state officially adopted their doctrine. Historically, the scholars more willing to cooperate with the state and assume official administrative positions have largely been classified as moderates. Unlike Imam Malik Ibn Anas (711–795 CE / 93–179 AH) and Abu Hanifa, the founder of the Shafiʿi school of jurisprudence accepted judicial appointments from rulers.

In addition, it is misguided to equate the rigidity of certain figures from the traditional and contemporary religious establishment with present-day

Islamist movements' justification of armed rebellion against Muslim rulers.[79] Even though some academics draw a straight line between the two and set both within the same historical tradition, there is a huge difference between the approach to "commanding virtue and forbidding vice" found in the work of Ibn Hanbal and followers of the traditions of the Prophet (*Aṣḥāb al-Hadith*) and the use of the same formula as a slogan and as a partisan ideological justification for violence against rulers or against those with different views.

Even for Ibn Hanbal, the principle of appealing to the Qur'an and Sunna against the tyranny of the ruler did not mean that violent rebellion was permissible in the name of jihad or otherwise. Ibn Hanbal did not believe in a new age of ignorance (*jāhiliyya*) nor in jihad against a Muslim ruler. He was not, as some jihadi Salafis anachronistically imagine, the Abu al-Aʿla al-Mawdudi (1903–1979 CE), the Sayyid Qutb (1906–1966 CE), or the Muhammad Abd al-Salam Faraj (1954–1982 CE) of his age.[80] In *Ṭabaqāt al-Ḥanābila* and in Abd al-Qadir Ibn Badran al-Dimashqi's (1864–1927 CE / 1280–1346 AH), later introduction to Hanbalism, we find interpretations attributed to Ibn Hanbal himself enjoining obedience to the imams and avoidance of civil war; Ibn Badran repeats verbatim the passage enjoining obedience to the righteous and sinful imam.[81] This version of Ibn Hanbal and his tradition is more of a precursor to the Salafism that advocates obedience and loyalty to rulers, represented by crude readings like that advocated by Muhammad Aman al-Jami (d. 1996 CE). The latter was a prominent figure at the Islamic University of Medina who opposed Brotherhood-style activism and founded al-Jāmi Salafism.

It is important to note that, contrary to these readings, Ibn Hanbal does set an authority above the ruler that can hold him accountable, even if he does not call for revolt against the ruler. Despite the ways these different streams of Hanbalism interpret Ibn Hanbal, he never wrote a book nor established a doctrine. In addition, Ibn Hanbal neither called for unconditional obedience to tyrannical rulers nor agreed to rebel against them. He was a simple narrator who kept distance from the rulers and politics, a path not followed by Hanbalis, including his sons. Put differently, while Ibn Hanbal feared the ruler and rebelling against him, he did not support obeying the ruler if that meant disobeying God. This disobedience was passive, not active.

Michael Cook (b. 1940 CE), a British scholar of Islamic history, elaborates on this point. He explains that Ibn Hanbal did not approve of Muslims seeking the help of the ruler or exercising political power to fulfill their obligation of "commanding virtue and forbidding right." Cook notes that Ibn Hanbal discourages the reporting of misdeeds of fellow Muslims to the authorities, i.e., the ruler (*sultan*). As he writes, "Ibn Hanbal is told by a disciple that one of his brethren is suffering greatly on account of the objectionable activities of his neighbours. They do three things: they drink liquor; they play lutes; and they commit offences which are coyly explained as having to do with women. The syndrome, once again, is wine, women and song. The victim, so the disciple reports, proposes to denounce them to the authorities (*sultan*). Ibn Hanbal disagreed; he should admonish and discourage them, but the authorities are to be left out of it."[82]

In general, the first Hanbalis did not clash with or confront sinners, believing that they were more powerful when performing the duty of forbidding vice. As Cook notes, they did not resort to, or cooperate with, authorities. In this picture of early Hanbalis' performance of their daily duties, two things are conspicuously absent—one implicitly, the other explicitly. Implicitly absent is any tendency for Hanbalis to seek out trouble in other parts of town. There is no indication that they attempted to carry out the duty in communities that were less sympathetic to their values. Indeed, they did not seek out Muʿtazilite preachers to revile and assault, raid brothels, or interfere in the pleasurable activities of the military and political elite. This is hardly surprising, as the Hanbalis were ill-equipped to confront the immoral majority; they could hardly dominate their own streets let alone those of others. Explicitly absent are the ruling authorities: Hanbalis sought neither confrontation nor cooperation with them, as Ibn Hanbal made it clear that one does not target the authorities when performing these duties, for their misdeeds are frequent and flagrant. As Ibn Hanbal puts it, one should not expose oneself to the sultan since "his sword is unsheathed." He was once consulted by a fellow Ahmad Ibn Shabbawayh al-Marwazi (d. 843 CE / 229 AH), who had arrived in Baghdad with the bold intention of commanding and admonishing the caliph; Ibn Hanbal discouraged him on the grounds of the risks he would have to flee.[83]

Early Abbasid attempts to impose the belief that the Qur'an was created caused puritanical thought to become dominant within parts of the religious establishment more independent from the state. The Abbasid caliph Jaʿfar Ibn Muhammad al-Muʿtasim Billah al-Mutawakkil (r. 847–861 CE / 232–246 AH) eventually renounced this doctrine and came to some agreement with the ʿulamaʾ who opposed Jahmism and the Muʿtazilas in order to placate the masses, win their support, and thus restore his authority in the face of the rising power of Turkic soldiers and their increasing encroachment onto the political authority and affairs of the caliph.[84]

To understand the dynamics between Orthodox Sunni puritanism and folk religion, it is useful to examine how the establishment and folk religiosity were similarly resistant to renewal and rationalist exegesis in this early period. Abu al-Hasan ʿAli Ibn al-Husayn al-Masʿudi (896–957 CE / 283–346 AH), the historian and traveler, wrote, "When al-Mutawakkil became caliph, he ordered an end to disputations and debates. . . . He ordered the people to submit and imitate (those senior to them) and ordered the hadith scholars to (disseminate) hadith and expound on the Sunna and the community."[85] Al-Mutawakkil bolstered his position with ordinary people by taking severe measures against monotheist non-Muslims living legally within an Islamic state (*dhimmīs*) from 937 CE / 325 AH. He used a cross-cultural, tyrannical, populist identity strategy to flatter popular sentiments. Muhammad Ibn Jarir al-Tabari (839–923 CE / 224–310 AH) writes

> Al-Mutawakkil ordered that the Christians and all other Dhimmīs wear yellow hoods (*ṭayālisah*) and *zunnār* belts, ride on saddles with wooden stirrups, affix two pommels at the rear of their saddles, and place two buttons on the caps (*qalānis*) of those who wore them, which were to be a different color from the cap worn by Muslims. . . . In addition, he ordered their renovated places of worship destroyed, and that one tenth of their residences be seized. If the location was sufficiently spacious, it was to be turned into a mosque. . . . [He] prohibited the employment of Dhimmīs in government bureaus and in official functions, in which they would have authority over Muslims. He prohibited their children from studying in Muslim elementary schools (*katātīb*) or being taught by Muslims. And he prohibited their displaying crosses on religious holidays such as Palm Sundays.[86]

Al-Mutawakkil's policies were similar to those allegedly pursued by Umayyad caliph Umar Ibn ʿAbd al-ʿAziz (r. 718–720 CE / 99–101 AH),[87] who was renowned for his piety relative to other Umayyad caliphs and his closeness to the religiosity of ordinary people. This Umayyad caliph prohibited the construction and renovation of churches; while some say he initiated these steps himself, others say these policies were attributed to him to give them legitimacy.[88] Either way, al-Mutawakkil followed his example fanatically, imposing sumptuary codes on non-Muslims and, in 855–856 CE / 241 AH, even ordering his fiscal administrator in Homs to "destroy the churches and places of worship in Homs, replace them with mosques, [and] to expel every single Christian from the city."[89] Prior to al-Mutawakkil, sumptuary laws were unprecedented in Islamic history.

TAWḤĪD: THE SINGULARITY AND UNITY OF GOD

Quintan Wiktorowicz (b. 1970 CE), an expert on Islamic movements, holds that the different Salafi currents, ranging from religious puritans to political or jihadi Salafis, are united by a common understanding of creed,[90] namely the singularity and unity of God (*tawḥīd*) and refusal to use human logic and reason to adjudicate details of doctrine. They share an aversion to theology and theological debates (*ʿilm al-kalām*) on issues of divine nature in general. These currents differ, however, in how they apply religious precepts to contemporary issues and problems. In general, different Salafisms agree that these differences are not creedal but instead connected to questions of strategy.[91] In short, the difference is one of politics not belief. In the language of Islamic jurisprudence (*fiqh*), they agree on theological and Shariʿa judgments (*tanqīḥ al-manāṭ*) but not on how these judgments are implemented in practice (*taḥqīq al-manāṭ*); in the language of classical logic, they agree on the concepts but not on the instances.

Proceeding from the principle of divine unity, the Salafisms of Ibn Abd al-Wahhab (and Ibn Taymiyya before him) reject the idea of human lawmaking because only God has the right to legislate. Ibn Abd al-Wahhab's famous tripartite definition of this concept requires Muslims to disavow the worship of false gods.[92] Since God is the sole legislator, accepting human-made legislation affords these policies a divine quality, and this implies the existence of another divinity (*al-shirk bi al-ulūhiyya*). al-Mawdudi, a scholar and Islamic activist in British India and later Pakistan, developed the principle of God's sovereignty (*ḥākimiyya*). Muslims are those who submit to God's sovereignty, relinquish their freedom and opinions to God, and "commit themselves to not managing the system of their lives in this world in any way other than in conformity with His precepts and commandments."[93] Note the similarity to the Kharijite slogan, "no judgment (*ḥukm*)[94] except God's."[95] Qutb, an Islamic scholar and leading member of the Egyptian Muslim Brotherhood, revised and helped popularize the principle of God's sovereignty across the Arabian Peninsula through Muslim Brotherhood émigrés who fled there from Egypt during the Arab Cold War between the Nasserite and the Saudi regimes.

All Salafisms reject the separation of religion and politics, as accepting this separation would relegate religion outside the sphere of political power and not only give man-made laws precedence over divine laws but also turn the latter into a freedom of conscience issue. For Salafism, the only sources of law are the Qur'an, the Sunna of the Prophet, and the consensus of the Salaf (*ijmāʿ al-salaf al-ṣāliḥ*). Using any other source constitutes an innovation threatening the principle of a single divinity of God (*tawḥīd*). This opinion is grounded in several hadiths, including the hadith of al-Irbad Ibn Sariya (d. 1295 CE / 694 AH).[96] Despite being rejected by several authoritative collections of traditions, this hadith is deemed authentic because of its widespread acceptance in the Muslim community. It states that

> The Messenger of God delivered an admonition that made our hearts fearful and our eyes tearful. We said, "O Messenger of God, it is as if this were a farewell sermon, so advise us." He said: "I enjoin you to fear God, and to listen and obey, even if a slave is made a ruler over you. He among you who lives long enough will see many differences. So hold on to my Sunna and the Sunna of the rightly-principled and rightly-guided caliphs; bite on it with your molar teeth. Beware of newly-introduced matters, for every new matter is an innovation and every innovation is misguidance."[97]

This hadith is considered spurious because there were no rightly guided caliphs at the time of the Prophet.[98] The phrase "rightly guided caliphs" was introduced later in the third century AH after the caliphate had shifted from the Umayyad to the Abbasids. Experts in Hadith have cast further doubt on its validity, noting that it has a weak chain of transmission. Specifically, one chain of transmission is broken and the other passes through an unknown figure, Abd al-Rahman Ibn Amr al-Sullami al-Himsi. Researchers concluded that, "Given the chains of transmission of the hadith, which either include an unknown transmitter, or do not follow the correct order, we consider it probable that the hadith is weak, and not correct in this transmission or text."[99]

All nonreformist Salafisms reject pluralism and equate it with disunity (*furqa*). This is not because they support unity in a general sense but because they support it as dictated by the principles of the Shariʿa as they understand them. Typically, the unity aspired to by Salafis causes anyone who expresses a different opinion either to split from or be ostracized by the movement, thus producing the exact opposite of the desired effect. But this does not, for them, preclude the existence of a single group that is right, compared with all the other groups, as found in the hadith of the "saved sect": "My community (*umma*) will split into 73 sects, all but one are destined for Hell. They asked, 'Which one?' He said, 'The one that emulates me and my companions.'"[100] Accordingly, since the fourth century AH, the Salafis (or more accurately, Ahl al-Sunna wa al-Hadith wa al-Athar) have claimed that they are the saved sect referred to in this hadith. Of course, other Islamic sects make the same claim.

All nonreformist Salafi currents believe that if Muslims give human reasoning precedence over the Qur'an or use it independently of the text, they will commit the sin of idolatry (*shirk*) and threaten the principle of tawḥīd. Nonreformist Salafis believe that the Qur'an came to save humanity from its pursuit of whims and desires, which, as in Hobbes' state of nature, leads to anarchy and war of all against all. Nonreformists do not trust humans' ability to reach agreement (or a contract) on how best to live in the world. They do not suppose the existence of a coexistence dictated by reason. For example, they believe that democracy constitutes anarchy and faithlessness (*kufr*). For them, the only way to most effectively run society is to follow a will superior to that of humans, embodied in the Qur'an and the Sunna and the (reimagined) practices of the Salaf, especially the rightly guided caliphs. Some take this as far as consistent emulation of those practices, even in habits and daily conduct that are neither related to religion nor to the administration of the community.

Nonreformist Salafis are typically hostile to culture and cultural production, although they often make use of cultural products for their own purposes. Their tendency to revert to the past is also apparent in their antipathy toward anything that falls outside their narrow definition of Islam. According to their narrative, the first examples of unacceptable innovation (*bidʿa*) appeared as Islam expanded across conquered lands and mixed with local native cultures. Nonreformists perceive the religious and cultural poverty of Islam's Arab birthplace as either simple and pure or rough and backward depending on the context. Today, extremist movements find it easier to spread simplistic and authoritarian beliefs among newly sedentary tribes with no deep-rooted religious traditions (compared to settled peasants and city dwellers). It is easy to spread such beliefs in these contexts but difficult for them to put down deep roots.

In the case of ISIL, Salafism has become a wrecking ball against culture, civilization, and history. In their quest to return to Islam's assumed "pure beginnings," they have made it their mission to destroy everything to begin again. They start by stripping Islam of any folk traditions and social institutions and delinking it from its cultural context. In this way, Salafism transcends cultural boundaries and local traditions, tending toward the globalization of Islam by connecting Muslims with an imagined community of true believers that represent the religion.[101] Globalization in this case becomes synonymous with cultural dilution. This abstract and culturally thin community is imagined as purely Islamic, a group of believers stripped of other affiliations and loyalties.

Philippe-Joseph Salazar (b. 1955 CE), a French philosopher, blames the West for failing to recognize that ISIL is an Islamic cultural/political movement with deep civilizational underpinnings that uses visual and digital technological innovations to promote its ideas. In his view, the West would better understand the rise of ISIL if it did away with "derision, dismissal, and denial" and understood that it is grounded in the "rhetorical ecology of Islam."[102] In fact, ISIL is fundamentally opposed to the totality of Islamic civilization in terms of law, philosophy, theology, history, literature, and art and has no deep roots in living tradition. Instead, it clings to selective saying and deeds of the righteous first Muslims as they imagine them.

Salazar argues that ISIL has been influenced by Western pop culture not in terms of content but of the means by which content is disseminated and consumed; ISIL borrowed these means (e.g., the Internet) to spread its own imagined culture and promote its caliphate. According to Salazar, ISIL transformed the nature of the Internet by weaponizing it. Before ISIL, the biggest fear about the Internet was the illegal pirating of content and the threat to user privacy. This, he argues, reflected a failure to grasp the true nature of the Internet and its lack of any moral dimensions. ISIL effectively connected with and attracted younger generations by means of their preferred medium, the Internet. This aspect is neglected by Western media, which portrays ISIL fighters as savages and barbarians or as mentally ill. In Salazar's view, the West does not recognize that these "barbarians" and "psychopaths" are using modern technology and professional (textual, audio, and visual) production techniques to communicate with each other and more effectively spread their ideas over social media. He deems ISIL the first global extremist organization to combine the culture and ideas of totalitarianism with modern information communication technology. In his view, if these technologies had been available to Marxists, the Soviet Union would have more effectively promoted Marxist thought and attracted additional broad-based support. Also, he argues that ISIL represents the first political culture to use modern means of communication with a defined aim and strategy.[103] According to Salazar, ISIL may be able to exploit the idea of waging jihad militarily to establish the caliphate; this factor might prove decisive in its success. However, even if the caliphate fails militarily, its cultural and rhetorical power will survive. The challenge in the long term will be to restore trust in the human sciences to combat the culture of "the caliphate."[104]

It is important to note that ISIL is not the only armed organization to smartly and effectively use the Internet. Other (non-Islamic) right-wing, religious, and extremist groups have successfully used the Internet to promote their ideals, secure resources, and mobilize communities. Salazar's arguments need to be enriched with an understanding of instrumentalism and a historical examination of how individuals with established secular and rationalist beliefs commit violent acts in the name of ideology. By focusing on instrumentalist approaches, we can understand how the Internet's functional characteristics are neutral toward heinous acts destructive to human societies and to the moral core of religions. However, this functionalism has completely modern motivations, since the Internet is both a tool and a source of knowledge. Since Internet users interact with ISIL's pictures and audio-visual messages, they participate in the production and dissemination of ISIL's messages and objectives. In this sense, ISIL is a modern movement, explicable in terms of modern history not a historical or creedal past of which it makes selective and strategic use.

In my view, the goal of establishing the caliphate was not the main attraction for potential recruits and supporters but rather sectarian conflict in Iraq and ISIL's military capacity. More important still was the collapse of the nation-state in Iraq and Syria, which created a vacuum of political and social authority. In fact, ISIL had already reached its apogee when it declared the reestablishment of the caliphate in 2014 CE. Shortly thereafter its power began to decline due to splits within the Islamist constituency whose allegiance it demanded. Islamist movements, particularly other jihadi militants, branded ISIL fighters infidels and actively challenged the organization's religious leadership, and the declaration of the caliphate further fragmented potential communities of supporters and provoked a spiral of mutual excommunication (*takfīr*) among the militants. Rather than bolstering the organization, establishing the caliphate thus became a source of weakness for ISIL.

Per Salazar, Salafism of this kind is thus not a matter of preserving traditions or heritage. Jihadi Salafism, in its various guises, often uses its conception of "pure Islam," indoctrination, and imposing social controls to destroy both traditions and heritage. Indeed, the centuries-long process of modernization and its incorporation into Western hegemony makes developed liberal democracies more closely tied to their traditions and heritage than Salafis or even than authoritarian Muslim states that have either severed or instrumentalized their links with tradition and heritage. From this perspective, the Islamic revival/awakening movement is a kind of "return" in and of itself, but not a return to traditional Islam and not to Islamic civilization. In fact, it is diametrically opposed to both, as demonstrated by the fact that it broke away from the four well-established Sunni schools of Islamic jurisprudence in favor of an inferior alternative lacking their solid foundations. Salafism does not acknowledge actually existing Muslim societies as Islamic, and it disparages their cultural and religious heritage. It acknowledges "religion" only as it conceives it, disconnected from real societies, and "purely" revealed. Likewise, it recognizes only the imagined Islamic community: the abstract Muslim community severed from any historical context and an imagined Medina depicted in cherry-picked hadiths, biographies, and tales of conquest. Jihadi Salafism's pure Islamic umma is an abstract holy community that has never existed and never will.[105]

Reformist Salafis also seek a return to "pure" Islam to cleanse it of impurities, innovations, and obsolete traditions. However, they aim to develop Muslim society and reconcile Islam with modernity so that modernization does not become a process of elimination of Muslim identity and culture. Returning to the original Islam is a means of purging it of elements of degeneracy, obstacles to progress, and a retrograde view of history. It aims to advance Muslim societies *within* Islamic civilization, not *outside* it, and within the cultural and national contexts of the believers. From this perspective, anything that hinders this reconciliation with modernity is a backward tradition that obstructs progress. Given the connotations that the term *Salafi* now carries, reformists are *metaphorical* Salafis.

REASON AND REVELATION

There was, then, a reformist appeal to the Salaf, drawing among others on Muʿtazilite sources and the traditions of Ashʿari theologians (*mutakallimūn*). This Salafism has been lost—or elided—with the rise of militant Salafi positions that are alienated from and hostile to both the Islamic cultural heritage and to renewal and modernization (democracy cannot be considered a modern development of the spirit of shūrā nor reconciled with it, and the mere mention of democracy is a slippery slope to heretical innovation and ultimately to kufr). In exegesis, however, what is typically meant by Salafism is the model presented by Ibn Taymiyya and by Ibn Hanbal's polemics against Jahmism and rationalist schools of thought, such as the Muʿtazilite school.

Ibn Taymiyya has important things to say about the clash of proof from reason with proof from revelation, on which he elaborates in the following passage:

> When it is said that two proofs conflict with each other, whether both are based on revelation, or both on reason, or whether one is based on tradition and the other on reason, it must be said that they must either be both definitive, both speculative, or one definitive and the other speculative. If both are definitive, it is not possible for them to be in contradiction, whether both are based on tradition or on reason, or one is based on reason and the other on tradition. All rational people agree upon this: the meaning of a definitive proof is certain, and its result cannot be false. Therefore, if two definitive proofs contradict each other, then two opposites are consistent, which is impossible: Moreover, if any allegedly definitive proof is believed to contradict another, then one or both of the proofs must not be definitive, or the things proved must not be contradictory; and if the things proved contradict each other, this prevents the two proofs conflicting. If one of the contradictory proofs is definitive and not the other, then the definitive proof must, rational people agree, be given precedence, whether it is derived from revelation or from reason, since a speculative argument is not a certainty. If both are speculative arguments, then one has to ask which is more likely, and that is given precedence, whether it is derived from tradition or from reason.[106]

The question is who decides which speculative argument takes precedence over the other. Here Ibn Taymiyya gives us a general rule: "If Islamic law and reason contradict, precedence must be given to Islamic law, because reason attests to the truth of Islamic law in all its propositions, whereas Islamic law does not attest to the truth of reason in all its propositions, and the truth of knowledge does not depend on every proposition of reason."[107]

In short, the function of reason is subordinate to the revealed text. Reason does not govern the revealed text but explains it, defends it, and may be used to deduce propositions from other concepts whose creedal truth is accepted, without reason determining their validity. As another source of inspiration for modern Salafism and a follower of Ibn Taymiyya stated, "I knew my Lord via my Lord, and if not for my Lord, I would not have known my Lord."[108] Salafis totally reject the process of deriving religious rulings by independent analogy (*qiyās*) when it dispenses with religious texts as the Ahl al-Ra'y (proponents of opinion) would do.

While Salafism rejects the use of reasoned opinion (*ra'y*) and rational preference (*istiḥsān*), Ẓāhirism—a school of Islamic jurisprudence—accepts logic and inference to understand texts but gives tradition precedence. For example, the theologian Abu Muhammad 'Ali Ibn Ahmad Ibn Sa'id Ibn Hazm (994–1064 CE / 384–456 AH), the leading proponent and codifier of the Ẓāhirī school of Islamic thought, entirely rejects the use of analogy. As far as Ibn Hazm is concerned, Shari'a contains everything we need to know about religion; analogy is unnecessary because anything not explicitly mentioned by God or His messenger is in principle permissible. This position also makes it possible to limit religious knowledge to the text, leaving reason unconstrained outside these limits; it allows cognitive secularization to take place by understanding and explaining issues and phenomena not mentioned in the text through human reason. This is Ibn Hazm's position with regard to *fiqh* (Islamic jurisprudence). When it comes to theology, he criticizes the inference from the observable to the metaphysical; since they are different in kind; to do so would be to draw an analogy between "the metaphysical and something of a different kind."[109]

This does not mean that the Shari'a is rigid and frozen. It is true that according to this conception reason does not govern Qur'anic revelation, but reason (including that of Ibn Taymiyya) has nonetheless operated and operates outside the manifest meaning of the Qur'an in legal and other matters.

In fact, nineteenth-century CE reformists' return to Ibn Taymiyya might be considered proof of the fact that one model of Salafism sees ijtihād as the other side of adherence to the fundamentals: Ibn Taymiyya in his rulings and fatwas attempted to revive ijtihād; he even faced imprisonment because of some of his bold, original fatwas (which have been adopted today in many Islamic countries), particularly regarding divorce. It is for this reason that many of his contemporaries describe him as a reformer (in his age) despite the fact that many opposed him for doctrinal reasons. In any case, he was neither the Ibn Abd al-Wahhab nor the al-Mawdudi nor the Qutb of his time.

The prominent Moroccan scholar, Muhammad al-Jabiri (1935–2010 CE), suggested that Ibn Taymiyya was inspired by Ibn Hazm's Ẓāhirism and Ibn Rushd's *Exposition of the Methods of Proof.*[110] Ibn Rushd, a foundational Muslim philosopher, follows Ibn Hazm in adhering to the manifest meaning of the text, supporting it by rational deduction and understanding meanings not necessarily from the literal meaning of words but from context—even if this demands a rereading of the whole Qur'an.[111] As such, the context is more important that the immediate meaning of words and analogy between similar things and consensus. While Ibn Taymiyya, Ibn Rushd, and Ibn Hazm were not against understanding the text based on consensus when it existed, they believed in different levels of consensus. Ibn Hazm saw a hierarchy of consensus and only accepted the consensus of the companions of the Prophet, excluding later generations. Ibn Rushd accepted the consensus of the companions and others alike; his book of legal theory entitled *Al-Ḍarūrī fī Uṣūl al-Fiqh* summarized and revised al-Ghazali's *Al-Mustaṣfā* to "purge" it of defects and incorporate legal evidence from the Qur'an, the Sunna, and the consensus of the community.

With respect to theological debates, in which Ibn Taymiyya, Ibn Rushd, al-Ghazali, and others participated, the dispute does not focus on the agreed principles of deduction but rather on the secondary issue of the meaning of the verses describing divine attributes. Are these verses to be understood in their manifest sense or interpreted allegorically? Ibn Taymiyya argues that the texts on divine attributes should be understood literally, given the consensus of the Salaf on the matter and the lack of evidence from the text itself that would mandate an interpretive reading. Meanwhile, Ibn Rushd argued that, in contrast to practical issues such as prayer and fasting, there is no consensus when it comes to questions established through reflection and reasoning, including knowledge of God and His names and attributes; in this he follows al-Ghazali and al-Juwayni. He concludes that the commoners (*al-'āmma*) should take the literal meaning of the text while the elite (*al-khāssa*) can consider the esoteric meanings. Despite Ibn Hazm's insistence on relying on the text and the outward meaning of the Qur'an and the Sunna (Ẓāhirism) in jurisprudence, when it comes to the divine attributes, Ibn Taymiyya paradoxically describes Ibn Hazm as a Jahmi given to allegorical exegesis.

How can we then accept that they all agreed that the understanding of the text depended on context, particularly since the question here is not concerned with the divine attributes but with innovation and reform? Perhaps al-Jabiri reached this conclusion because he considered the reasons for the revelation of particular verses (*asbāb al-nuzūl*) relevant to be the context, even though jurisprudence distinguishes between the context and the reasons for the revelation.

Al-Jabiri, who devoted himself to writing an interpretation of the Qur'an during the first decade of the twentieth century CE, was not a pioneer in this regard but was attempting to apply this approach to an overall reading of the Qur'an. Many before him believed that understanding the text must rely also on the specific circumstances under which a particular verse was revealed and not the general sense of the terms or sentence. However, given the absence of a full and reliable historical record, these circumstances are not always known or definitively ascertainable. Stories relating the context for revelation were themselves orally circulated for centuries before being written down,[112] and sometimes the Qur'an itself is the source for the specific circumstances. This means that, since it is rarely a matter of historical fact, establishing the context for a particular verse's revelation is itself no more than a form of interpretive exegesis.

Study of biographies of the Prophet can also reveal additional historical and social contextual information beyond the immediate circumstances under which a verse was revealed.[113] These biographies, in particular, can provide detail on the existence of a custom that seemed socially beneficial or on the codification of things that the Prophet did not object to. Ibn Hazm recorded an example: the Prophet based the call to prayer on a vision that one of his companions, Abdullah Ibn Zayd Ibn Tha'laba (d. 653 CE / 32 AH), had seen in a dream. Similarly, Abdullah Ibn Jahsh (d. 624 CE / 3 AH), the Prophet's brother-in-law and companion, was the first to allocate one-fifth of the spoils to the Prophet after the raid on a caravan of Quraysh at Nakhla between Mecca and al-Ta'if, a practice in conformity with the custom of the pre-Islamic tribal system toward the tribal sheikh.[114] The verse on the one-fifth share confirmed this. However, the rule remains that the divine revelation in its essence is a prophetic message and not just a series of political responses to specific circumstances. The verses with rulings and laws are far less common in the Qur'an than verses on faith and morality.[115] Clinging to literal responses to specific circumstances marginalizes the deep religious element of the prophetic message.

Regressive Salafis do not see the difference between verses given as an answer to particular issues under specific historical circumstances and spiritual and moral religious verses. They are all understood literally, and they are all applicable for all times and places. Nor do they clearly differentiate between verses concerning *'ibādāt* (worship) and those concerning *mu'āmalāt* (practical aspects of life), a distinction that even Ibn Taymiyya made. It is impossible to understand the latter kind of verse without reference to sociohistorical context.

This kind of Salafism refuses to grant precedence to logical or rational deduction in interpreting verses of the Qur'an. Instead, it relies on *atharī* interpretation (based on narration of the sayings and deeds of the prophet) that is not reasoned, explanatory, or implied.[116] It eschews the understanding of monotheism (*tawḥīd*) in terms of belief according to the various sects of theologians (*mutakallimūn*), including the Ash'ari, Māturīdi, and Mu'tazilas. It breaks with these schools regarding the rules of inference, the sources of evidence, the hierarchy of evidence, and the general approach taken. Indeed, Salafism confronts them directly, particularly the Mu'tazilas. Salafis, as the trend of the People of the Hadith (Ahl al-Hadith), associated the Mu'tazilas with Jahmism, considering both a single entity with varying degrees of adherence to Jahmi doctrines.[117] This was also one of the reasons for the violent physical and intellectual struggle between the Hanbalis and the Shafi'is, who were closely associated with creedal Ash'arism. This pushed the Hanbalis, the Ash'ari Shafi'is, and what remained of the Mu'tazilas to declare each other infidels in the second half of the fifth century and the beginning of the sixth century AH. According to al-Ghazali, who clearly referred to this conflict and condemned it, "Every group calls its opponents infidels and accuses them of disbelieving the Prophet."[118]

For the Salafis, the texts of the Qur'an and the sayings of the Prophet are clear and unambiguous. The role of Muslim scholars and jurists is restricted to explaining the prescriptions and proscriptions of the Shari'a found in the Qur'an and Sunna. There is no room for interpretive difference or religious pluralism. Although differences in Islamic jurisprudence are theoretically acceptable, those who express different opinions are attacked relentlessly. Nonetheless, the biggest source of conflict is creedal disagreements. But this does not diminish the importance of Muslim scholars and jurists. In fact, it heightens their importance, as evidenced by the fact that even the most extremist jihadi Salafist movements, like Jabhat al-Nuṣra in Syria and later ISIL, need the fatwas of their Shari'a experts (*shar'iyyūn*) to justify their practices; similarly, they revere Muslim scholars and jurists and dig through their writings for quotations that justify their positions and actions. This is why these groups' Shari'a manuals typically consist of a brief paragraph outlining the idea followed by a long series of citations from the Hadith and quotes from jurists they endorse, ranging from Ibn Hanbal to Ibn Taymiyya and Ibn Qayyim. They also cite jurists of the other schools (Hanafi, Maliki, and Shafi'i) if the selected citations support their position.

This tradition goes back to the spirit of the early writings of the Wahhabis. While these works consider the Qur'an and the Sunna to be the source of all truth, they extract it not by means of interpretation—which they reject—but by reference to the literal meaning as set out and explained by the Muslim jurist they endorse:

> Ibn Abd al-Wahhab's work became, in appearance, a work where the author's voice was absent. The truth has already been provided; the author has only to lay out the sources and supply them with a few glosses, termed *masā'il* (issues), without regard for the meaning of that expression in the Islamic tradition. The Wahhabi text thus consists of citations, surrounded by glosses whose key characteristic is silence and a failure to derive meanings. . . . This is because additions and investigations are tantamount to a human intervention in the message (*balāgh*), and the message is the prerogative of a prophet acting with divine guidance. If the reader compares this with the formulation of structurally similar positions in the works of Ibn Taymiyya, he will see how Islamic thought had been stultified in eighteenth-century Najd, and how it had lost all the aspects that gave Islamic history its vitality.[119]

Chapter 2

ON APOSTASY

CONTEMPORARY CONSERVATIVE PURITAN SALAFIS OFTEN REFER to jihadi Salafis as Khawārij because of their indiscrete and reckless engagement in takfīr—the act of branding individuals as infidels, including rulers and in some cases even religious forces with dissenting opinions. Contrary to the typical orthodox Muslim conception of faith as something that "increases and decreases. It increases through acts of obedience and decreases through acts of disobedience,"[1] the Khawārij were quick to declare that their opponents were infidels on the grounds of evildoing or sin, thereby collapsing the distinction between disbelief (*kufr*) and evildoing. Khawārij considered faith an indivisible combination of conviction, words, and deeds; the absence of one meant the absence of all. Committing a grave sin, such as theft or adultery, was thus tantamount to apostasy, and unrepentant perpetrators of such sins were to be fought and killed. In contrast, Hanafis divided faith into internal conviction (*al-taṣdīq bi al-qalb*) and external verbal profession (*al-iqrār bi al-lisān*) with no mention of deeds and no provision that allowed the sincerity of such professions to be questioned.

Murji'ism began as a neutral position on the conflict between the Khawārij and the competing supporters of the rival caliphs ʿAli and Muʿawiya, all of whom accused one another of being unbelievers.[2] Murj'ites considered all parties to be believers, thought that obedience to both ʿAli and Uthman was obligatory, and refused to rule conclusively on individuals' fates in the hereafter because only God has the right to judge and therefore all questions of this kind must be deferred until Judgment Day.[3] The name *Murj'ite* is derived from *yurji'*, which means to postpone or withhold. As a result, Murj'ites refused to declare anyone as an infidel regardless of their sins so long as they openly professed Islam, and they famously proclaimed that "obedience does not avail when combined with disbelief; sin does not harm when combined with belief."[4] Murj'ites' unifying aversion for declaring individuals infidels appeared in the first major Murj'ite text written by Hasan Ibn Muhammad Ibn al-Hanafiyya (d. 718 CE / 100 AH). Murj'ites continued to shy away from declaring individuals as infidels even after the ascension of the Umayyad caliphate, which they accused of "deviation" from the right path, and at some points rebelled against.[5]

Although this principle later unraveled, only to be contained in the process of Sunnization,[6] it was also adopted by some rationalist schools, such as the Māturīdis. The Ash'aris likewise took a similar position on the relationship between sincere conviction, words, and deeds. In addition, the Murj'ite position was popular with rulers because it postponed their being held to account for their actions until after death; their reckoning was with God, and not the concern of their subjects (the masses and the clergy). Because the declaration of a ruler as infidel is the only way to justify rebellion against him (*khurūj*), Murj'ism provided no religious warrant for rebellion and ensured obedience. Several early classical works report that the caliph al-Ma'mun said that "Murj'ism is the religion of kings."[7]

Both Salafis and Twelver Shi'a reject the Murj'ite view that faith is only a matter of professing doctrine openly because they believe that the Qur'an links word and deed explicitly.[8] However, they also reject the Kharijite principle on declaring individuals infidels. For Salafis (and Sunnis generally), this declaration requires definitive scriptural proof that an action amounts to an absence of faith and warrants banishment from the community; the Khawārij view that committing a grave sin makes someone an infidel thus puts them beyond the pale. While this is the main point of disagreement between Salafis and Khawārij, they do agree that Muslims proven to have made statements amounting to faithlessness are apostates who must either repent or be killed. Some hold that apostates should be killed without being given the opportunity to repent because Salafis make no distinction between faithlessness and apostasy, except in the sense that there are "original" disbelievers (*kafirūn*) who have never embraced Islam and apostates who once professed Islam but later renounced it. Both types of disbelievers are subject to the same provisions on inheritance, punishment, and so on.

In theory, all Salafi currents agree that there are three mitigating factors that can prevent someone from being declared an infidel. The first is ignorance: a Muslim who is ignorant of religion cannot be declared an infidel. For example, a Muslim ruler may be excused for misunderstanding certain religious provisions, interpreting them contrarily to their apparent or external (*ẓāhir*) meaning or being misled by advisors or religious scholars. The second is coercion: someone who says or does something contrary to Islam under duress cannot be held responsible for their actions. The third is well-intentioned error or error that is entirely accidental. For example, a person cannot be declared an infidel if they suffer a slip of the tongue in a moment of extreme joy and say, "O God, I am Your lord and You are my servant," or if they do something amounting to faithlessness out of absent-mindedness, forgetfulness, or ignorance. Indeed, someone who rules on a particular issue contrary to God's revelation but who believes in the Shari'a and accepts in principle the obligation to enforce divine commands is guilty of unintentional sin (*'āṣin wa-fāsiq*) and is not considered an infidel or an apostate. In *Issues of Imam Ahmad Ibn Hanbal, Narration of Ishaq Ibn Ibrahim Ibn Hani al-Nisapuri* (*Masā'il al-Imam Aḥmad Ibn Ḥanbal, Riwāyat Isḥāq Ibn Ibrāhīm Ibn Hāni' al-Naysabūrī*), Ibn Hani says

> I asked [Ibn Hanbal] about the hadith of Tawus [and] what he had meant when he spoke of faithlessness that does not place you outside the community. Ibn Hanbal responded, "That is found in this verse: 'Whoever does not judge according to what God has revealed, those are the unbelievers (*kafirūn*)' (5:44)."[9]

As such, giving a ruling contrary to what God has revealed while still believing in Shari'a and the obligation to enforce it is a lesser form of faithlessness, or failure to act in the correct way (*fisq*). Only in the view of some Khawārij do unintentional failures and breaches (*ma'ṣiya*) constitute greater forms of faithlessness.[10]

However, the Egyptian Islamist jihadi organizations that have combined political religiosity with Salafism (and other jihadi organizations influenced by them) have reversed the principle of "excuse by ignorance" and replaced it with "ignorance is no excuse." For them, those who ignorantly engage in faithlessness are apostates since they have already received the Islamic message and the relevant information is readily available. This development shows the influence of the modern state's legal maxim that *ignorantia juris non excusat.* Indeed, contemporary Salafisms are modern even in their endeavor to root themselves in the past and their efforts to frame themselves as a faithful perpetuation of the ancient Salafi understanding. While rejecting positive or man-made law as an alternative to Shariʿa, they treat Shariʿa—which originally meant "path," with Islam in general being the path paved by Muhammad—as a ready-made body of positive law imposed from above that regulates society regardless of whether individuals are aware that it is in force. Similarly, the ideological concept of God's sovereignty (*ḥākimiyyat Allah*)—whose roots are already present in the Wahhabi *Najdi Essays*—mirrors the concept of sovereignty in constitutional law as the supreme authority and the last reference in issues of legislation.

While jihadi Salafism does not explicitly declare that the Muslim masses are infidels, in practice it does so implicitly by rejecting the "excuse of ignorance." Even now, there is still significant debate among Salafis over whether the Shiʿi community as a whole or societies as a whole can be declared infidels. Following in the footsteps of al-Qaeda-affiliated leaders like Abu Musʿab al-Zarqawi (1966–2006 CE) and Ayman al-Zawahiri (b. 1951 CE) and Salafi theoreticians like Abu Muhammad al-Maqdisi (b. 1959 CE), ISIL's religious officials (*sharʿiyyūn*) consider all Shiʿa to be infidels and refuse to grant them the benefit of ignorance. This stance is not rooted in literal textual interpretation and cannot be understood without taking into consideration the sectarian civil war that took place in Iraq after 2006 CE / 1426–1427 AH.

It is useful here to recall that, unlike jihadi Salafis, prominent scholars who came to be considered Salafi authorities did not declare entire communities to be infidels. For example, Ibn Taymiyya did not pronounce the Ismaʿili masses to be infidels; instead, he believed that only the Nizārī leaders should be killed, not the commonfolk. While Ibn Taymiyya branded the beliefs of the Twelver Shiʿa as blasphemous, he did not consider either their leaders or commoners to be infidels because their leaders interpreted the Qurʾan allegorically; he even cites various Shiʿi texts showing their external and internal faith. Similarly, some views ascribed to Ibn Hanbal, a narrator retrospectively considered a juristic and theological authority for Salafis, indicate that he only approved of the killing of the "preachers of the heretic innovations" (*'mubtadi'a'*). Other views ascribed to him approve the killing of various kinds of theologians considered heretics by him, such as Jahmites, without asking them to repent.

However, most Salafi currents still hold that only individuals and not societies can be branded as infidels. Individuals can only be branded as infidels if there is conclusive evidence and they have been offered ample opportunity to defend themselves. For example, the courtroom testimony of Salih Sarriyya (1936–1976 CE),[11] one of the first modern jihadists, indicated that he made a clear distinction between the declaration of individuals and communities as infidels. Sarriyya made the same distinction in his *Essay on Faith*, where he discusses how to determine whether a country should be considered part of the Abode of Islam (*Dār al-Islām*)[12] or the Abode of War (*Dār al-Ḥarb*) based on their laws. According to Islamic just war theory, it is only permissible to wage war on countries categorized within the Abode of War. Sarriyya argues that, while the territory of all nominally Muslim societies should be categorized as being in the Abode of War, not all who live in these societies are infidels.[13] This is a traditional distinction conceptually well-grounded in the juristic principles of takfīr declaring someone an infidel, even if overzealous application tends to erase the difference between the individual and society and between absolute and specific takfīr, as explained in the previous chapter.[14]

In addition, Salafi currents agree that the mitigating factors preventing the declaration of individuals as infidels should apply in some contemporary cases. Because the process of evaluation itself requires human judgment in each case, it is subject to change depending on individuals' understanding of the context. Wiktorowicz offers the following example: if rulers replaced Shari'a knowing that this act is un-Islamic and implemented "non-Islamic law because they no longer believe in Islam, [Salafis] would unite in condemning them as apostates (although some would still weigh the consequences for Muslims and whether declaring these rules as infidels would create a lesser or greater evil)."[15] Whether Muslim "perpetrators of innovation" are declared infidels depends on whether they realize that their actions are wrong, they defend their actions as right, or their actions constitute a particularly odious innovation.

ISIL has shifted away from making this distinction to declaring that their enemies and entire societies are infidels. ISIL's broad proclamation of groups as infidels was inspired by Ibn Abd al-Wahhab's concept of the "nullifiers" (*nawāqiḍ*) of Islam (under the influence of radical contemporary Salafis of the Arabian Peninsula)—beliefs that place you beyond the pale of true Islam—all of which concern doctrine. Through its monopolization of doctrinal truth, ISIL believes that moral scruples are not to be observed when dealing with infidels; as such, it is permissible to betray, lie, trick, steal from, and kill infidels in the name of Islam. By contrast, the Khawārij considered sin blasphemous. Indeed, they believed that being religious was not devoid of moral considerations; the Ibadis among them even rejected enslaving and killing and forbid intermarriage with Muslim opponents.[16]

Both al-Zarqawi and ISIL adopted theories from al-Muhajir's book *Points in the Jurisprudence of Jihad*—also called *The Jurisprudence of Blood*—as central justification for eschewing moral standards when waging jihad. Al-Muhajir's more extreme fatwas include rulings that prioritize the fight against the "near enemy" (apostate Muslims), deem all Shiʿa to be infidels, and legitimize suicide operations, assassinations, beheadings, and violent terror tactics. Al-Muhajir relied particularly heavily on the writings of Ibn Taymiyya, Ibn Qayyim, Ibn Abd al-Wahhab, and the Najdi Salafi ʿulamaʾ. However, he also drew eclectically on any Islamic expert or jurist (*faqīh*) who justified bloodshed, regardless of whether they were Hanbali, Hanafi, Shafiʿi, or Maliki. Although al-Muhajir's book was first published after the Second Battle of Fallujah (2004 CE), al-Zarqawi had already used al-Muhajir's theories to justify suicide operations to cadets at a training camp in Afghanistan and had even invited al-Muhajir himself to give Shariʿa classes at the camp.

Salafis rely heavily on the Hadith—the collection of traditions containing sayings of Prophet Muhammad—to interpret, tailor, and apply the general provisions of the Shariʿa to rulings on particular cases. As such, the hadiths, with all their flexibility inherited from the early generations of Muslims, thus become a methodology for adjudication. Since the body of prominent Hadith does not always have a clear solution to a specific issue, the solution is to use fabricated hadith that meet the needs of the users and the occasion in a different historical period rather than using reason to extract a ruling from the values or general aims of the religion. These spurious hadiths were made up by jurists or political authorities or were drawn from popular culture. For example, while al-Farra' claims in *Ṭabaqāt al-Ḥanābila* that Ibn Hanbal's companions reported that he had memorized 700,000 (or even a million) hadiths,[17] al-Farra' included only 30,000 hadiths in his compendium (*musnad*), and even fewer if the repetitions are excluded.[18]

Historically, those who supported this method of relying on hadiths when deriving rulings were called Ahl al-Hadith, as opposed to those who supported deriving rulings based on reasoning (Ahl al-Ra'y). It is not a coincidence then that Abu Hanifa, the founder of the Hanafi madhab and a prominent jurist of Ahl al-Ra'y, recognized the authenticity of only a few dozen hadiths. Although supporters of Ahl al-Hadith collectively opposed those who supported Ahl al-Ra'y, they disagreed over the authenticity of certain hadiths. In fact, the Ahl al-Hadith scholarly stream among narrators that emerged at the end of the second century and the beginning of the third century AH was not homogeneous, and the Ahl al-Sunna wa al-Hadith associated with Ibn Hanbal and his companions, which became the most influential among Salafis, was only a Baghdadi group of the Ahl al-Hadith. While Ahl al-Hadith collectively prioritized the Hadith, the contents of their reports (*akhbār*) differed, causing conflict. More importantly, they typically disagreed on how to characterize a given situation, and thus how to deal with it and which hadith to cite in support of their position.

In our current time, jihadi Salafis continue to disagree on how to characterize the present situation: Is this an era of *jāhiliyya* (pre-Islamic ignorance) or an era of Islam? Should Muslim-majority territories be considered part of the Abode of Islam, the Abode of War, or a composite of both? Should the caliphate be restored now? To what extent does the Hadith establish criteria for a state to be ruled by an imam? Disagreement over these issues is argued by different applications of the Qur'an and Sunna to reality, but this does not mean that the disagreement stems from this difference in understanding the text that is used to justify each position. For example, while some jihadi Salafis argue that using heavy destructive weapons against infidels is justified because the Prophet used a catapult (*manjanīq*) against the people of al-Ta'if, others argue that this analogy does not hold. Still others point to the political innovation in Ibn Taymiyya's Mardin fatwa, which develops the concept of "mixed domain" (*al-dār al-murakkaba*) and legitimizes the Mamlūk's assault on the city of Mardin and their capture and enslavement of its inhabitants.

The Mardin fatwa was (and still is) frequently cited by jihadi Salafis, including the Egyptian Islamist group Jamāʿat al-Jihad, and Saʿid Hawwa (1935–1989 CE), a Syrian Brotherhood jihadi. Faraj, a leading ideologue of Jamāʿat al-Jihad, writes that when Ibn Taymiyya was asked "whether the town of Mardin, which was governed according to the provisions of Islam before being over taken by leaders who implemented blasphemous laws, was in the Abode of War or Abode of Peace (Dār al-Silm), he answered that it was a mixed case: it was not in the Abode of Peace, where the rulings of Islam apply, nor in the Abode of War, whose people are infidels. Rather, it formed a third category, one in which Muslims should be dealt with as they merit and non-Muslims as they merit."[19]

Egyptian Islamist takfīr trends that emerged in the 1960s and 1970s CE held that there were three rules underpinning the declaration of someone as an infidel. First, ruling and legislating contrary to the divine revelation constitutes polytheism (*shirk*) because it allows the state the right to legislate amounts to worship of something other than God. Second, anyone who adheres to certain tenets of Islam while disregarding others is an infidel because Islam is an integral whole. Third, mere faith is not sufficient, as the sincerity of a person's belief is known to God alone. However, individuals' religiosity must be manifested through actions that can be judged in this world rather than in the next. In this sense, Egyptian jihadi Salafis are not preachers but persecutors. As the slogan has it, believers must be convinced in their soul, profess it with their tongue, and act according to the fundaments (*al-iqrār bi al-janān wa al-qawl bi al-lisān wa al-ʿamal bi al-arkān*). These three rules of declaring someone an infidel are all straightforwardly derived from a single overarching principle: there is no allowance or space for individuals unconvinced of the basic axioms.

By contrast, Islamic movements that reject declaring individuals as infidels and believe in peaceful proselytism are more interested in juristic thinking that concerns society's interests and its actual conditions or whether modern democracy corresponds with or can be adapted to the classical concept of consultation (*shūrā*). At the very least, these groups continue to develop jurisprudential/juristic thought and adopt rational and less extreme interpretations in their response to questions and challenges.

In his book *Jihad: The Absent Commandment* (*Al-Jihad: Al-Farīḍa al-Ghā'iba*), Faraj argued that jihad is a duty incumbent on every Muslim (*farḍ ʿayn*) even in a modern Muslim country like Egypt, which he called an infidel state and thus part of the Abode of War. To justify his assertation, Faraj cited Ibn Taymiyya's aforementioned fatwa that deems Mardin a "mixed domain" and thus able to be attacked. At the time, Mardin was under Mongol rule.[20] Although both the city's inhabitants and occupiers professed the Islamic faith, Mardin was governed according to the Yasa legal code, which Ibn Taymiyya attributed to Genghis Khan, not the Turks or the Mamlūks, whose own legal code he had legitimized through other fatwas. But it must be recalled that the Mamlūks under whom he lived were at war with the Mongols and the Franks (Firanja, as the Muslims called the Crusaders). Ibn Taymiyya's fatwas cannot be understood outside the context of war.

Faraj argued that since the Muslim rulers are apostates, they should be judged more harshly than the other infidels. Faraj also stressed that younger generations must be taught that the fight against the rulers of Muslim countries will facilitate the fight against Zionism and colonialism.[21] This is reminiscent of the slogans of the Arab radical left of the 1950s and 1960s who stated that the road to Palestine runs through Amman, or Beirut, etc., meaning that overthrowing Arab regimes and liberating the Arab people is a precondition for the liberation of Palestine.

To justify their doctrinal positions, Islamist jihadi movements selectively pick Qur'anic verses and interpret them out of context and without regard to the meaning of the text. For example, these movements agree that "Muslims were ordered to fight people only regarding the external performance (*ẓāhir*) of Islam and insofar as its rights may be secured from them. At the same time, God has barred them from what lies beyond: what is in the heart and what is hidden behind closed doors."[22] However, they appeal to contradictory verses to reinterpret those that uphold religious freedom, thereby expanding on the aforementioned rulings on the "nullifiers" of faith. To suggest that there is no compulsion in matters of faith, these movements cite verses such as "There shall be no coercion in matters of faith. Distinct has now become the right way from (the way of) error" (2:256) and "(O Prophet,) exhort them; thy task is only to exhort: thou canst not compel them (to believe)" (88:21–22). Simultaneously, they draw on the following verse to assert that compulsion is possible and legitimate, even obligatory, in the outward manifestations of religion: the Prophet said, "I have been ordered to fight against the people until they testify that there is none worthy of worship except God and that Muhammad is the Messenger of God." They also point to the verse, "And fight against them until there is no more oppression and all worship is devoted to God alone" (8:39). It is important to note that even though this verse refers to Arab polytheists during war, Islamist jihadi movements assert that it applies to Muslims.

Consequently, the jihadi Salafi interpretation of judgment, reward, and punishment by God in issues of religion (and the Wahhabi interpretation before them) reads as follows: God judges internal faith, while the apostasy and the enforcement of external manifestation of religion is the duty of those who take this responsibility on themselves, the jihadi Salafis, and the state that they intend to turn into a Shariʿa state.

Jihadi Salafis further justify their restriction of freedom of religion and religious practice by reinterpreting verses about the emergence of Islam. For example, they assert that in the early period of Islam, "when conquest demanded by political circumstances became a religious obligation given theoretical articulation by the jurists, who deemed it . . . jihad in the 'path of God,' those who had entered into Islam under duress became Muslims as far as (the jurists) were concerned. Formal religiosity remains the outward guarantor of order, and that is what any religious community needs."[23] However, the formation and expansion of Islam was more pluralistic, vibrant, and open to theological disputes than these movements acknowledge. Furthermore, since Muslim societies were established and modernized and the concepts of the human, the individual, and the citizen were developed, Islam's essence, ethical content, and its aspects of faith have indisputably become more easily reconciled with freedom of belief.

Jihadi Salafis' reinterpretation of Qurʾanic verses border on the absurd and abuse the essence not only of Islam but of faith. Indeed, these movements' doctrinal position on the compulsory outward manifestation of religion suggests that hypocrisy is not a problem; as long as people practice religion outwardly, it does not matter if in their hearts they are infidels (this issue is left to God's consideration after death). For example, they interpret the following verse in inverted fashion to mean that a person's choice to believe or disbelieve is a personal and private one: "And say, 'The truth comes from your Lord; so whoever will, let him believe, and whoever will, let him disbelieve'" (18:29). According to these movements, what matters most for society is to be outwardly religious. Individuals who are sincere believers but disagree with jihadi Salafis' interpretation of outward religious obligations and duty makes one an apostate to be fought. Although jihadi Salafis agree that only God may judge individuals' inner belief and hold their souls accountable, they believe they are justified in holding individuals responsible for how they outwardly practice Islam. Another Qur'anic verse that they reinterpret in inverted fashion is "And had thy Lord so willed, all those who live on earth would surely have become believers, all of them" (10:99). They assert that this verse justifies their political religiosity and judgment, thereby subordinating God's will in comparison to their declaration of enemies as infidels.

Islamist jihadi movements' interpretation of religion and religiosity is devoid of spirituality and marginalizes ethics, free choice, and faith. By prioritizing formal displays of religion and ostentatious shows of devotion and piety, individual responsibility for action, opinion, and belief becomes meaningless. As such, it is difficult to reconcile these movements' position with any version of democratic culture. While some of these movements may adopt democratic procedures and partially liberalize, they object to democracy's moral foundations that emphasize individual choice, the autonomy of the individual will, and the individual's right to a protected moral system that he or she believes in. In addition, these movements tear down the ethical function of religion that is most appropriate for pluralism and the democratic system. In a democratic system, the majority and/or their representatives legislate, which stands contrary to these movements' belief that God alone legislates. For them, everything is subsumed under their principle of monotheist faith; democracy is a form of idolatry to be fought. Even if individuals act unanimously, they do not have the right to "permit the forbidden" or "forbid the permitted." According to these movements, no loyalty is owed to the state if it is not Islamic, regardless of whether Islam is mentioned in the constitution. However, jihadi Salafists typically permit conspiracy from inside the state and enlistment in the army or other state organs if it serves the cause of jihad. Muslims do not need permission from their parents to embark on jihad to fight infidel tyrants (*ṭawāghīt*). In general, they think that they represent the Muslim community (*jamā 'at al-Muslimīn*), not a community of Muslims (*jamā'a min al-Muslimīn*).

Jihadi Salafis view faith as not only believing in the entire revelation—in God, Judgment Day, the afterlife, and the prophets and messengers—but also ruling in accordance with their specific understanding of the Shari'a. Indeed, believing in God alone and bearing witness that there is no god but God and that Muhammad is His Prophet does not make someone part of the Muslim community; it does only if he submits to the method and law derived from God's words and the Prophet's (the facts to which he has borne witness); he who does not submit to them is an infidel.[24] Sarriyya and other jihadists did not interpret this as meaning to submit to the divine attributes as elaborated in the text, the accounts of Hell, the torment in the grave, or the joys of Heaven, etc. In their view, these are turns of phrase to keep religion uppermost in people's minds, the details of which are inconsequential; the Prophet's companions were not worried about these questions, and it was only during the era of intellectual decadence in Islamic history—which they object to—that these theological issues became central concerns.

As such, these movements' doctrinal position reflects a religious fundamentalism that is uninterested in the concerns of the theologians, ascribes little importance to spiritually and the occult, and goes beyond the Prophet, his companions, and Salafism. This is a point of similarity with religious reformism. While supporters of these movements are aware of demons, angels, Heaven, and Hell from what is written in the Qur'an and Sunna, they accept these metaphysical matters wholesale on faith; any further elaboration on issues beyond the human capability to understand are an "innovation to be fought."[25]

Different Salafi movements fundamentally disagree over a broad spectrum of issues, including political strategy and implementation; lately these disputes have reached the point of division and mutual declarations of infidelity. Because declaring individuals or communities as infidels can only be about doctrine, jihadi Salafi factions make nondoctrinal issues doctrinal ones; the imamate for example is a doctrinal issue only in Twelver Shi'ism, while ISIL turned the imamate and the oath of allegiance (*bay'a*) to a caliph into a doctrinal issue in Sunnism too. Other jihadi Salafi movements disputed this thesis when ISIL asked them to swear allegiance to Abu Bakr al-Baghdadi.

Some Salafis shun politics and restrict their activities to preaching, emphasizing the manifest meaning of the text, and promoting adherence to the outward display of religiosity. Other Salafis engage with politics, starting with admonitions and nonviolent engagement; the spectrum of difference runs all the way to jihadi Salafism, which advocates violence. Moreover, while most Salafis—and most other Islamic movements—agree that Islam forbids the deliberate targeting of noncombatant civilians, some jihadi Salafi jurists have justified the targeting of Western noncombatants like those working in Iraq by arguing that they were directly assisting the American occupation forces. In this case, they draw on Qur'anic verses and hadiths concerning those who help the enemy in wars against the Muslims to prove that civilians are legitimate targets. This kind of Salafism has been influenced by (or has influenced) Islamist political movements, including certain Brotherhood currents and jihadi formations. We should remember, of course, that tracing ISIL's genealogy and intellectual origins does not mean that it is necessarily the product of those origins and influences. ISIL is not just an idea or a text. It is a social phenomenon that is the product of historical circumstances, both social and political.

To explain the variations within Salafism, let us take the example of Muhammad Nasir al-Din al-Albani (1914–1999 CE), a Salafi scholarly authority opposed to both nonviolent and violent political activism. The "apolitical" al-Albani belonged to the "scholarly Salafism" (*Salafiyya ʿilmiyya*) trend, which opposed rebellion against the Muslim ruler regardless of whether he ruled tyrannically. Al-Albani's strict adherence to the Salaf inspired a variety of jihadi Salafi movements, including groups that ended up advocating violent action. For example, he inspired al-Jamāʿa al-Salafiyya al-Muḥtasiba. While this group focused on nonpolitical action, the group's leader Juhayman al-Utaybi (1936–1980 CE), who led the bloody attack and occupation of the Grand Mosque in Mecca on November 20, 1979, eventually gave it a messianic tinge (Mahdism, believing in the return of the Mahdi). He heavily criticized the House of Saʿud (Al Saʿud) for not adhering to the principles of correct religion and for deviating from the Salafi path advocated by Ibn Abd al-Wahhab.[26] Al-Albani also influenced al-Maqdisi, who became one of the most important theorists of jihadi Salafism; al-Filastini, the theorist of the Algerian Fighting Islamic Group (al-Jamāʿa al-Islāmiyya al-Muqātila) and one of the most extreme ideologues of violent jihadi Salafism; and Jaysh al-Islām, one of the armed Islamic factions that fought in the Syrian Civil War.

Al-Albani also inspired well-known nonviolent conservative Salafi scholars. He became an authority in Hadith; for many Salafis, arguments become a matter of "God said," "the Prophet of God said," and "al-Albani said." Al-Albani was not averse to inciting the Saudi religious establishment and "those in power" to discipline opposing Salafi scholars, as he did with the Syrian Hanafi Abd al-Fattah Abu Ghuddah (1917–1997 CE), whom he accused of being "an enemy of the faith of Ahl al-Sunna wa al-Jamāʿa."[27]

Conservative puritan Salafism does not consider itself a political movement or an organization of any kind, even if it forms what might be described as a fraternity. Puritan Salafis present themselves as the true Muslims, guardians of the creed, and defenders of monotheism and the way of the Salaf. Given their focus on creating and disseminating a pure understanding of Islam, they tend to avoid mixing with non-Salafis, whom they consider heretical innovators. At a minimum, they advocate avoiding social contact with non-Salafis—even if they are family members—and refuse to engage in any dialogue with non-Salafis since it may cause them to doubt their faith. For them, knowledge is essentially found in Islamic sources, and to believe otherwise—for example, by drawing inspiration from reason as a primary source of proof—is to cast doubt on the sovereignty of Islam, leading to innovation or nonbelief.

As such, fanatic puritan Salafis isolate themselves from nonbelievers, even calling on Muslims in the "lands of faithlessness" (e.g., Europe) to leave so as to avoid the influence of "corrupt" lifestyles, citing a hadith that forbids living among open polytheists (although some read this saying of the prophet as applying to those living among them in time of war and thus referring to soldiers, and others read it as a justification of the Prophet's emigration, *hijra*, from Mecca to Medina). Those who choose to remain mostly isolate themselves within their own communities, part of the imagined global community of true Muslims. Rather than nationalism, patriotism, or nationality, puritan Salafis are united by creed. This principle of emigrating to a place where it is possible to worship freely and the dogmatic imitation of the Prophet's deed even led al-Albani to issue fatwas telling Palestinians to leave Palestine (including Jerusalem) because it is no longer in the Abode of Peace and, as he wrote, because "weak and humiliated" people may lose their religion "in the long term." He ultimately recanted this position due to the shocked condemnation it received.[28]

Followers of puritan Salafism disagree with political and jihadi Salafis because they reject any involvement in antiregime political activity. Because no political parties existed during the time of the Prophet, and no demonstrations, sit-ins, or revolutions occurred against the rulers, individuals should not be involved in these political activities. Instead, the faithful should only offer admonishment and recommendations.

Puritan Salafis commonly accuse Salafis who join political organizations of being misled by the Muslim Brotherhood. In particular, the Saudi leadership exploits this tendency to accuse the Brotherhood of being responsible for the politicization of Salafism or even of being responsible for events like 9/11,[29] which the Muslim Brotherhood condemned. They have failed to grasp that Salafism has produced currents that, although they interact with and have been influenced by political-religious movements (or what is wrongly termed political Islam), are nonetheless part of the Salafi (particularly Wahhabi) tradition, and not only the Qutbist tradition in the Brotherhood. These movements have in fact influenced each other.

Chapter 3

RELIGIOUS ASSOCIATIONS AND POLITICAL MOVEMENTS

THE EMERGENCE OF SALAFISM IS MOST CLOSELY ASSOCIATED WITH interpretations that can be traced back to Ibn Hanbal, who "revived the creed of the Salaf and fought in their defense."[1] In the seventh and into the eighth century AH (thirteenth to fourteenth century CE), Ibn Taymiyya revived the Hanbali creed by reproducing Ibn Hanbal's Salafism, adding to it and applying it to derive new positions on the issues of his day. In the eighteenth century CE, a new form of Salafism emerged in the Arabian Peninsula with Ibn Abd al-Wahhab. Unlike Ibn Taymiyya, Ibn Abd al-Wahhab identified Salafism with Hanbalism. Some Salafis consider this a third revival. Ibn Abd al-Wahhab's alliance with Ibn Saʿud meant that the Kingdom of Saudi Arabia adopted Wahhabi ideas and institutionalized them in the state apparatus through the Council of Senior Scholars and its various officials who controlled education and other socialization policies. Due to the symbolic influence that Saudi Arabia enjoyed, thanks to Mecca and Medina and its rising economic influence from oil revenue, it was able to spread Wahhabi ideals through proselytizing organizations.

However, before Wahhabi Salafism swept eastward and westward and permeated local Islamist movements,[2] the term *Salafism* was associated with quietist Salafi associations and movements in Egypt and the Levant, which did not directly participate in any forms of political action. For the most part, these groups received their funding either from local donors or from institutions working to spread the Salafi message abroad and thus were financially independent from both the state and official religious establishment and from Saudi Arabia's provision of financial support—and its efforts to "Islamize" Muslims by turning them into Wahhabi Salafis (at least in the beginning). These organizations advocated a "committed" lifestyle dedicated to the duties and outward displays of religion, taught people how to pray correctly and fulfill their other obligations, and spread Salafi culture through distributing copies of the Qur'an, religious literature, and other educational activities.

In addition, the approach taken by some of these associations—particularly those active among the urban masses outside the Arabian Peninsula—demonstrates that there was not a sharp division between Salafism and Sufism when it came to religious revival. Sufism is a mystical form of Islam that emphasizes the inward search for God. For example, the Jamāʿat al-Tablīgh wa al-Daʿwa—which was to become a Salafi organization in the broad sense of the word—first emerged in Indian Sufi circles, beginning with the Chishti order and then spreading to other orders of Sufism like the Naqshbandīs, Qadirīs, and Suhrawardīs.[3] As it spread throughout the Indian subcontinent, these Sufi orders confronted and reacted to other forms of popular religiosity; building on a long-established conviction to propagate the "correct Islam," it ultimately began to espouse a form of Salafism. Even though one of the defining features of Wahhabi Salafism was a hostility toward Sufism that sometimes went as far as accusing Sufis of polytheism and declaring them as infidels, Indian Sufism's "Salafi" tendency was further entrenched by contact with Arab and Saudi Islam.

To compete with Sufism, early Salafi reformists established associations in urban centers to provide an outlet for religious enthusiasm. These associations included the Young Men's Muslim Association and the Islamic Guidance Society, which appealed to the intelligentsia and had branches in Egypt, Syria, and Iraq. Gibb, an Orientalist historian and expert on Arabic literature, described these associations as follows: "It is true that these societies sometimes seem to stress outward loyalties rather than the inner religion; but, as instruments of modern apologetic and the maintenance of the tradition of worship, they occupy at present a special place in the religious life of the Muslim East."[4]

It is important to note that this type of Salafism was not necessarily Hanbali. Instead, this Salafism began as an effort to familiarize the masses with the religious principles and the fulfillment of religious obligations and commandments;

over time, it transformed into a puritanical call to impose a particular lifestyle on communities. For example, contrary to a popular religiosity that promoted good neighborliness, this type of Salafism sought to impose dhimmī-tude—a permanent state of subjection and discrimination that can only be escaped by conversion—on non-Muslim citizens and prohibit social contact with them. In addition, Salafism challenged various manifestations of modernization at the state level and sought to impose social control on liberties, especially in art and literature. Various organizations in Egypt like al-Gamʿiyya al-Sharʿiyya, the Jamāʿat al-Tablīgh wa al-Daʿwa,[5] the Islamic Daʿwa Society, Anṣār al-Sunna al-Muḥammadiyya, and the Good Islamic Ethics Society sought to promote a particular puritan religiosity among the masses by institutionalizing Salafism. While these organizations were not political parties, most of them disseminated a Salafi culture that was relatively hostile toward ideologies, political parties, modern lifestyles, and mixed education for males and females (so-called imported ideas), thereby restricting popular culture and turning it against any renewal other than its own. Some of these Salafi groups abstained from politics, tolerated moderate forms of Sufism, and advocated submission to whoever the ruler (*walī al-amr*)[6] might be. Other groups, while not overtly political, served as a sanctuary for Islamic activists; still others received direct support from political-religious movements.

Sustained efforts to publish and distribute Salafi scholarship in the early twentieth century CE illustrates the extent to which this early form of popularizing Salafism and reformism overlapped on some issues and diverged on others. For example, Anṣār al-Sunna al-Muḥammadiyya encouraged and supported publishers, like al-Maktaba al-Salafiyya, in producing new editions of early Salafis, specifically Ibn Taymiyya and Ibn Qayyim al-Jawziyya. Indeed, the famous reformist Abduh was one of the first to take an interest in publishing certain of Ibn Taymiyya's works, as illustrated by his *Averting the Conflict between Reason and Revelation* and *The Way of the Prophetic Sunna*.[7] However, other associations like the sharʿiyya Society, led by Mahmoud Muhammad Khattab al-Subki (1858–1933 CE) (an Ashʿari Maliki scholar), disagreed significantly with Ibn Taymiyya, Ibn Qayyim, and the Wahhabi Salafi school, going so far as to call them misguided infidels. Dār al-Manār—another Egyptian publisher, which published the *Al-Manār* journal—even published a book by Salih Ibn Mahdi al-Muqbili, a Yemeni Zaydi Sheikh, because of its Salafi reformist spirit.[8]

From the onset, establishment scholars active in these associations often responded to secular, liberal, and even religious renaissance intellectuals in a Salafi fashion. For example, Muhammad al-Khidr Husayn (1876–1958 CE), an Islamic scholar, littérateur, researcher, poet, and founder and chair of the Islamic Guidance Association, wrote a refutation of ʿAli Abd al-Raziq's (1888–1966 CE) famous *Islam and the Foundations of Government*.[9] Published in 1925 CE, Abd al-Raziq's book suggested that there was no need for a caliphate and that Islam had minimal relevance to the specific nature of political systems (i.e., that there is no Islamic system of rule). Other scholars wrote similar responses to Taha Husayn's *On Pre-Islamic Poetry*, which argued that some pre-Islamic poetry was inauthentic; many interpreted this as saying that parts of the Qur'an itself could be historically inaccurate for the same reasons. Both books were highly controversial; in addition to al-Khidr Husayn's refutation of Abd al-Raziq's book, Rida publicly attacked both books. In particular, the ferocity of the attacks on Taha Husayn forced him to remove the offending chapters from his book and reissue it under a new title, *On Jahili Poetry*, which was ultimately banned, and he faced legal action.

The most ubiquitous type of Salafi association does not fall under any the models of religiosity mentioned previously but instead intersects with them through the culture it seeks to propagate. Take, for example, Egypt's Sharʿiyya Society,[10] founded in 1912 CE by al-Subki.[11] It propagated a religion "free of innovations and superstitions," organized Qur'an memorization classes, was active in charity work, and provided social services. While the Society adhered closely to the Associations Law and avoided involvement in politics, its declared aims illustrate its Salafi credentials: "fighting innovations and superstitions that have become so prevalent as to be considered [true] religion and observing virtue and the upright law and the guidance of the Prophet, despite the seductions of false civilization."[12] Salafism, in the sense previously formulated, cannot necessarily be traced back to Ibn Taymiyya or Ibn Hanbal. Nor is it limited to a specific current like Wahhabism in the sense of war on innovation and the return to the "upright law and the guidance of the Prophet."

In his *Fatwas of the Imams Silencing the Innovators*, al-Subki presents an "endless" series of traditions containing the sayings of Prophet Muhammad that condemn innovation. Could the Prophet have been so concerned with innovation at a time when the primary aim was to establish a new mission?

How could innovation have been so widespread to become a theme of so many assumed hadiths when Islam itself was still so new? It is as if there were so many novelties at the time of the Prophet and his companions that they perceived every new thing as a heretical innovation, which can't be true of course. That wasn't the time when every heretical innovation was an aberration, and every aberration led to Hell. Al-Subki's position, which he elaborates on in *The Way of the Salaf*, is an Ash'ari position that relies on hermeneutics (*ta'wīl*), allegorical interpretation, an approach that Ibn Taymiyya and the Wahhabis have vehemently rejected. In fact, al-Subki comes close to calling the Wahhabis infidels and refuses to call them Salafis, stating that the Prophet's companions (*Salaf*) are "innocent of them" (*minhum barā'*).[13]

What is important to note here is the definition of innovation as heretical not only because it contravenes the Qur'an and the Sunna but also because "it goes against the understanding of the Prophet and his companions ." In *Fatwas of the Imams*, al-Subki cites Azhari scholars from the four traditional schools of jurisprudence, like Ibn Hajr al-Asqalani (1371–1449 CE / 773–852 AH) and Ibn Hijr al-Haytami (1503–1566 CE / 909–974 AH). As such, al-Subki does not take a unique Salafi position against popular religiosity; instead, his arguments reflect a traditional scholastic position found in classical books from the early years of Islam. Indeed, the Shi'i 'ulama' have developed similar lines of argument on issues of ritual mourning (*taṭbīr*) and other practices disliked by their scholars and reformers. Here, the Salafi and scholastic positions on popular religiosity intersect. As such, some Salafi associations acted as intermediaries between the religious establishment and popular religiosity by spreading "correct Islam."

It is important to note that some researchers do not agree with this broad perspective on Salafism, particularly with how its interaction with different forms of religiosity produced hybrid movements. For example, Richard Gauvain—an academic expert on the Middle East—highlights that the Shar'iyya Society (al-Gam'iyya al-Shar'iyya) was mistakenly considered Salafi because its educational courses were similar to that of Salafi organizations.[14] Gauvain thus maintains that Egypt's main Salafi organization should not, in fact, be classified as Salafi. The Society is labeled as Salafi because it rejected innovation and emphasized technical accuracy in worship. In addition, the Egyptian government ordered the merger of the Shar'iyya Society with the more "truly" Salafi organization Anṣār al-Sunna al-Muḥammadiyya in the late

1960s CE, as they viewed the latter's more radical thought as a threat. al-Fiqqi, a student of Rida, established Anṣār al-Sunna al-Muḥammadiyya in 1926 with the goal of spreading Ibn Taymiyya's teachings on monotheism and to refute the claims of heretical movements, particularly Sufism in all its forms. Anṣār al-Sunna al-Muḥammadiyya enjoyed good relations with the Wahhabi clergy in Saudi Arabia. Ultimately, this merger led to cooperation and comradeship between the two.

Although many Western scholars distinguish Egypt's Salafi organizations from political-religious movements like the Muslim Brotherhood on the grounds that most Salafis are apolitical, Gauvain argues that this distinction is inaccurate as Anṣār al-Sunna al-Muḥammadiyya and other Salafi groups are highly politicized.[15] Egyptian Salafis often categorize the political attitudes of a Salafi sheikh as more inclined toward a "Qutbi" jihadi or puritan "Madkhali" perspective. Gauvain notes that a "Cairo-focused investigation into the meanings of Qutbism and Madkhalism . . . is nevertheless necessary" since individuals frequently employ these terms. He also notes that these labels "were first coined and make most sense in Saudi Arabia, where a third, arguably apolitical (but not antipolitical) position is upheld by most Islamic jurists, including Ibn Baz and Ibn al-Uthaymin." However, Gauvain argues that the usage of these terms might differ across the Egyptian and Saudi contexts because Egypt does not implement Shari'a while Saudi Arabia does. Moreover, some of these organizations—particularly Anṣār al-Sunna al-Muḥammadiyya—had a problematic and antipathetical relationship with the Egyptian government; as such, any expression of allegiance made to then-president Hosni Mubarak was an invitation for accusations of "political obsequiousness (i.e., Madkhalism)."[16]

As Gauvain asserts, there was no strict division between these associations and political organizations. Indeed, although these "apolitical" organizations shunned involvement in politics because it was corrupting and endangered their mission (*da'wa,* or call), it was not taboo for them to assume a political stance. Islamist political activists joined these societies not only as a legal cover. This at least partially explains why, after the 2011 Egyptian revolution, the Salafi group of Alexandra quickly established a political party called al-Nour. Al-Nour, among other political parties associated with "apolitical" Salafi groups, participated in the parliamentary elections, competing against the Muslim Brotherhood as well as secularist, nationalist, and liberal parties. Al-Nour did not hesitate to stand by a military coup against an elected president (a coup that the Kingdom of Saudi Arabia also supported). As such, it seems that Salafi organizations do not believe that abiding by elected democratic institutions constitutes disobedience to the ruler or creation of chaos (*fitna*).

Salafis' call to return to the sayings of the Prophet, his companions, and religious fundamentals was not a reaction to modernity in general but instead a push for self-preservation in the midst of specific types of modernization that rapidly engulfed Arab and Muslim countries and resembled internal collapse. Such calls for a return to the wellspring of Islam have appeared across history as a recurring (but ever-changing) pattern of renewal (*tajdīd*). They appeared with Ibn Taymiyya and Ibn Qayyim under Mongol and Crusader pressure after the collapse of the Abbasid caliphate and again after the fall of the Ottoman Empire. While in each case the nature of the renewal—the form, functions, and role of the return to the past—is radically different, they are linked by their interaction with historical conditions; in order to preserve an assumed collective self, they advocate a return to the lives of the forefathers (the Salafism of popular Islam) or the intellectual precepts of the great jurisprudents of the past (juristic Salafism). It is important to note that this is not an independent line of intellectual development in which every fundamental Salafi jurisprudent produces the same school of thought centuries later. Indeed, no independent history of thought produced jihadi Salafism, and no single tradition carried from Ibn Hanbal through to Ibn Taymiyya and Ibn al-Qayyim and then directly to Salafi societies in twentieth-century CE Egypt or to the Manar School. Major political and cultural developments, changes in lifestyle, and social crises and upheavals motivate new jurisprudential and juristic thinking, which in turn look for jurisprudential and juristic sources that might give legitimacy. These movements then retroactively project themselves as a continuation of those traditions, making it appear as though they are simply their offspring.

In the 1980s CE, many scholars produced histories of jihadism that outlined a genealogy beginning with Ibn Taymiyya and passing through Qutb to the jihadis as if they were connected by a historically autonomous fundamentalist trend that culminated with al-Qaeda. For example, Israeli Orientalist Emmanuel Sivan (b. 1937 CE) begins his 1985 CE book on "radical Islam" with Ibn Taymiyya's declaration that Muslim Mongols were infidels because they followed their own legal code rather than Shariʿa.[17] Sivan connects Ibn Taymiyya to al-Mawdudi and the concept of the new age of ignorance (*jāhiliyya*) followed by Qutb,[18] who he then links to movements like Islamic jihad and al-Takfīr wa al-Hijra. Ibn Taymiyya's declaration of the Mongols as infidels was not endorsed by other jurists, who had tolerated the Mongol's legal code (Yasa) before Ibn Taymiyya under the Seljuks and Ayyubids and continued to tolerate it after him under the Mamlūks and Ottomans. From an epistemological perspective, Sivan ignores the political context of Ibn Taymiyya's rulings on the Mongol's legal code. Specifically, because Ibn Taymiyya was an ally of the then–Mamlūk sultan, who had his own legal code and was warring against the Mongols, some of his opinions were politically motivated. Nevertheless, many Orientalists (and also Islamists) strip historical context in order to frame ideological development as a fixed linear historical trajectory.

When al-Qaeda emerged, scholars directly linked the group to Wahhabism, which had been mentioned rarely in the past. For example, the 9/11 Congressional Commission's official report stated that "Osama Bin Laden and other Islamist terrorist leaders draw on a long tradition of extreme intolerance within one stream of Islam (a minority tradition), from at least Ibn Taymiyya, through the founders of Wahhabism, through the Muslim Brotherhood, to Sayyid Qutb."[19] Of course, reference must be made to a phenomenon that has recently become central to international politics: the proliferation of jihadi Salafi movements in the Arab region after the end of the Soviet-Afghan war in the 1980s CE. The organizations established by the "Afghan Arabs" returning to their home countries laid the groundwork for the second generation of jihadi Salafi groups, some of which are classified as al-Qaeda affiliates and some as more extreme splinter movements.

Before al-Qaeda was indigenized in certain countries, it was relatively distinct from home-grown Islamist movements shaped by local social conditions. By directly confronting the US-led new world order, al-Qaeda formed a military and ideological center for jihad. It called for the use of violence against the US without regard to geography, showing itself to be a product of globalization. We find this in the profiles of the 9/11 attackers: they were culturally and socially "modern men," whose religiosity was ideological. This religiosity served as a definition of identity against an unjust alienating world dominated by the powerful, resembling a search for meaning by alienated individuals instead of traditional religiosity with its inherited functions.

This general rule does not apply to all individuals drawn to al-Qaeda in their countries. Some were attracted to it as a movement fighting the Americans worldwide. For example, the Yemeni regime took a tolerant stance toward jihadis who returned after fighting in Afghanistan because it wanted to avoid confrontation with their tribes and it also wanted to retain funding from the West in the fight against al-Qaeda. While these jihadis did not fight against the ruling regime, they were active against socialists and Westerners, which proved problematic for the regime. In many cases, Yemeni jihadis remained socially rooted in their tribes. While many young men had Islamist or global motivations, their desire to join al-Qaeda was often shaped by their local affiliations and conflicts, social milieu, and psychological constitution. Individuals who joined ISIL were similarly influenced by their home country and environment, financial incentives (e.g., salaries), and once ISIL captured regions of Syria and Iraq, fear.

While individuals' social background cannot comprehensively explain the trajectory and motivations of those who join groups like al-Qaeda, it can help explain the public attitude toward such actions and the constituencies and origins of these radicals. Studies show that alongside social history, there is a more specific history concerning the trajectories of these movements' leaders. Three features of these trajectories are commonly identified.[20]

First, many jihadi Salafi leaders receive their initial Islamist political education through participation in movements like the Muslim Brotherhood, as was the case with al-Takfīr wa al-Hijra and part of the Jihad Group, both of which began as Brotherhood splinter movements. They were unable to reconcile themselves to what they considered inconsistencies in the Brotherhood's ideology, its readiness to compromise, its attempts to influence Muslim rulers and not topple them, and its party politics. Similarly, these leaders may have learned from educated middle-class relatives who belonged to the Brotherhood and strongly identified with imprisoned and prosecuted figures of the Brotherhood. However, many jihadi Salafi leaders began in apolitical puritan Salafi associations before being influenced by Islamist political movements or particularly formative experiences like volunteering for jihad in Afghanistan.

Second, some individuals have been driven to extremism by an intense personal experience of injustice—for example, fighting against the Americans in Iraq or, during that period, spending a long time in American prisons in Iraq, as well as spending time in Syrian prisons. This is particularly common when, after this experience, they are exposed to the influence of people close to them who are charismatic and religiously ideological. Since not everyone who experiences injustice or torture turns to religious extremism and advocates violence, it is also important to consider an individual's personality, sensibilities, and background.

Third, the historical record indicates that founders and leaders of jihadi Salafi groups do not necessarily come from poor or rural backgrounds. For example, key figures like Faraj and Aboud al-Zomor (b. 1946 CE)—both leaders of the first Jihad Group in Egypt—were solidly middle class. The same applies to current members and leaders of al-Qaeda, which influenced its distinct character as an elitist global organization. Indeed, the socioeconomic and educational background of those who carried out the 9/11 attacks did not fit Western experts' preconceived ideas of who carries out suicide operations. François Burgat (b. 1948 CE), a French political scientist and a Middle East scholar, stated that "various field surveys do tend to converge in proving that no such thing as a typical socioeconomic profile of the 'partisan of Muslim-speak' exists. Everywhere, the sociology of the Islamist field lends weight to an identical depiction of reality: that of the social diversity of the actors and the fragility of any solely socioeconomic explanation for their commitment. Everywhere, the sociological study of the Islamist terrain demonstrates one fact: the sociological variety of activists and the weakness of the purely socioeconomic explanation for their commitment."[21]

THE MUSLIM BROTHERHOOD AND QUTBISM

In 1954 CE the Egyptian government cracked down on the Muslim Brotherhood, imprisoning many members and causing others to flee to the Gulf states (particularly Saudi Arabia), Algeria, and Yemen. In these countries, Brothers who worked in education alongside Sudanese and Syrians had a significant influence on younger generations. These members' exile facilitated the spread of the Brotherhood model. Interactions between members and locals in Saudi Arabia and other Gulf states produced various syntheses of Brotherhood (especially its Qutbist strand) and Wahhabi ideas, each of which took different forms depending on the level and type of Brotherhood and Wahhabi Salafi influence.[22] These different syntheses drove Saudi Islamists toward a politicized but more moderate Wahhabi Salafism. These new streams influenced Islamist currents in Egypt, Syria, Palestine, and the Maghreb and left an impact on some aspects of popular mass religiosity via preachers, Salafi organizations, and communications technology.

Within the Brotherhood itself, founder Hasan al-Banna's (1906–1949 CE) eclectic approach—which claimed to be Salafi, Sufi, and reformist—ultimately triumphed. Al-Banna's model drew on the eclecticism of the reformists by emphasizing the idea that the Brotherhood is the cornerstone of an all-encompassing Islamic life. In order to respond to modernists and liberals, al-Banna placed the concept of an "all-encompassing," or "broad-tent," Islam at the heart of his vision, adding mass party loyalty and the pragmatic pursuit of the society's aims for good measure. Al-Banna's continuity with the reformists is embodied in his upbringing, which was influenced by reformist Islamic revivalism. The first Islamic movements to emerge in this atmosphere centered on questions of cultural revival and jihad in the broadest sense (from individuals' struggle against whims and lusts in order to consolidate Muslim identity, to gradual transition to rule according to Shariʿa after the re-Islamization of society and the struggle against Westernization and Christian missionaries). Al-Banna himself was close to Rida. His father also produced an edited version of Ibn Hanbal's musnad.[23]

Conversely, Qutb's totalitarian method, which he developed more than three decades after the establishment of the Brotherhood in the context of prosecution by an authoritarian secular regime, was less successful and largely found expression either in organizations outside the Brotherhood or in Brotherhood splinter organizations. Qutb's strict dichotomies between an eternal and trans-spatial Islam and new jahiliyya and between the party of God and the party of the devil (which prefigured Bin Laden's (1957–2011 CE) idea of Dār al-Īmān and Dār al-Kufr) were alien to the Brotherhood's gradualist approach to building the Islamic State.[24] Using an approach transcending Qutb himself (but lacking his sophistication), Qutbist organizations used the theory of the new age of ignorance to brand Muslim societies and rulers as infidels.[25] As did Ibn Taymiyya before him, Qutb viewed the age of ignorance as an un-Islamic moral and social condition rather than a past historical age. Ibn Taymiyya, agreeing that the age of ignorance was originally a state of ignorance and not necessarily a historical period, writes in the introduction to his work *Iqtidāʾ al-Ṣirāṭ al-Mustaqīm*, "Some companions of mine asked me to comment on the origin of this question, given its great benefit. A great many people have been so troubled by it that they themselves have entered *a kind of ignorance* [emphasis mine]. So I wrote down what occurred to me then."[26] But these ideas concerning individual *jāhilī* (ignorant) feelings and behavior are essentially different from Qutb's inflated concept of the new jahiliyya that became the intellectual basis for authoritarian jihadi movements, including those that emerged from the Muslim Brotherhood and who consider whole Muslim societies as living in a new stage of ignorance, a fact that justifies isolation from this kind of society and jihad (in the narrow sense of war against the infidels). We find this same approach in the work of the Yemeni Salafi scholar al-Wadiʿi, who in a book of fatwas titled *Attack of the Cassette Tapes on the People of Ignorance and Sophistry* describes society as jāhilī, but not in the sense of its being faithless (except for those who abandon prayer). Al-Wadiʿi goes on to describe the same society as one that loves the good, before adding that it is incumbent on Muslims to combine self-isolation with missionary work (i.e., to detach themselves from the wicked but to interact with society for the purpose of the call).[27]

From 1969 CE onward, the rising popularity of the Qutbist approach among some younger Muslim Brotherhood members pushed the organization to distance itself from Qutbism. The second supreme guide, Hasan al-Hudaybi (1891–1973 CE), published an essay titled *Preachers, Not Judges* refuting Qutab's age-of-ignorance argument. In addition, al-Hudaybi's essay sought to refute the takfīri current and, to a certain extent, the ḥākimiyya current that reinterpreted al-Mawdudi's concept of God's sovereignty in takfīri jihadi terms. Aligning with the traditional Egyptian Brotherhood position, al-Hudaybi saw the Brotherhood as "a community of Muslims" and not "the community of Muslims," even if it tried to incorporate other Islamic movements into its organization. He advocated the Brotherhood method of building the Islamic state by starting with the gradual education of the individual and then spreading to society then the government, while accepting that society is Muslim and that one is Muslim simply by articulating the two professions of faith, even if forced.

The Muslim Brotherhood continued its political trajectory as an organization opposed to Qutbism, showing a great willingness to work within the framework of competitive political systems. In Egypt, Yemen, Jordan, Bahrain, and Kuwait, the Brotherhood branches have participated in and competed with other Islamist organizations in institutionalized political systems. Although the Brotherhood has renounced violence and accepted political accommodation with society since the late 1960s CE, authoritarian regimes have nevertheless continued to accuse the Brotherhood of extremism. Indeed, since the July 2013 coup in Egypt, Arab regimes have engaged in intense efforts to eradicate the Brotherhood. However, although some major Brotherhood and post-Brotherhood organizations like al-Nahda in Tunisia and the Justice and Development Party in Morocco have accepted the principles of democracy, including the idea of the peaceful transition of power, it is important to note that the Brotherhood members have not been totally immune to Qutbism: depending on the circumstances and the nature of the leadership, they have oscillated between a more radical and a more moderate approach.

Importantly, takfiri movements do not keep entirely to the text: the concept of God's sovereignty, so central to Qutb's thought, does not appear in any sacred text (unless al-Mawdudi's writings are considered sacred). Indeed, it is an "innovation," if we employ Salafi terminology. From prison, al-Hudaybi warned members of the Brotherhood that the concept of God's sovereignty did not appear in the sayings of Prophet Muhammad or in "any verse of the Qur'an." He went on, "In our proper research in hadiths of the Prophet, we have not found a single one that contains this word, nor is it attributed to the Almighty.... People are thus making a term that does not appear in the Qur'an or the Sunna of the Prophet into the foundation of their doctrine."[28]

In any case, both al-Banna and Qutb rejected the understanding of revival and progress embraced by modernist thinkers of their times who stressed that the path to revival was "clear, evident, and straight without deviation, singular without multiplicity. In short, it means taking the path of the Europeans, for us to be their peers and partners in civilization, the good parts and the bad, the sweet and the bitter, what is loved of it and what is hated, what is to be praised and what is to be faulted."[29] Like many other liberal, leftist, and nationalist modernists, Taha Husayn was not hostile to Islam and received an Arab-Islamic education. Similarly, Egyptian liberals like Lutfi al-Sayyed (1872–1963 CE) and Muhammad Husayn Haykal (1888–1956 CE), author of *The Life of Muhammad*, simply believed that an Arab renaissance required an acceptance of the main factors behind Western progress.

Writing at the same time, al-Banna responded to the same question of cultural renaissance but in terms of "a modern Eastern renaissance... a glorious Eastern form."[30] For al-Banna, such a renaissance would be impossible without Islam as "doctrine and worship, homeland and nationality, religion and state, spiritualism and action, Qur'an and sword."[31] It would also be impossible without taking the debate over Egypt's identity (Islamic or secular, traditional or modern) to the masses.[32] To attract the masses, it would be necessary to specify that the target community was Islamic, Arab, Salafi, Sufi, and reformist. Al-Banna and his supporters assumed that all Egyptians who rejected Westernization would accept a combination of moderate forms of Salafism and Sufism, which was already a reality for many Egyptians. However, from the 1920s until 1952 CE, Egypt had witnessed a struggle between "Eastern" and "Western" schools over whether Egypt belonged to the Orient or to Europe via a shared "Mediterranean culture" rooted in the ancient formative contribution of Pharaonic Egypt to Mediterranean civilization.[33] While Taha Husayn argued for the view that Egypt should be viewed through a Western prism as part of the Mediterranean basin and the "Near East" as opposed to the "Far East," al-Banna advocated the Eastern stance, with a strong emphasis on Islamic identity. Issues of identity can thus arise even within a society that is considered homogeneous in terms of religious doctrine and ethnicity. Tribalism and sectarianism can emerge and stir up conflicts in Muslim society. The issue does not depend on religious homogeneity but on the concept of citizenship, integration policy, and the politicization of identity by colonialism and later by ruling regimes and their opponents.

When we plunge into the world of activist political Islamists, we have to give up the search for an imagined Islamist "intellectual purity." Consider the internal reality of the fraternal world of communist movements, which has been quite different from an ostensible Bolshevik purity. Also consider the world of Arab nationalist movements, the practice of which has been far removed from the ideologues' slogans; in internal struggles for power, Arab nationalist ideals have ceded pride of place to sectarianism, tribalism, regionalism, party advantage, and clientelism, all of which are antithetical to those ideals. The world of political activism brings us face to face with the practical reality of politics as an arena of social and ideological power struggles aimed at mobilization marred by contradictions, aspirations for leadership, and conflicts. Even when, in the heat of their preoccupation with founding and constructing new identities, these movements have rejected the use of Western terminology (in any language), they have not obtained intellectual purity but only indicated disposition. These rejections have not had an impact on the terms that have not translated but rather spelled out their impact on those who have refused to translate them.

Through the very act of rejection, the ostensibly authentic becomes ineluctably bound up, even obsessed, with the same concepts it deems new and alien. The alien element dominates in an inverted manner, whether translated into Arabic or not. The newcomer comes to dominate the passive recipient because the latter does not engage nor interact with it in authentic self-confidence. The choices are either passive rejection or passive acceptance. In this sense, Salafism is a vehicle of the inadequacies and impediments of Arab modernity.

Hichem Djait (1935–2021 CE), a prominent historian, argues that "the Islamic movement is not, deep down, religious, nor is it so from the perspective of intellectual religious culture, since its intellectual foundations are weak. It wanted to go beyond reformist syncretism and to confront political and legal secularism, as well the submission of leaders and statesmen to foreign influence. Yet to resist the injustice of these influences required engaging seriously with the world of modernity, as China and Japan did."[34] *Reformist syncretism* refers to Salafism, and here it does not mean actually going back to the Salaf in the sense of a manifestation of true Islamic culture. It does so only in selective, imaginary terms and through literal interpretation of the text combined with modern concepts and reactions and through its negative interactions with the specific kind of modernization to which Salafis' societies have been exposed and projected interpretations of what the Salaf said—all in the context of responses to contemporary adversaries.

This is not simply a matter of accepting Western science broadly or acknowledging the West's superiority in scientific fields but of recognizing the Western sciences as simply techniques, tools, and skills to navigate in the modern world. Unlike the Ottoman state's chief cleric (*shaykh al-Islam*) and his Islamic legal experts who rejected modernization legal reforms (Tanzimat) and unlike the early Wahhabis (who similarly opposed the codification of Islamic jurisprudence along the lines of modern regulations), Islamist movements accepted technologies of modernity and some of its institutions. This includes the later Qutb, an iconic figure for Islamic extremism's confrontation with the West. By contrast, Wahhabis from central Saudi Arabia agonized over whether to permit the use of telegraphs and radio, eventually doing so only when requested to by the king (and after a broadcast of Qur'anic verses had won many of them over, apparently convincing them that this could not be the voice of the devil); the same applied to bicycles, cars, and other new technologies.

It is no surprise that jihadi Salafist followers of Qutb's thought adopted this instrumental approach to Western science and technological development, as many graduated from faculties of medicine, engineering, or the sciences. Nor is it a coincidence that most of them come from a background in the hard sciences rather than from the social sciences or humanities, whose scholars tend to be influenced by rationalist thinking about society, even if to a limited extent. jihadis accept Western sciences only instrumentally as tools separate from the values that accompanied their creation, from the Enlightenment to the application of the scientific method in dealing with social and historical questions. More recently, jihadi theorists like Abu Mus'ab al-Suri (b. 1958 CE) and Abdullah Ibn Muhammad have reframed concepts in strategic studies and terminology from political science as instrumental tools.

ISLAMIST MOVEMENTS AS MODERN MOVEMENTS

The structure of the Muslim Brotherhood (and some modern jihadi groups) is thoroughly modern and echoes the organization of the Leninist party. Under al-Banna, who considered consultation with party bodies as advisory and nonbinding, the Brotherhood grew to resemble Leninist democratic centralism. For example, the role of the supreme guide is structurally similar to the secretary-general in a Communist party. As a whole, the organization of the Brotherhood historically followed a tightly bound intellectual, political structure based on a membership organized into "families" (*usar*) mirroring Communist party cells (although recent reforms have introduced many changes to internal organization).[35]

Qutb's vision of the close-knit political movement is no different from the Leninist concept of the vanguard party in its democratic centralist form, where voicing an opinion is permitted but only with absolute commitment and adherence to the commands of the amir of the group.

There is a more important consideration to add to our examination of these groups' authenticity and purism: their Islamic revivalist project itself would not have advanced—or even come about in the first place—without contemporary Western terminology and concepts. For example, Islamist jihadi movements have implicitly adopted concepts like the idea of a partisan political or ideological party taking power over and administering a society through state institutions, among many other terms related to mass politics and modern governance.

An Islamist movement that emerges in the context of modernization and the nation-state is not simply following a fundamentalist script that has been playing itself out again and again ever since Ibn Hanbal, Ibn Taymiyya, or Ibn Abd al-Wahhab. Even if fundamentalisms or calls for a return to the fundamentals recur in times of crisis, thus forming a pattern, they are still movements and currents that are part of a given historical and sociopolitical context. They emerge within the framework of a modern nation-state—with army, flag, symbols, mass society, public sphere, media, political platforms, and power structure, which they hope to influence or even remove and replace. Indeed, the concept of ḥākimiyya itself is really just a theological inversion of the Western concept of sovereignty.

All contemporary Salafi movements—be they reformist, jihadi, or otherwise—are modern in the sense that they are ideological movements that have emerged from and are shaped by the pressures of the modern world and use modern means to organize. It is no coincidence that Ishaq Musa al-Husayni (1904–1990 CE), author of one of the first works on the Muslim Brotherhood, titled his book *The Greatest of the Modern Islamic Movements*.[36] In the same vein, it is impossible to appreciate Qutb's writings without understanding the alienation of the Eastern intellectual within Western civilization, the modern state, the role of the charismatic leader and/or vanguard party and mass mobilization (as in the case of Nasser), the position of an intellectual humiliated in the prisons of a modern authoritarian surveillance state, or the emergence of class-based nationalist ideologies. In Qutb's development of a universalist, totalitarian alternative to communism, liberalism, and nationalism, we need to consider his critiques of modern capitalist society, his emulation of and response to Marxism and socialism, and his answer to emergent nationalist movements in the Third World influenced by Marxism and secular nationalism. Neither this debate—which took place in the 1960s CE—nor Qutb's various arguments and examples can be understood outside this context. During this period, Qutb still found socialism attractive enough to publish his *Social Justice in Islam* (1954 CE).

Other Brotherhood theorists of that period attempted to combine socialism and Islam. For example, Mustafa al-Siba'i (1915–1964 CE) distinguished his 1959 CE book, *Socialism of Islam*, and its principles of social justice from contemporary secular socialism and communism. In his arguments about how to develop Islamic solutions to modern problems, al-Sibaʿi heavily relied on the broad objectives of Shariʿa, which made him unique among Brotherhood ideologues of his time. For example, he publicly defended the 1950 CE Syrian constitution, a semisecular constitution that stipulated Islam as the religion of the president but not the religion of the state and that specified Islamic jurisprudence as a major source of legislation but not the main source. He urged Islamic peoples to draw up similar constitutions for their own countries.[37] Al-Sibaʿi was one of the earliest Brotherhood thinkers to recognize the possibility of transforming it into a working party along the lines of today's al-Nahda in Tunisia or the Justice and Development Party (AKP) in Turkey.

In his book *Islam Slandered among Communists and Capitalists*, the renowned Egyptian scholar Muhammad al-Ghazali (1917–1996) argued that while communism was theoretically sound, it had not been around long enough to judge its success. He added that the idea of public ownership in communism was an extension of the Islamic concept of endowed land (*waqf*). In his 1951 book *Thus We Know*—written in response to Muhammad Khalid's *Thus We Begin*—al-Ghazali attempted to harness the radicalism that had begun to spread within the Brotherhood, energized by the fierce social struggle against Ottoman officials and landowners and by the national liberation struggle against the British. Meanwhile, the Salafism of the Arabian Peninsula was still far removed from these developments.

In the case of social political phenomena, like the Islamist movements, there is no such thing as an intellectual development independent of historical, political, and social contexts. While modern activist Islamist thinkers draw on the foundational works of Ibn Hanbal, al-Ghazali, Ibn Taymiyya, Rida, and al-Mawdudi as part of what we might call a Salafi theoretical tradition or what Western and Arab publishers like to market as fundamentalist Islam,[38] Islamic thought has been shaped by its confrontation and interaction with issues like communism, socialism, capitalism, and liberalism and nationalist authoritarian secular regimes. For example, the shift from the Salafism of Rida to that of al-Banna and the Muslim Brotherhood shows a marked stagnation and stultification of the vitality of Islamic thought in that period, as well as a political shift that cannot be explained by ideas alone. To understand this shift requires a logic that goes beyond the study of ideas in themselves to an understanding of how sociopolitical movements influence the ideas that they advocate for and the study of the specific historical conditions that produce them. In the same vein, it is impossible to understand organizations like al-Qaeda and ISIL without examining US hegemony after the Cold War, the occupation of Afghanistan and Iraq, the rise of Iranian power in Iraq, Lebanon and Syria in the aftermath of the Israeli occupation of southern Lebanon (1982 CE) and the American occupation of Iraq (2003 CE), the growth of political sectarianism in the Arab region after the Iranian revolution, the fomenting of the Sunni-Shiʿi issue, and the crisis of the Arab state and its increasing reliance on violence against the Arab uprisings, among other factors.

Viewed from this perspective, the intellectual transition from Rida to al-Banna is a natural one taking into consideration the modernization of Egypt, the British protectorate, the emergence of nationalist and leftist parties, secular movements, paramilitary youth movements and scouting organizations, Christian missionary activity, and—last but not least—the abolition of the caliphate in Istanbul. It is documented in the relationship between the two men, their work together on the journal *Al-Manār*, al-Banna's emulation of Rida's interpretation of Qur'anic verses, his takeover of the journal after Rida's death,[39] and al-Banna's view of himself and his Brotherhood as Rida's disciples. Like Rida, al-Banna opens his exegesis with the eclectic statement that "the Qur'an is [to be] interpreted in a way that is Salafi, traditional, civic, contemporary, didactic, social, and political."[40] The political requirements of a political party and mass movement overcome ideological consistency. This is not an intellectual but rather a political, organizational transition wherein the logic of the political movement quickly influenced ideas. Ideological political parties, especially mass or would-be mass parties, cannot avoid syncretism in respect of the relationship between ideas and reality and between "theory" and practice (the ideologies of secular parties are frequently called theories).

Al-Banna's *Memoirs of the Mission and the Missionary* and other sympathetic biographies suggest that he had an acute lifelong anxiety about the impact of modernity and Western culture on Egypt, a country on the margins of modernization and still colonized through patronizing custodianship and British administration of the Suez Canal. Al-Banna was born into the lower middle class as it was shaken to its core by the transformations of the modernization process imposed from above. Following in his father's footsteps, he began his professional life as a watchmaker, adept at the reverse engineering required to take a watch apart and put it back together again. Angry at what he felt to be an increasingly Westernized and Christianized society, he became a member of the Society for Prevention of the Forbidden (Jam'iyyat Manʿ al-Muharramāt); later, in his first job in Ismaʿilia, he encountered direct colonialism and Western privilege, leading him to conflate modernity with colonialism. Note that while a member of the association, he was also involved in the Husafiyya Sufi order in Damanhur, which for him presented no contradiction.

While studying in Cairo, al-Banna began to view the city as a battlefield between the Camp of Debauchery (Muʿaskar al-Ibāḥiyya) and the Camp of Islam (Muʿaskar al-Islāmiyya). This dichotomous mode of thinking requires an opposing camp that is defined by and redefines Islam. As such, the Brotherhood's ideological deployment of Islam takes shape via its juxtaposition with other camps. Like other angry political prophets seeking to change humanity, society, state, thought, and practice on the basis of a single principle, al-Banna believed that after World War I, a "wave of debauchery swept ever faster over souls, opinions, and ideas in the name of freedom of thought and over conduct, morals, and action in the name of personal freedoms. [It became] a tidal wave of atheism and licentiousness so powerful and overwhelming that nothing could stand before it, helped along by developments and circumstances."[41] His anger at depravity and atheism persisted throughout his life, illustrating how formative these psychological and moral experiences were for both his personality and his mission.

The young al-Banna was motivated primarily by search for identity and meaning in the face of what he believed was the collapse of traditional social structures at the hands of emergent cultural forms. He stated, "I was extremely pained by this. . . . I found some relief by sharing these feelings with many sincere student friends. . . . I also found comfort in visiting the Salafi Library . . . where we would meet with the believer, religious fighter, activist, scholar, and Islamic journalist al-Khatib."[42] He would later write that "only God knows how many nights we spent discussing the state of the Muslims and the sad path that the Muslim umma had come to in the various aspects of its life. . . . We were so upset by where we had ended up that we would be brought to the brink of tears."[43] While this suggests that al-Banna was inclined toward reformism, his statement also illustrates that he strongly resented the status quo, felt threatened by modernity and interactions with the "other" in the colonial context, and felt a bitter failure stemming from the unfulfilled aspirations for independence at the end of World War I. These feelings were compounded by the collapse of the Ottoman state and their dashed hopes that Mustafa Kemal Atatürk (1881–1938 CE), president of the newly formed Turkish republic, might usher in a Turkish Islamic renaissance inclusive of Arabs and a joint struggle against the colonial mandates in the Arab east. Instead, Atatürk abolished the caliphate and began a radical campaign of Westernization aimed at establishing a political system based on a secular nationalist ideology.

While reformists at the time engaged with existing regimes when necessary, they had not advocated establishing a political party with Islam as its ideology. However, another angrier and more emotive current had now emerged from the premise that the collective self, identity, and religious morality were under threat. An even more dramatic shift occurred with Qutb, who was deeply averse to modernity and experienced a severe spiritual crisis intensified by his romantic character (well-attested by his pre-Islamist writings) and his experience of modernity as an alienated intellectual for two years in the US. Qutb was persecuted and imprisoned by a regime whose secular-nationalist ideology enjoyed mass support that verged on leader worship (and which Qutb believed amounted to polytheism). The Brotherhood had become a mass political movement that advocated gradual Islamization while compromising with the authorities. In response, Qutb called for an emotional break with society reminiscent of Ibn Abd al-Wahhab's doctrine of "loyalty and disavowal" (*al-walāʾ wa al-barāʾ*),[44] which urged Muslims to rise above and treat with contempt (*istiʿlāʾ*) a degenerate, ignorant society.

To understand the distinction that Qutb made here, we must remember that al-Banna did not believe that Arab life before Islam was pure evil. For example, al-Banna cited premonotheistic Babylonian, Canaanite, and Phoenician civilizations as key parts of Eastern identity against a Eurocentric historiography that pretended Western superiority, which was particularly common in European racism of the 1940s CE. In addition, rather than opposing the reformism of al-Afghani, Abduh, or al-Kawakibi, al-Banna saw the Brotherhood as an extension of their reformist tradition, albeit through the lens of Rida and from the perspective of a populist mass movement. His work took place in the context of the separation of the caliphate from the sultanate and its subsequent abolition as well as conflicts between conservatives and modernists, pro-Easterners and

Westernizers, and Islamists and liberal Egyptian nationalists. As such, al-Banna aimed to rehabilitate and unify the meaning of Islam so that Salafis, Sufis, sports enthusiasts, and good Samaritans could all find what they were looking for through religion, while preserving Salafi opposition not to Sufism in general but to extreme Sufi rites. Al-Banna sought to build an Islamic society, then an Islamic state. From the unification of the Islamic states would emerge the state of the caliphate, the ultimate end goal. This was not an immediate political agenda.

Qutb's branding of Muslim society as *jāhilī* (living in a pre-Islamic stage) recalls Ibn Abd al-Wahhab's *Matters of Jahiliyya*,[45] written 150 years prior in a context far removed from the urban landscape of the Arab states and the challenges of colonialism. Although calling someone jāhili is not the same as declaring them an infidel, Qutb's understanding of the age of ignorance (*jāhiliyya*), however, resembled and even suggested the branding of societies as infidel. At least some of his disciples interpreted Qutb in a manner that subsequently brought them closer to Wahhabi takfīri ideology. Qutb even described Muslim mosques as temples of this age of ignorance, as illustrated in his interpretation of Sura Yūnus (10:87): "And [thus] did We inspire Moses and his brother: 'Set aside for your people some houses in the city, and [tell them], "Turn your houses into places of worship, and be constant in prayer!" And give thou [O Moses] the glad tiding [of God's succor] to all believers.'" Qutb interprets this verse as follows:

> This experience, which God presents to the company of believers as an example, is not particular to the Israelites; it is a pure experience of faith (*tajriba īmāniyya maḥḍa*). The believers may one day find themselves hunted down in the ignorant (*jāhili*) society, when persecution is rampant, tyranny overbearing, the people corrupt, and the environment rotten—as was the case under Pharaoh at this time. Here God guides them to do several things: to isolate themselves from the age of ignorance with all its corruption, filth, and wickedness—where possible—and to rally together, as the righteous and pure company of believers, to purify and vindicate itself, to train and organize itself, until God's promise to it is fulfilled.
>
> [They are told to] avoid the temples of ignorance—to take the houses of the Muslim company as mosques where they may feel insulated from the ignorant society, where they can worship their Lord correctly, and through that same worship engage in a kind of organization in an atmosphere of pure worship.[46]

Before this there was a qualitative break in the flow of history between Ibn Taymiyya and the revivalism of Rida and the reformists, imposed by modern civic life. This break can only be explained by the impact of Ottoman modernization, especially during the Tanzimat period, and the impact of colonialism and world trade on the Arab world. As such, we cannot think of Salafism as an uninterrupted linear tradition stretching back to Ibn Hanbal. Indeed, Ibn Hanbal's understanding of Islam is not compatible with the rational "progress-oriented" Salafism of the Reformers of the nineteenth and twentieth centuries CE, and it is morally incompatible with the behavior of jihadi Salafi takfīri movements like ISIL, as he forbade open and proud displays of violence and the mistreatment and killing of prisoners, even in the case of Byzantine Christians. Moreover, as we discussed previously, Ibn Hanbal opposed declaring Muslim rulers as infidels.

It is impossible to understand modern calls for an ideological "return" to religious fundamentals and to the Prophet and his companions without considering the ramifications of modernization and the colonial period and without taking into account how closely associated progress, modernity, colonialism, and Christian civilization are in the minds of the people who found themselves belonging to what came to be considered and treated as an "inferior" civilization. As put by the Algerian intellectual Malik Bennabi, it is not simply that the persecuted are "figures from the past," so atomized and stagnant as to be "colonizable." They are what he calls *l'homme post-almohadien*,[47] children of a decayed civilization who evoke past glories, identities, and golden ages in order to confront modern civilization. These people might have given those who embraced Western civilization a chance had modernization been more successful. However, its failures—combined with colonizers' hypocritical refusal to accept Eastern modernity as a peer in its own social context and insistence on dependency—showed them that their fears were well-founded.

While this is the case for Salafi movements that emerged in the shadow of colonialism, the nation-state, and modernization, it was not true of Ibn Abd al-Wahhab, whose message spread in the peripheries of Saudi Arabia and aimed to revive the "true faith" among the tribes, whose experience didn't include colonialism or the nation-state, and whose religiosity was very fragile.[48] However, after the purging of al-Ikhwān,[49] the fanatic elements who insisted on the "pure" teachings of Wahhabism, the Saudi dynasty subjugated the religious component of their system to political power and indisputably took advantage of modernity and the tools provided by the Saudi state. Despite its early premodernism manifested in its reluctance to accept even technological novelties, Wahhabism's regional expansion was part of the crisis of modernization, as it was facilitated by the same crises of Arab urban life mentioned previously.

I sympathize with critiques of the argument that contemporary Islamist movements are simply reactions to failed modernization or challenges to dwindling social conditions. This argument assesses these movements' attitudes toward Western civilization from a Western perspective. However, this argument fails to recognize that these movements are rooted in what they believe to be an intellectual tradition contiguous with the culture and community religiosity. In my view, Islamist movements are modern movements that emerged from and in reaction to the problems of actual modern society, rejecting it ideologically while making instrumental use of its products. While the causes that they champion are modern, they respond to the causes in what they think is the authentic language of an "unpolluted" superior past.

While Islamist movements must be examined as a product of existing cultural and historical contexts, those who speak of an ideological, political return to religion or the unity of religion and state do not necessarily assume that these societies had previously abandoned or broken with Islam before "returning" to it. Indeed, there is not a single serious scholar, Orientalist or otherwise, who claims that calls "to return to religion" assume that people had abandoned it. It is true that religiosity ebbed among the urban masses in the 1970s CE, but in general Muslims today are much more religious (in the sense of observance and knowledge of religion) than they were before modernization. At the same time, they are more secular in their relationship to their social and natural environment and to the human body. However, Islamic movements' call to return to religion is a call for mobilization in support of a political religious ideology. Specifically, Islamic movements seek to transform an imagined retrogressive utopia already present in popular religiosity (since the time of the Prophet and the rightly guided caliphs) into a program for a political movement (with Shariʿa as a body of law to enforce, the rule of the Prophet and the rightly guided caliphs as a state, consultative body (*shūrā*) as a parliament or senate, and the prophetic succession as a self-sustaining Islamic system of rule). This "return" is accompanied by the phenomenon of mass religiosity previously unknown in the context of popular or folk religiosity. It is important to note that there can be no return to Islam as religion and state (*dīn wa dawla*)—as stated in the Brotherhood's and other Islamist movements' slogan—because this will not be feasible in the future and Islam has never been "a-religion-and-a-state" in the past. The state projected on the past by this formula is a modern concept of a secular nature, even if it uses religion as an ideology.

Prison split the Muslim Brotherhood into two groups. One group decided on tactical dissimulation (*taqiyya*) and declared loyalty to the Nasserite regime under duress. The other group rejected this course of action and rallied around Muhammad Qutb (1919–2014 CE) (Sayyid Qutb's brother).[50] Considering themselves to be the true "community of Muslims," they declared Egypt's rulers and society as a whole to be infidels and accused their brethren of making peace with an infidel government. Inside the prison, one subgroup of Brotherhood members even declared another group to be infidels.[51]

Ahmad Ra'if (1940–2011 CE), who was imprisoned alongside the young Shukri Mustafa (1942–1978 CE), founder of the extremist Takfīr wa al-Hijra, documented this split. At this point, Mustafa was an eighteen-year-old with a difficult family situation; he did not know why he had been jailed and had minimal knowledge of Islam and no political inclinations whatsoever. Ra'if states that Mustafa turned to religion, with his hatred of the regime and society growing as a result of the torture he endured while in prison.[52] He further claims that, on the authority of Muhammad Qutb, Mustafa declared the government to be disbelievers, and that it was not he who was saying this but the Qur'an.[53] The seeming modesty of attributing a thought not to oneself but to the text—"It is not me who is saying this but God Himself"—is a well-established discursive strategy used by Salafi Islamists to silence their opponents. The pretense of modesty can be one of the worst kinds of arrogance.

At this time, the idea that the Brotherhood represented not *a* community of Muslims but *the* Muslim community began to gain popularity among some Brotherhood theorists. For example, Hawwa—a leader in the Muslim Brotherhood's Syrian branch—wrote that "all the evidence indicates that this community (i.e., the Muslim Brotherhood) is in all respects the closest to being the Muslim community," and thus he concluded that it was illegitimate for a Muslim to avoid it or to leave this community after joining it.[54] Mustafa Mashhur (1921–2002 CE), the then-supreme guide of the Egyptian Muslim Brotherhood, denounced this argument as "a false claim and a fabrication" and an "individual opinion" that did not reflect the Brotherhood's view.[55] The subject is likewise discussed at length in al-Hudaybi's *Preachers, Not Judges*, which characterizes the Brotherhood as *a* community of Muslims that does not declare other groups infidels. Al-Hudaybi argued that only individuals could be declared infidels and then only under strict conditions. Describing an act as ignorant did not amount to faithlessness or apostasy. Ahl al-Sunna do not equate every sin with faithlessness but they do believe that those who declare sins lawful are infidels.[56]

UTOPIA

Salafism does not only take refuge in the literal meaning of texts; it also appeals to an imagined version of life in Medina in the time of the Prophet and the rightly guided caliphs. Whenever there arises a need for a social utopia or ideal within the prevailing religious cultural framework, many point to early Muslim society in Medina as an example of a vanished golden age in an era of fragmentation, decline, and dispersal. The biography of the Prophet—first written down and circulated more than 150 years after his migration from Mecca—and stories transmitted by early generations and attributed to the Prophet and his companions inspired Salafism's idea of Medinan life.

Importantly, there are significant differences between the vitality of Islamic debates on the Sunna and its status in the second century AH and the sterility of the debates about the Sunna in contemporary political Salafist discourse. For example, Hanifa had strict conditions for accepting stories of the Prophet and a flexible approach to opinion and interpretation, while the Shafiʿi and other scholars accepted more dubious hadiths as legally on par with the Qur'an as long as there was no clear contradiction with Qur'anic verses. Since the details of many Islamic religious rites are not given in the Qur'an, but instead in reports passed on in the Sunna or in Islamic practice, some Islamic jurists went as far as to argue that the Qur'an needs these reports more than they need the Qur'an.

Not all religious utopias are revolutionary. While some are simply a moral ideal of popular religiosity, others are enacted by individuals living in small communities according to the correct interpretation of God's teachings that aspire to be a harmonious alternative society. However, some religious utopias have become political ideological programs that certain Islamist movements seek to impose on society. The trend of implementing religious utopias as political programs would have remained marginal were it not for the partial collapse of the Iraqi and Syrian states, which facilitated the spread of political sectarianism and barbaric violence. ISIL did not invent the sadistic and violent strategies it has so effectively transformed into ritual and spectacle. Indeed, tyrannical regimes paved the way for this development, mastering the art of violence no less horrifically than ISIL. Although it is far more common for state regimes (mostly since the twentieth century CE) to enact violence behind closed doors, in the beginning of the Syrian revolution the ruling regime even filmed and distributed its violent acts in order to intimidate people and deter them from participating in protests.

By acting out Qur'anically prescribed punishments, beheadings, and slave markets that were the embodiment of the prophetic era, ISIL has turned a would-be utopia into a bloody nihilistic nightmare. In its attempt to establish a state based on the prophetic model, it has created a kingdom of punishment that is the exact opposite of a utopia. To justify its brutal acts, ISIL cites verses that threaten "torment in this world" for infidels and apostates at the hands of the believers before divine torment in the hereafter. ISIL has repeatedly argued that while torturing prisoners and mutilating and desecrating corpses is "reprehensible" (*makrūh*), in Islamic legal terms they are not forbidden. To justify this stance, ISIL (and al-Qaeda in Iraq before them) often cited al-Tawba, "Fight against them! God will chastise them by your hands, and will bring disgrace upon them, and will succor you against them; and He will soothe the bosoms of those who believe" (9:14).[57] They claim that God will chastise (torment) infidels in this world through the hands of believers. After 9/11, it became common for Arab intelligence officers—particularly the Syrians and Jordanians—to use this verse when training in coordination with the US to illustrate how "terrorists" think.

Not all utopias are future utopias. Plato's utopia was social harmony manifested in a primitive society in a prehistoric state of innocence. This view is entirely compatible with later attempts to imagine a future utopia that might restore this lost harmony regardless of whether this loss is due to alienation from human nature, the appearance of religion, or the emergence of private ownership, a class-based society, or the state. All utopias share the desire to restore social harmony and reintegrate the individual into the collective. Utopias are typically based on the idea that there is essentially one human problem to solve and the solution will inevitably bring about harmony.[58] This kind of imagined harmony has never prevailed in any ancient community. In these respects, the religious salvationist utopia resembles the secular salvationist utopia, of which F.A. Voigt wrote, "It projects into the *past* what *never was*, it conceives what *is* in terms of what is *not*, and the *future* in terms of what can *never* be."[59]

When utopia is presented as a political ideology that strives to restore organic harmony to the collective, it inevitably depends on carriers who are willing to fight against the different "other," whether this is manifested in the autonomy of the individual or the distinction of religious, national, and cultural minorities. Exactly who this "other" is depends on how this ideology defines the abstract identity of their community. While modern utopias have largely drawn on scientific theories and solutions, religious utopias rely on faith to create a sacred social order whose implementation is a divine duty. When faith is used as the basis of social order in a religious utopia, the movements seeking to create this utopia are not satisfied with establishing an isolated society for the righteous; they seek to save society as a whole. When religious movements are influenced by modern revolutionary discourse, they can transform into salvationist revolutionary movements with totalitarian programs. For example, Sayyid Qutb was influenced by modern ideals, which provided totalitarian solutions for saving society from the crisis of capitalism and modernity. As such, he rejected existing reality and drew on Islamic civilization and religious precents to propose imaginary utopian alternatives that he believed to be fact.

In terms of the return to a harmonious community, it is difficult to overlook the similarity between organizations like ISIL and movements such as the Khmer Rouge in Cambodia. While the Khmer Rouge sought to create a classless agrarian peasant society, ISIL aimed to establish the caliphal state. Contrary to the Khmer Rouge, ISIL did not succeed in taking control of an existing state; however, it was able to establish a parallel state apparatus that opposed the status quo international order on the geographical margins of existing states. The two movements are also similar in their determination to remold society on the basis of predetermined specifications, reject pluralism, eradicate those deemed different, and use extreme violence to do so.

From the perspective of both religious and secular conservative thought, utopias are impossible to create. Conservatives have a deep-seated aversion to utopias that require a revolution or depend on revolutionary change in human nature. This is common to all conservative philosophies and religious establishments. Just as conservative secular thought is inimical to secular utopianism, conservative Islamic thought (e.g., nonpolitical puritan Salafism) is hostile to other movements' attempts to impose Islamic utopias (e.g., ISIL).

Political Islamic movements draw on ideals deeply rooted in the popular imaginary of Islamic societies and their collective memory of the prophetic mission, the rule of the rightly guided caliphs, and the justice of the pious. But this alone explains nothing. An ideal does not, by itself, transform those who are committed to it into political activists, nor does it spontaneously metamorphose into a program for jihad. Whether religious political movements can transform this ideal into an ideological tool depends on existing social and political agents. Activist political religiosity involves a feedback loop; activism itself influences the form that religiosity and belief takes. And herein resides the relationship between the political and the ideological: ideological partisan movements, Islamic or otherwise, are more like ideological 'brotherhoods' or sects wherein members frequently express their doctrinal or activist affinity.

The tradition of positioning the ideal in the past appears prominently in Ibn Taymiyya's work. Ibn Taymiyya believed that not only temporal distance from Medinan society but even geographical distance from the city itself constitutes a move away from the original social ideal. Geographical distance means mixing with other cultures and civilizations, which he believed led to heretical innovation.[60] But Ibn Taymiyya did not make his objective the implementation of a utopia.

Salafis argue that Ibn Taymiyya's book of Islamic creed (creed of Wasitiyya), *Al-'Aqīda al-Wāsiṭiyya,* emerged at a time when foreign "nations assailed Muslims on all sides" against a background of "contemporary materialist ideas and other corrupt beliefs, a shortage of Islamic scholars, and ignorance becoming so widespread that right became wrong and wrong became right, innovation became Sunna and Sunna became innovation; idolatry became monotheism and monotheism became idolatry."[61] It is important to note that the same period that this Salafi author believes "lacked knowledge" is the source of much contemporary scholarship, including works on grammar, literature, language, law, theology and doctrine, and Qur'anic exegesis. Salafi attempts to classify this period of Islamic history as decadent were certainly ideological. Taha Husayn, in his introduction to Abu al-Khayr Muhammad Ibn Abd al-Rahman al-Sakhawi's classical history of Medina, *Gems in the History of the Holy City of Medina*, found much to praise about this era.[62]

The Medinan utopia is, of course, retroactively juxtaposed with the present "decadent" reality. Ibn Taymiyya argues that only an uncompromising imposition of Shariʿa law can suppress the various manifestations of this geographical and temporal distance from the original ideal society. But that "ideal society" of the Medina was not governed according to the Shariʿa, rather Medina produced the Shariʿa. The Shariʿa was not a preexisting system imposed on Medina.

This way of thinking has promoted the popular perception that Shariʿa law is a series of commandments and ready-made rulings found in the Qur'an and the traditions and sayings of the Prophet and his companions. However, even from the perspective of how Hanbalis themselves practice Islamic jurisprudence, this perception is totally incorrect. Just as the liberal conception requires people to accept a constitution, Ibn Taymiyya's perspective requires that people perceive Shariʿa as a set of rules that must be enforced. Constitutional principles are protected from change, amendment, and replacement by ordinary legislative procedures, as if they were sacred. Of course, unlike the Salafi conception of the Shariʿa, constitutions include procedures for changing them in exceptional circumstances and due to historical development. If Shariʿa was viewed as sacred in this sense, there would be no problem. However, those who insist on the sanctity of Shariʿa believe it is divine and must be enforced. This is the task of the "one who renews religion for the umma," according to their understanding of renewal (which means restoring it to the past—a curious kind of renewal).

This is why Ibn Taymiyya goes into great detail on the administrative, judicial, and commercial functions of the ruler and his responsibility to maintain Qur'anically prescribed punishments, stating that "right can only be enjoined and wrong prevented through the punishments provided for by the Shariʿa; God deters by the power of the rule (*sultan*) what he did not deter by the Qur'an, and maintaining the punishments is an obligation for rulers. This is done by punishing [those who] abandon their obligations or engage in forbidden acts."[63] In Ibn Taymiyya's view, the ruler is responsible for halting the historical decline away from the ideal utopia. To do so, the ruler must act in service of the Qur'an and compel those for whom faith is an insufficient deterrent. The state here rules in the service of God. In practical terms, the state's divine right is encapsulated in this function: to deter using its political power what God has not deterred by the Qur'an. Ibn Taymiyya certainly did not think by doing that a retrospective utopia would be implemented, and he could not and did not need to observe that this utopian past was constructed retroactively and had never existed.

Alternatively, the ruler's deterrent role arises from the fact that that God does not deter certain things through the Qur'an;[64] therefore, there are things that the sultan or amir must do in pursuit of what is right. By this logic, the ruler can use his authority to decide, legislate, and force compliance with other matters not mentioned in the Qur'an; that is, in modern terms, the state's duty. While Ibn Taymiyya's words stress the ruler's service to religion, they can also signify a beginning of a distinction between religion and state. However, since this differentiation (state and religion) was first consolidated, a gradual historical shift has taken place whereby religion has come to serve the state even as the state claims to serve religion.

There are always two sides to this differentiation: the imposition of religion by the state (theocracy) and the state's use of religion (authoritarian autocracy that uses religion). In both cases, the state imposes appropriate policies in spheres where religious provisions are absent or incomplete. We cannot expect Ibn Taymiyya to see these possibilities existing in the religion-state dichotomy that made the desire for the Medinan ideal completely obsolete. Like in other works on the creed and Islamic jurisprudence before his era, Ibn Taymiyya had nothing distinctive or unique to say on politics according to the Shari'a (*al-siyāsa al-shar'iyya*) that had not already been said by earlier jurisprudents. The Islamic civilization, like any other civilization, maintained a distinction between religion and political power in the practice and self-consciousness of political power even when the prevailing culture was religious, and before the emergence of the modern state. Along with other phenomena, I consider these distinctions part of a process of historical secularization that predates the concept and reality of secularism (in the sense of separation of church and state or the state being neutral in religious affairs, leaving religious decisions to individuals, and understanding phenomena according to their own internal laws rather than mystical or metaphysical powers). In the tenth century CE, the caliph's religious authority became distinct from the temporal authority of the generalissimo (*amir al-umarā'*); a similar distinction is made between the

Islamic jurisprudents and the sultan. This differentiation was both social and legal. Indeed, these developments were even cited by Turkish jurisprudents when the sultanate was separated from the caliphate by parliamentary decree in 1922 as evidence that this separation had existed historically in both Islamic jurisprudence and reality. This argument paved the way for the later abolition of the caliphate.

Chapter 4

WAHHABISM IN CONTEXT

IBN ABD AL-WAHHAB GLORIFIED THE IMAGINED MEDINA AS described in the traditions and sayings of the Prophet by comparing his own times to the age of ignorance that historically preceded the Prophet. Among other things, this comparison involves an implicit claim to prophecy, or at least a comparison of his mission with that of the Prophet, leading a campaign calling people to Islam during an age of ignorance. As long as revivalist Salafis are battling the age of ignorance, then the Qur'anic prohibition on coercion in matters of faith ("Distinct has now become the right way from [the way of] error" [2:256]) does not apply to them. So long as the world is in the age of ignorance, there is the need for a new jihadi prophetic mission to show the truth afresh. Both Ibn Abd al-Wahhab and his successors effectively monopolize mediation between God and man by striking down every innovative mediation between God and man found in this new age of ignorance. It is as though they represent a new prophetic mission to revive the pure and "true" or "upright" religion that stands in opposition to a popular religiosity replete with innovations.

This implicit claim to prophecy-like mission boils down to three main implicit presumptions that were naturally denied by Ibn Abd al-Wahhab and his followers. The first is understanding present reality as the age of ignorance. An extensive literature proceeds methodologically from the premise that it is an age of ignorance in order to develop the concept of jahiliyya, to be distinguished from both its original use and its later simple or ordinary use as a word describing individual misdeeds and sins. For example, Ibn Abd al-Wahhab himself wrote a book titled *Matters of Jahiliyya.*[1] The second is the claim that, even though the Prophet has communicated his message, right has not become clear from wrong, implying the need for a new jihadi prophetic mission. The third is abolishing intermediation between God and man, a core feature of popular religion that Salafis call innovation and polytheism. Wahhabi Salafism is obsessed with abolishing any intercession or intermediaries between God and man to ensure that it monopolizes this mediation. While popular intercession is worship, rites, probably holy men (saints), and even sacred places and things, Salafis' intercession focuses on following and obeying someone who knows better, who understands God's will! Even though Wahhabis came up with the idea of "polytheism by obedience" (*shirk al-ṭāʿa*), they still exchange one intermediary for another.

Those who discuss a new age of ignorance inadvertently impose their message on others without realizing that it constitutes an implicit claim to be a new prophetic mission. They create political movements that resemble sects in the Weberian sense. For the most part, those who belong to the religious sect consider not only other sects to be errant but also the majority of the population. They consider themselves strangers in a world of ignorance: religion began as a stranger and will be a stranger again, "so blessed are the strangers, who cling to my Sunna when my Muslim community turns corrupt," as the saying goes that the Salafis attribute to the Prophet. Ultimately, radical Salafi Islamists believe they are both strangers and the saved, while everyone else is ignorant.

Since Ibn Abd al-Wahhab seeks to go back to the simple, valid Islam derived from the principle of absolute monotheism, he rejects innovations, intermediaries, and adherence to the schools of jurisprudence. He lists six fundamental principles of his Islamic revival: (1) monotheism and the return to God alone, excluding any partners, which implies an end to division among sects; (2) unity in religion; (3) obedience to those in authority;[2] (4) God alone granting knowledge—no one but He has knowledge of what is hidden, whether in the future, beyond direct perception, or in the realm of the metaphysical (*al-ghayb*); (5) rejection of those who claim sainthood; and (6) combat with other sects such as the Shiʿa, the Khawārij, the dervishes, the Sufis, the Ashʿaris, and the religious practices of the Turks (he emphasized that the Ottoman sultan was a false caliph).[3] As such, following a particular school of Islamic jurisprudence and blindly imitating Muslim scholars is a heretical innovation.

Ibn Abd al-Wahhab widened the scope of alleged innovations to incorporate not only unauthorized forms of worship but also personal conduct. In fact, some of his followers have imitated the Prophet in every tiny detail of dress and appearance, considering anything less than copying the Prophet's personal behavior to be an objectionable innovation. Previously, they disliked using the phrase "Our Lord Muhammad," lest it be a pretext for polytheism. In addition, they detested swearing by objects and venerating the dead and the demolished structures built over graves; they also viewed the celebrations, music, drums, and pipes of the Hajj processions in Ottoman times as a heretical innovation. They even opposed the practice of covering the Kaʿba—the building at the center of Islam's most important mosque in Mecca—with cloth and neglected its curtains until they became rags. They thus brought their society and Islamic jurisprudence to such a state that even changing the coverings of the Kaʿba was later considered a positive development.

The Prophet was born and raised in the pre-Islamic Arabian Peninsula. He was a man of his time in terms of his dress, personal daily conduct, and how he greeted people. Throughout history, jurisprudents and Muslim scholars have distinguished between that which constitutes revelation, legislation, or desirable practice on the one hand and the habits of the Arabs and the Prophet's personality on the other; the latter two are not considered part of the revelation and have no legal force. As such, by insisting that people imitate the Prophet as a man, Ibn Abd al-Wahhab and those who fought innovation were, in fact, creating new innovations at the expense of the spiritual and moral message of the prophetic mission itself.

Wahhabism would not have been able to triumph in the Peninsula without forming an alliance with at least one major tribe. The same is true of other revivalist movements from the Arab region, such as the Mahdists and the Sanusis, who stressed the recognition of a tribal leader, his progeny, and inherited leadership. Ibn Khaldun (1332–1406 CE / 732–808 AH) had already stressed that tribal *ʿaṣabiyya* (tribal solidarity)—the major driving force of the tribe to seize power from decadent rulers whose own ʿaṣabiyya has weakened due to decay caused by the luxuries of the rule itself and urban life—is usually assisted by the adoption of a religious mission.[4] The Wahhabi religious doctrine proved to be an "extremely useful tool in the conquest of the Arabian Peninsula"[5] by the Saudis. The pact between Muhammad Ibn Saʿud and the Ibn Abd al-Wahhab was sealed in 1744 CE / 1157 AH and in 1746 CE / 1158 AH they started their jihad.

Ibn Abd al-Wahhab ought to have seen tribal dynastic rule as an innovation (compared with the rule of the caliphs in Medina). Indeed, some of the Prophet's companions rejected the heir of the first Umayyad caliph, Yazid Ibn Muʿawiya (647–683 CE / 26–64 AH), on the grounds that this was an innovation. However, Ibn Abd al-Wahhab recognized Muhammad Ibn Saʿud and his heirs as imams in 1774 CE / 1188 AH after the principality of Riyadh fell into the hands of the Saudis in 1773 CE / 1187 AH.

Wahhabi biographers reproduce the conversation between the two men as follows: "[Ibn Saʿud] said to the Sheikh: I give you power and protection.' Then the Sheikh said to him, 'I give you glad tidings of glory, power, and decisive victory. This is the word of monotheism, to which all the messengers have called. He who adheres to it, practices it, and champions it will rule the people and the land. You can see that all of Najd has fallen into shirk and ignorance, dissent and conflict, and infighting. I hope you will be an imam for the Muslims to rally around, and your progeny after you will be imams in turn.' The Imam [Ibn Saʿud] welcomed and greeted him, offering him refuge and support."[6]

Until the start of the state-building process after the increase of government revenues from oil exports,[7] during the Saudis' third attempt to unify the Arabian Peninsula,[8] the latent tension between the Wahhabi religious mission and the tribal political power was not clearly identifiable. Subsequently, the mission recognized the political legitimacy of the imamate, emphasized by the phrase "king of the people and the land." Rather than reproducing the jurisprudence of the Prophet and his companions, this structure reproduces that of the sultanic rule. While the caliph of the sultanic state ceded all authority beyond the walls of his palace to the sultan, Ibn Saʿud became the "imam" of a heritable "imamate," with the progeny of Ibn Abd al-Wahhab inheriting the position of sheikh. But this tradition did not long survive the development of a state bureaucracy, as the various posts of the religious establishment became occupied by jurists and scholars from different tribes and families, who became state employees, or "civil servants." Ibn Abd al-Wahhab's and Ibn Saʿud's alliance and allegiance was based on the idea that it would be the sheikh who would declare jihad and decide on issues of peace and war. In this sense, Ibn Abd al-Wahhab was in real terms the imam and Ibn Saʿud was the amir. But when Ibn Abd al-Wahhab withdrew from public life in 1773 CE / 1187 AH, the imamate became exclusively Ibn Saʿud's, and the role of the sheikh's heirs became that of religious leadership and legitimization of the ruler's acts.[9]

In the early days of Islam, the Prophet, who was the imam, was the preacher and ruler. After the Meccan era, during which the Prophet was preaching, not ruling or fighting, converting to Islam became not an individual but a tribal act in reality, as entire tribes became Muslim simultaneously, starting with al-Aws and al-Khazraj in Medina. As became clear during the first council convened to debate who should be the Prophet's successor, tribal structures remained dominant.

Wahhabism may have inspired many Islamic rebel movements due in part to its strategic geopolitical location, including rebellions led by Sayyid Ahmad Khan (1817–1898 CE / 1233–1306 AH) and the Shariʿatulla movement against the Moghuls, Sikhs, and the British in India, the movement led by Algerian Sheikh Muhammad Ibn ʿAli al-Sanusi (1787–1859 CE / 1201–1276 AH) in Libya, the Mahdi movement in Sudan, and other revolutionary groups in the heart of Africa.[10] Despite Wahhabism's possible influence, this was not a network of fundamentalism or Salafism.

In his study about Muhammad Hayya Ibn Ibrahim al-Sindhi al-Madani (d. 1750 CE / 1163 AH),[11] John Voll (b. 1936) notes that Ibn Abd al-Wahhab was one of his students during his stay in Medina. Wahhabism is seen as a part of a wave of Islamic revivalism stretching from Indonesia to Morocco; this wave did not always take Hanbali form as it was shaped according to the prevailing country context. While Voll acknowledges that Ibn Taymiyya's Salafism influenced Ibn Abd al-Wahhab, he argues that Ibn Taymiyya's teachings were not the main influence on the Hanbalism of the contemporary Eastern Arabs in the eighteenth century CE. Wahhabism was influenced by other sources; for example, despite the fact that he was a Hanafi connected to Naqshbandī Sufism, al-Sindhi instilled a hostility to veneration of saints and to innovation in Ibn Abd al-Wahhab.[12] Al-Sindhi was part of a broader network of Muslim scholars that extended throughout the eastern Arab world and central Asia. For example, Abu al-Tahir al-Kurani (1670–1733 CE / 1081–1145 AH), one of al-Sindhi's teachers, also tutored Shah Waliullah al-Dahlawi (1699–1762 CE / 1111–1176 AH), a well-known Islamic scholar in India.[13] Before him, both Sheikh

Yusuf Abd al-Mahasin Tajul Khalwati (1626–1699 CE / 1035–1110 AH), who led a revolt against the Dutch in Indonesia before being exiled to South Africa, and Abd al-Ra'uf al-Sinkili (1615–1693 CE / 1023–1105 AH), who led the Sufi Islamic revival movement in Sumatra, were tutored by al-Kurani's father, Ibrahim Ibn Hasan al-Kurani (1615–1690 CE / 1023–1101 AH), a famous teacher of that time in Medina.[14] Out of the twenty-four members of this "network" of scholars, not one was a Hanbali; most were Shafi'i with several Malikis and Hanafis. Among these men's pupils, some went on to lead Sufi orders and revivalist movements in their own countries.[15] So the revivalist wave was not a Hanbali Salafi wave, and Wahhabism was an exception.

The only Hanbali pupil Voll mentions is Muhammad al-Safarini (1702–1774 CE / 1114–1188 AH) from Nablus, which was one of the minor centers of the Hanbali school in the Arab world.[16] Natana DeLong-Bas believes that, although Ibn Abd al-Wahhab's writings neither show that he was a follower of Ibn Taymiyya nor that Ibn Taymiyya was the main component in his education, he must have used Ibn Taymiyya as a reference and source.[17]

Ahmad Dallal (b. 1957 CE), a historian and expert in Islamic Studies, notes that diverse individuals and groups have been mistakenly linked to Wahhabism, including the Indian Muslim revivalist Barelvi as well as the Association of Young Muslims (Subbanu al-Muslimīn) of West Africa. Many studies of modern Islamic thought assumed that the revivalist movements that emerged from the mid-eighteenth to the mid-nineteenth century CE constituted a single homogeneous body of fundamentalist thought, despite having different organizational styles. Dallal notes that this fundamentalist mode shares themes with Wahhabi thought because it emphasizes "abiding by the Qur'an and the Sunna, return to origins, revival of independent interpretation and hadith studies, rejection of innovation and imitation (*taqlīd*) in matters of law, and rejection of the excesses of Sufism." Dallal argues that the assumption that these revivalist movements were homogeneous led many to wrongly conclude that Wahhabi thought influenced India's Islamic scholar al-Dahlawi, West Africa's Usman Ibn Fodio (1754–1817 CE / 1167–1232 AH), and North Africa's al-Sanusi, an Arab Muslim theologian and founder of the Sanusi mystical order.[18] Dallal asserts that Wahhabism and these movements are radically different, particularly because the former is considered the "antithesis of everything the Islamic eighteenth century stood for." Since Ibn Abd al-Wahhab focuses on the issue of faithlessness, Dallal notes that it should be the basis of comparison between these movements and Wahhabism.[19] Indeed, Ibn Abd al-Wahhab stood out in his reckless declaration of individuals as infidels.

In any case, the Wahhabi tendency to declare individuals infidels clashed with popular and establishment religiosity outside the Arabian Peninsula. Laypeople and religious scholars alike rejected Wahhabi accusations of faithlessness and critique of their traditional religiosity as impure. An example of this was Damascus Muslim scholars' response to letters sent in 1810 CE / 1225 AH by Sa'ud Ibn 'Abd al-'Aziz to the governor of Damascus, Kunj Yusuf Pasha (r. 1807–1810 CE / 1221–1225 AH), whom he thought was still in office. The Muslim scholars of Damascus rejected Ibn Sa'ud's call to become Muslims (which implied that they were infidels) and affirmed that they were followers of the prophetic tradition. They also rejected his invitation to send representatives of the four schools of jurisprudence to debate with Wahhabi scholars. Moreover, they branded Wahhabis as Khawārij: "Right has become distinct from error. The Truth has come to light, and the Truth is more worthy of being followed. Beyond the truth, there is only error. . . . As for the sins we have been tested with, they are not the first bottle to break in Islam. They do not exclude us from Islam, as the misguided Kharijite sect claims. . . . God says that good deeds erase bad ones." Their response letter continues: "God says that the Bedouin Arabs are the most infidel and hypocritical and least worthy to know the bounds of what God has revealed to His Messenger; since you are Bedouin inhabitants of the wilderness, a Najdi sect, a faction of the [false prophet] Musaylima, your belief is a heretical innovation, an invention of people ignorant of the imams of the religion of Ahl al-Sunna wa al-Jamā'a. You are an iniquitous sect of Khawārij."[20] As such, the Wahhabis were not received in Mesopotamia and the Levant as conquering heroes as they had hoped.

Wahhabism did not spread far beyond the Arabian Peninsula, except for border tribes' seasonal raids into rural and settled areas in the Levant. As Dallal notes, Wahhabism was the exception in the eighteenth century CE rather than the rule, especially after the Saudis were defeated by the Ottomans and the Egyptian army for the second time in 1818 CE / 1233 AH. Interaction with European colonial interests at the beginning of the twentieth century CE revived the movement and the Saudi-Wahhabi alliance, which was later further empowered by oil discoveries and the integration of Saudi Arabia into the global economy.[21]

However, several tribes on the geographic margins of Mesopotamia and the Levant did join the Wahhabis as they supported their raids on urban centers and were easily able to accept their culture. Two aspects of Wahhabism, in particular, appealed to certain Reformers and elites after abolishing the caliphate: the element of simplicity and the return to the fundamentals of religion and the fact that the Arab aspect of Wahhabism resembled an Arab uprising against the Ottomans, who were now seen as Turks by some opponents of the ruling officers of the Committee of Union and Progress. Note that some Arab Reformers and elites openly called for the restoration of the caliphate to the Arabs, and many of them were disappointed by Sharif Husayn (1865–1935 CE) of Mecca and his sons.[22]

A condescending attitude toward existing folk religiosity is inherent to Salafism and is not limited to Wahhabism. In the twentieth century CE, Salafis who volunteered for jihad in Afghanistan expressed similar aversion toward the popular religiosity practiced by their hosts. For example, al-Suri—a Syrian ideologue of the Islamist jihadi stream—reported critically the frustration of Arab jihadi Salafis with the locals' practices and traditions in Afghanistan, describing the tension between jihadi Salafis and the Taliban (which adopts the Hanafi madhab and the Māturīdi doctrine). More known and obvious is ISIL's repugnance to popular religiosity and its attempts to impose new forms of religiosity onto communities in Syria and Iraq. Unable to create a grassroots base in the countryside or the cities where deep religious traditions persist, ISIL's support base has been limited to recently settled clans. Even in such cases, the clans have not necessarily been influenced by ISIL's religiosity but rather by political considerations.

The problem in the case of eighteenth-century CE Najd, as Ibn Abd al-Wahhab saw it, was not only innovations and false tradition but lack of religiosity and widespread idolatry. Ultimately, the brevity and directness of the letters that Ibn Saʿud sent to tribes and villages before attacking them appeared like a call to a new religion. According to a contemporary French officer, Ibn Saʿud would send a messenger holding the Qur'an in one hand and a sword in the other, bearing a succinct message recorded and translated in various forms: "From ʿAbd al-ʿAziz to the tribe of . . . greetings. Your duty calls you to belief in the book I am sending you. Do not be pagans like the Turks who ascribe partners to God. If you believe, you will be saved. Otherwise we will fight you unto death."[23] This was the impression emerging among foreign scholars writing about Wahhabism at the beginning of the nineteenth century CE; this impression was so strong that it required clarification: "It is not a new religion, but the religion of Muhammad himself in its original simplicity. For this reason, it had all the qualities of a religious reformation. It shunned traditions, emphasizing morality, rather than the creed, as paramount. Hence the similarity between Wahhabis and Protestants. The Wahhabis added morality to the concern for the creed, and their creed is pure monotheism."[24]

However, we have provided evidence to affirm that Wahhabism is not a new religion, because the tone taken by Ibn Saʿud might suggest to the foreign observer such a suspicion. While the letters of Ibn Saʿud to the tribal and district leaders are reminiscent of the letters of the Prophet to the tribes and kings, the Prophet's letters to the tribes and kings did not contain a threat of death or fighting and they were to Byzantines and Persians, not to Muslims seen as polytheist apostates.

The contemporary European perspective of the emergence of Wahhabism has been influenced by the history of Protestantism. Protestants believed that adherence to the text and rejection of intermediaries and inherited traditions—including rival interpretations of the text itself—would provide greater space for true Christian faith. Contrary to the delusions of those who practice esoteric interpretation or hermeneutics (*taʾwīl*), Wahhabis believe that not everything can be found in the text. This means that it is necessary to seek knowledge of order and laws outside the text. This belief confuses a desired potential with reality and has led some contemporary European observers and Arab reformists to admire Wahhabism. "Herein lies the reason for the poverty of Turkish legislation, which tries to rely on interpretation of the Qur'an by each according to his fancy. The Turks take the Book with them wherever they go, believing that it contains in uncontestable fashion all details of knowledge and art. . . . This tradition makes the Turks forever ignorant, but the Wahhabis, who are today as ignorant as the Turks were yesterday, have opened the way for enlightenment by abandoning blind imitation."[25]

This same logic links the secularization of knowledge to Protestants' individual reliance on the text rather than the contrived interpretations of the religious establishment. In my view, this is not a necessary link; many Protestant sects have isolated themselves, lived strictly by the text, and shunned worldly explanations of phenomena, while others have tried to dictate their religious understanding of true Christianity by force. Enlightened Protestantism did not emanate from the internal dynamic of the reform itself but through interaction with the development of the modern state, science, and the bourgeoisie. Moreover, nominalism, which encourages empirical scientific research into specific phenomena, is connected to the Franciscan transformation within Catholicism and not Protestantism. Its theoretical assumptions concerning the actual particulars and the theoretical universals resemble those of Ash'arism, not Hanbalism or Wahhabism. And, empirical research did evolve in the context of Muslim civilization. Roger Bacon, Francis Bacon, Galileo, Copernicus, and Kepler were not Protestant, and the scientific and industrial revolutions were not brought about by a religious reform. However, Protestantism has contributed to the emergence of the modern individual by positioning the believer as responsible for his actions in front of his creator without intermediaries. The relationship between this religious culture and the atomization and deconstruction of communities by industrialization/modernization and the relation between the interaction between science and religious reform on the one hand and modernity on the other is a different story. Here we can speak on Protestant impact. But there is no direct path from religious reformation to enlightenment.

In advocating a return to the literal meaning of the text, Wahhabism does not deny the text's comprehensiveness or its ability to provide answers for everything. In addition, Wahhabism does not advocate reasoning independent of the text or understanding things by their own internal laws. Rather, the return to the plain meaning of the text formed part of a puritanical Salafism directed (selectively) toward the past and not the future. The Wahhabis do not go back to the past in search of an intellectual renaissance or a reconciliation of religion and modernity; instead, they advocate a return to an imagined past to restore it. Over the course of more than two hundred years, Wahhabi Salafism has failed to make room for an enlightenment and has actively obstructed any such development. Its version of adherence to the plain meaning of the text as it defines it has neither permitted interpretation within religion nor enlightenment outside it. Even the slightest social reform in later Saudi Arabia has had to go through a conflict with Wahhabi Salafism.

Wahhabis do engage in interpretation. Specifically, they use the literal meaning of the traditions and sayings of the Prophet and his companions to interpret the literal meaning of the Qur'an while rejecting rational inference. They are not fundamentalist in the classic Islamic sense of fundamentalism; they have no independent method of applying the fundamentals of jurisprudence to derive new legal rulings like those of the founders of the jurisprudential schools. The highest status that Wahhabi scholars can obtain is that of a legal authority within the schools of jurisprudence (mujtahid within the madhab), never transgressing the limits set by the founding legal authorities. In this, they usually imitate Ibn Taymiyya, who was a juristic innovator in his day, particularly regarding his rulings on divorce, for which he was imprisoned.

I do not entirely reject the comparison between the beginnings of Wahhabism and those of Protestantism. Martin Luther (1483–1546 CE / 888–952 AH) and Ibn Abd al-Wahhab do share similarities, like fundamentalists do, especially in their rebellion against the religious establishment, their readiness to declare opponents as infidels, their strict imposition of outward religious practice on the masses, and their willingness to appeal to princes for assistance (a practice totally opposed by Ibn Hanbal, for example). For Wahhabism, this meant rebelling against the Ottoman's centralized and hierarchical religious establishment, although the Wahhabis ended up referring to their grand mufti ʿAbd al-ʿAziz Ibn Baz (1912–1999 CE) as "His Excellency the Father" (*Samāḥat al-Wālid*), a title very similar to that of the pope.

WAHHABISM, ISLAMIST MOVEMENTS, AND TWO DIFFERENT MEANINGS OF JAHILIYYA

One example of the projection of modern concepts onto the historical record is scholars' attempts to portray Hanbalism as the origin of Wahhabism. While political sociologist Sami Zubaida (b. 1937 CE) does this, he has attempted to refute the claim that there is a genealogy linking Hanbalism with modern radical Islamist movements (from which he rightly excludes early Wahhabism) and its challenge to the separation of religion from state.[26] From Zubaida's perspective, Wahhabism differs from modern radical political Islamism in terms of its tribal character.[27] It began as a puritan Islamic revivalist movement and ended up as a dynastic monarchy.

Conversely, Abdelwahab Meddeb (1946–2014 CE) not only considers Wahhabism a species of "political Islam" but also dedicates most of his book on political Islam to it.[28] For Meddeb, Wahhabism is the continuation of an

Islamic tradition that runs from Ibn Hanbal through Ibn Taymiyya to Ibn Abd al-Wahhab. In reality, while Ibn Abd al-Wahhab conceived the Prophet and his companions through Ibn Hanbal, Ibn Taymiyya did not, as he disagreed with Ibn Hanbal on several points. Drawing such a line forces Meddeb to view a decline in the historical development of ideas, just as the Salafis themselves conceive history of Muslim civilization. However, in this case, it is the history of Salafism from Ibn Hanbal to Ibn Abd al-Wahhab in decline, which would be true if such a chain of succession existed. Meddeb firmly adopts an epistemological approach based on comparison of root and branch, thereby branding Wahhabism as a degenerate version of its origin,[29] which is true according to this model.[30]

The key difference between Meddeb's and Zubaida's analysis is that Zubaida's 1989 CE book, *Islam, the People and the State,* predates the rise of al-Qaeda, while Meddeb's book was published after 9/11. These books illustrate how current affairs shape research agendas and perspectives. Prior to 9/11, scholars refused to see Wahhabism as part of the modern landscape of political Islam (i.e., the militant activism under such intense study in the 1970s and 1980s CE). After 9/11, scholars asserted that Wahhabism is the fountainhead of modern fundamentalism and the most dangerous movement in Islam. This illustrates how Islamic intellectual currents are classified not only according to the taxonomy of religious phenomena and mode of religiosity but also according to contemporary political developments. As such, it is necessary to review the history of studies on Islamic political movements (or Islamism) with an eye to understanding how they are characterized differently depending on the political motives and contexts.

Just as contemporary religious fundamentalism is rooted in the internal and external critique of the conservative religious establishment and the shift from popular religiosity to mass religiosity, so too is contemporary rebellious Wahhabi Salafism. Influenced by political Islamist religiosity, Wahhabi Salafism has broken free of the control of the Wahhabi religious establishment—which it considers a puppet of Al Saʿud—and seeks to hold the Saudi state accountable for implementing Wahhabi teachings. Rather than accepting the practices and laws of the Kingdom of Saudi Arabia as the worldly embodiment of Shariʿa, both reformists and takfiri Salafis in Saudi Arabia now use Wahhabism to hold it accountable. Although Ibn Abd al-Wahhab did not represent an activist political Islam in the sense used by academics today, the twentieth-century CE

Wahhabi type of Salafism became a key component of the ideology of many activist movements. In fact, Wahhabism was initially a minor trend with an austere puritanical understanding of religion.

The onset of the Arab Cold War between the Saudi bloc and Egypt in the 1960s and the West's political exploitation of the struggle to fight Arab nationalism and communism enabled Wahhabism to become a systematized Salafi creed propagated by preachers and well-financed Salafi societies and systematized in Shari'a departments in Saudi universities that attracted Islamist scholars and students from around the Muslim world. As the ideological backbone of a wealthy state with an integrated religious establishment, Wahhabis controlled educational curricula and the regulation of worship and social behavior. In addition, Saudi Arabia's increasing oil wealth facilitated the spread of this brand of Salafism to many regions in the Islamic world, a development that was welcomed by the US. At that time, Western countries had thrown their weight behind Islam as a bulwark against communism and radical Arab nationalism; the Saudi ruling elite made regular use of its connections to serve the agendas of its American and other Western allies. Saudi Arabia thus became a center for the political-ideological export of Wahhabism, and it created centers in countries like Pakistan. This explains the official Wahhabi sponsorship of the Pakistani Jamaat-e-Islami. (Note that the founder of this Islamic movement, al-Mawdudi, identified with the Saudi religious establishment and helped establish the Islamic University in Medina).

This historical record is well established. Indeed, once Wahhabism became a liability for the West and for the social structures and lifestyle brought about by affluence and modernization in the Kingdom itself, Saudi Crown Prince Muhammad bin Salman (b. 1985 CE) explicitly restated these facts, admitting that the Kingdom had exported Salafism by investing in religious schools and mosques abroad "when allies asked Saudi Arabia" to confront Soviet influence in the Islamic world.[31] He did this to fend off the charge that extremism spread from Saudi Arabia, even if that meant admitting that the Kingdom had obediently implemented policies favored by West.

In the 1980s and 1990s CE, Saudi Arabia spent nearly US$75 billion to promote the Wahhabi model through financially supporting Islamic associations and centers, the construction of mosques, and other activities. Saudi Arabia's vast financial capacity turned Wahhabism into a global ideological network that influenced modes of religiosity in other countries. Additionally, these global interactions reshaped Wahhabism in Saudi Arabia itself. Once a Salafi religious movement with a popular dimension, Wahhabism became an official religious establishment subordinated to the state. However, this means that Wahhabism has now developed two radically different faces. On the one hand, there is the politically "moderate" (religiously intransigent) religious establishment with its popular-religious following, its preachers, its curricula, and its associations, all of them marked by a puritan devotion to religious duties, social issues, and appearances. On the other hand, there is a politically militant jihadi Salafism that claims to return Wahhabism to its origins. While the first is apologist, obeys the regime, produces religious justifications for its policies, and has been gradually marginalized by the regime's political and civil institutions, the second attracts those aggrieved by state policy within a mass society. This first type of Wahhabism included critics like Salman al-Odeh (b. 1956 CE) and other members of the awakening (*Ṣaḥwa*) in the 1980s who rejected Saudi dependency on the US after the Iraqi occupation of Kuwait, moved toward more open and reformist positions, and ended up being prosecuted by the regime. The ex-Ṣaḥwa activists and religious scholars who became Reformers can be considered a third trend.

During the 1960s CE, the emergence of al-Jamāʿa al-Salafiyya al-Muḥtasiba (JMS) in Medina challenged the Wahhabi establishment in Saudi Arabia. JMS was influenced by Syrian Islamic scholar al-Albani's belief that the Wahhabi creed needs to be purified of certain misconceptions and innovations. This group was also acting to protect their creed from the potential "damaging influence" of other groups newly emerged in Saudi Arabia, like the Egyptian Muslim Brotherhood and Pakistani Jamāʿat al-Tablīgh.[32]

However, a greater challenge to the Wahhabi establishment was the growing popularity of the Islamic awakening (*Al-Ṣaḥwa al-Islāmiyya*) in Saudi Arabia during the 1980s CE. Its ideology was mixture of the Salafi-Wahhabi traditions and political views of the Muslim Brotherhood. In comparison with the "ideological threat" of al-Albani, this movement made his ideas and popularity seem like a lost opportunity to bolster the country's religiopolitical status quo. To counter the Awakening movement, the ruling family financially and institutionally supported the emergence and spread of the Jāmiyya movement toward the end of the 1980s, as it emphasized al-Albani's disengagement from politics, which was convenient for the Saudi ruling family. Subsequently, al-Albani became the third most influential scholar of the modern global Salafism, alongside Ibn Baz and Muhammad Ibn Salih al-Uthaymin (1925–2001 CE).[33]

The fragmentation of Wahhabism illustrates that when a Salafi-type religious movement transforms into an establishment that supports the ruling regime state, and is supported by the state, it will spawn a dissident Salafism motivated by many factors, including resentment of the gap between ideology and practice. This dissident Salafism points to the gap between propagated religious discourse and practice to explain various injustices and mobilize grassroot support. However extreme the contradictions, in an era where authoritarian rule is met by demands for freedom and rule of law, any mass movement must ultimately establish a position on democracy: Is it a series of demands or a system of government? The need to address civil rights and democracy has fomented divisions within Islamist movements. This division has not happened in a vacuum. Demands for democratization intersect with issues like the wholesale declaration of society as infidels; the characterization of Muslim-majority countries as being part of the Abode of Islam, the Abode of Faithlessness, mixed domain as per Ibn Taymiyya's Mardin fatwa, or an age of ignorance; legitimization of the use of violence against Muslim rulers; and other debates that accompany the Qutbite current in the Muslim Brotherhood.

Contrary to conventional wisdom, Ibn Abd al-Wahhab was the first person to use the term *age of ignorance* to refer to a societal and mental state in the modern age and not a historical period prior to Islam. Historically, the word *ignorance* had been used in passing to describe a particular human trait, referring to the gravity of a particular sin to be addressed. For example, in one story the Prophet warns Abu Dharr al-Ghifari (d. 651 / 653 CE / 31/32 AH), "You are a man with jahiliyya in you;" in another story he describes the condition of the Bedouin Arabs as one of ignorance. Ibn Abd al-Wahhab took the term *age of ignorance* and the associated Islamic rulings out of pre-Islamic history and applied them first to Bedouin communities in Najd and later to other Muslim societies. In fact, he extended the concept, outlining more than one hundred phenomena that constitute ignorance, all of which he considered innovations devoid of Islamic legitimacy in the areas of creed, worship, and action. In addition, he included protected religious minorities (*dhimmīs*) and Sufis in the ignorant category alongside polytheists.

For Ibn Abd al-Wahhab, ignorance was a set of beliefs and practices that, while prevalent in pre-Islamic history, still persisted in Arab society eleven centuries after the emergence of Islam. It is not a new ignorance but an extension of the old ignorance in the Arabian Peninsula.

In the language of early Islam, the *age of ignorance* referred to a sort of anarchy marked by the absence of authority or leadership; notably, Ibn Abd al-Wahhab emphasizes the absence of a state or a ruler to be obeyed as a feature of early Islam's conceptualization of ignorance. For Ibn Abd al-Wahhab, his contemporaries were "worse than the heretics (*zanādiqa*) of the tribe of Quraysh" in "their disobedience to rulers."[34] This is a long way from Qutb and al-Mawdudi's concept of ignorance.

Also notable is that the historian and geographer al-Mas'udi, used the term *age of ignorance* to refer to a lack of rulership. This usage is closer to an important aspect of the Prophet's and companions' understanding of *age of ignorance* as unruliness. In his *Meadows of Gold and Mines of Gems*, al-Mas'udi states that "there are those that are in ignorance because they do not have a king."[35] At other points, he links ignorance with the absence of binding, revealed laws. Here, the basic principle is that there should be arrangements, institutions, and customs that organize social life, the opposite of this being ignorance—something similar to the state of nature (in its negative sense of raw, primitive, and violent) in philosophical political thought in Europe in the seventeenth century CE. This is not to deny that scholars who lived before al-Mas'udi characterized the concept of ignorance differently, using it in passing to refer to Islamically unacceptable customs and behaviors that they noticed. For example, the Islamic scholar Muhammad Ibn Isma'il al-Bukhari (author of the famous hadith collection *Ṣaḥīḥ al-Bukhārī*) lists four traits of ignorance, including the rending of garments, the slapping of cheeks over the dead, and the questioning of genealogy. The term was also applied in the context of the Prophet's wives in the Qur'an: "Do not flaunt your finery in the manner of the jahiliyya" (33:33). Ultimately, the broader meaning of *ignorance* encompasses the absence of the means to regulate moral and behavioral values, that is, the absence of an organized society. In the view of late thinkers like al-Mas'udi, the transition from ignorance to Islam in the case of the Arabian Peninsula was a transition from a state of anarchy to a state where there was authority, namely a leadership who could enforce divine law. For authors hailing from the golden age of Islamic civilization like al-Mas'udi, laws did not necessarily have to be Islamic. In this sense, the term *ignorance* not only stood in opposition to the term *Islam* but had come to mean the absence of a ruling authority or kingship that is capable of enforcing law and order.

BETWEEN EARLY WAHHABISM AND CONTEMPORARY JIHADI SALAFISM

If the modern concept of ignorance emerged in an Arab context, its theoretical elaboration comes from al-Mawdudi, an Islamic jurist and scholar in British-occupied India. Al-Mawdudi considered ignorance to be a model of life opposed to Islam's model and its vision of the key issues. He used the term metaphorically to describe the condition of the Muslims and to confront Western philosophy and concepts of God, humanity, the universe, and life. As such, al-Mawdudi thus identified several kinds of ignorance: pure ignorance, like that of Western civilization; the ignorance of polytheism, like that of the Arab polytheists and Muslims who maintain polytheistic practices such as seeking the intercession of the dead and visiting the tombs of saints; and the ignorance of monasticism, like the error of the Christians and some Muslim Sufis.

Beginning in the mid-1970s CE in Egypt, the dichotomy between ignorance and divine sovereignty paved the way for movements that willingly declared communities infidels to emerge from the bosom of the Muslim Brotherhood. As seen in *Jihad: The Absent Commandment* by Faraj, the founder of the Jihad Organization, and in *Preachers, Not Judges*, by Supreme Guide al-Hudaybi, this period generated important debates about the legitimacy of using political violence to change the system of government and enforce the rule of the Shariʿa.

In the late twentieth century CE, these movements spread to other countries, accelerated by the return of the Arab Afghans and the emergence of a second generation of jihadi Salafis and other forms of violent Islamist movements. The logic of movements like al-Qaeda is based on Qutb's method of simultaneously declaring Muslim societies as ignorant and unfaithful if they did not follow his understanding of the "nullifiers of monotheism" (as reformulated by al-Mawdudi on the concept of monotheism set forth in Ibn Abd al-Wahhab's *Najdi Essays*). While Wahhabism pushed popular religiosity in a more puritanical direction, it did not present a revolutionary totalitarian theory like the one proposed by Qutb, based on al-Mawdudi's theory of the Islamic state as embodied in divine sovereignty, but it was satisfied by a sultanic rule that applies the Shariʿa. The concept of divine sovereignty was the point of departure for early jihadis' return to the Salafism of Ibn Taymiyya and Wahhabi Salafism, rather than the other way around, and it led Salafism to be reconceptualized in jihadi takfīrī terms.

As in the case of the Bedouin, whom he fought and saw as true polytheists, Ibn Abd al-Wahhab declared the leadership of these communities as infidels (*takfīr muʿayyan*). While Qutb discussed a general condition of ignorance, he did not emphasize proclaiming specific people infidels. However, in Qutb's thought, we find the theory of the solid foundation (*al-qāʿida al-ṣulba*), which was the group of companions that kept Islam alive when large parts of the Arabian Peninsula turned apostate after the death of the Prophet Muhammad. This brings us back to the theory of the new prophetic jihadi mission. For Qutb, the "solid foundation" was a vanguard, a revolutionary group of believers, that would violently eradicate irreligious tyranny (*ṭāghūt*) from the world. Their divine efforts would be distinguished by their direct relationship with the Qur'an (before its message became adulterated with philosophy and produced theology foreign to the spirit of Islam, etc.). The Muslims of the solid foundation, according to Qutb, understood the Qur'an neither as culture nor as a theological theory but as commandments to be followed. Even when they were in direct contact with ignorance, they remained emotionally isolated from it.[36]

Under the leadership of al-Zawahiri, Egyptian Islamic jihad initially adopted the Qutbist idea of waging war against the infidel Islamic regimes as a proxy for fighting the "far enemy." al-Qaeda subsequently reversed this stance, instead targeting "remote enemies" on whose support the survival of infidel tyrannical regimes (*ṭāghūt*) depends (the USSR in the case of the Afghan regime, serving as the prototype). This logic led it to directly fight the US, "the head of faithlessness," as the backer and protector of ṭāghūt regimes in Muslim countries who are to be treated like apostates. To justify this fight, these movements cite Abu Bakr (the first caliph) and Saladin, who defeated the Shiʿi Ismaʿili Fatimids before liberating Jerusalem from the Franks. Of course, they forget that Saladin was an Ashʿari in creed—and therefore a misguided innovator from the perspective of contemporary Salafism—who was close to the Nizārī Ismaʿilis and had Imami figures in his administration. Indeed, some of Saladin's greatest chroniclers, including Abu Tayy al-Halabi, were Shiʿa, and his sons openly accepted and acknowledged his Shiʿi sympathies and patronage of major Sufis like Ibn Arabi.

While a Qutbist logic inevitably shaped the shift from one enemy to another within a series of enemies of Islam, the Wahhabi component held greater influence over the second generation of jihadi Salafi ideologues like al-Maqdisi, al-Filastini, and the Shari'a officials of ISIL, particularly in terms of imposing a particular way of life. Illustratively, they now cite Ibn Abd al-Wahhab more frequently than Qutb, and jihadi Salafi theorists teach their students the same curricula that was taught in Saudi schools until recently.

> The founder of Wahhabism could easily declare those who disagreed with him infidels; points of doctrinal disagreement were nullifiers of religion. He believed that his creed was the Islam in its original simplicity, not one school of jurisprudence among others but the religion itself. It is easy to identify the continuation of this tendency among other violent Islamist movements that also see themselves as representing the upright religion in its entirety rather than belonging to a particular school of jurisprudence; they believe that they have found their way to Islam's simple essence, cleansed it of its impurities, and become entirely coextensive with it. Naturally, this is not reformist Salafism. To further illustrate this tendency, there is a story in Ibn Abd al-Wahhab's biography that, after having gone into seclusion for eight months, he came out to the people with a small book, saying, "With God as my witness, I follow the example of this book; I say that what is written in it is nothing but the truth." A man named 'Ali Ibn Rabia, who was a leading figure of Banu Tamim from the tribe of Banu Sa'd, arose . . . and took the book and looked through it from beginning to end. Then he handed it back and said, "This is true, so explain to us how to behave according to it." . . . Ibn Abd al-Wahhab said to him, "The way to propagate this matter is through advice and beneficence." 'Ali Ibn Rabia said, "And if it does not happen in this way?' He said, "By the sword." He said to him, "How can one who does not follow it deserve death?" He said, "Because he is a polytheist infidel." He said, "Is that what you say?" He said, "Yes, that is my belief."[37]

From the outset, Ibn Abd al-Wahhab's mission was distinguished by his willingness to impose his creed by force and fight infidels and apostates. He considered the Bedouin to be infidels like those who were first ignorant of Islam, writing that

> In the two *Ṣiḥaḥ*,[38] the Prophet says, "I have been ordered to fight against the people until they testify that there is none worthy of worship except God and that Muhammad is the messenger of God, and until they establish the prayers and pay the *zakat*.[39] And if they do so then they will have gained protection

> from me for their lives and property." . . . This is God's plain writ for the common simple man, and this is the word of God's messenger. . . . The community of Muslim scholars in our times say, "One who says that there is no god but God is a Muslim, whose property and life is protected, not to be declared an infidel or fought against." They even say this about the Bedouin, who deny the resurrection and the laws and claim that their false Shariʿa is God's truth."[40]

As such, the Bedouin are infidels because they prefer the adjudication of tribal custom to the rule of divine law. Ibn Abd al-Wahhab continues, "The Muslim scholars of the age acknowledge all of this and say, 'There is not even an iota of Islam in them.' . . . They have said that someone who declares a Muslim an infidel has committed an act amounting to faithlessness. For them a Muslim is someone without an iota of Islam, but who declares 'There is no god but God.' Yet he is very far from understanding it and meeting its requirements in terms of knowledge, belief, and action."[41]

However, there is a vast difference between Ibn Abd al-Wahhab, who considered obedience to the ruler central to any organized Islamic society, and "modern" jihadi Salafis who declare rulers infidels and justify revolt against them on the grounds of divine sovereignty. Although early Wahhabism revolted against the Ottoman sultanate, whose control of Najd and other internal regions of the Arabian Peninsula was very loose, it has since integrated into and legitimated the rule of another dynasty. However, this dynasty has managed to contain radicals' attempts to make the mission superior to the state. Note that the first Saudi project was unable to expand into regions of the Peninsula controlled directly by the Ottomans or the British, while the third and final sally successfully occupied the Hijaz only after the collapse of the Ottoman Empire and the withdrawal of British protection from the Sharifs.

We start, therefore, with four key elements of Wahhabism: purifying the faith by returning to the Qur'an and Sunna of the Prophet and his companions, as they are imagined by the Ṣiḥaḥ hadith collections and Salafi narrators; declaring that those who disagree with Ibn Abd al-Wahhab's ideals are infidels—particularly in the Bedouin social environment; fighting to impose the mission and forcing adherence to it; and, after the institutionalization of the mission under the Saudi dynasty, linking these elements with obedience to the ruler. From the very beginning, the central pivot of Ibn Abd al-Wahhab's ideals was simple absolute monotheism and its embodiment in social life in accordance with his Salafi understanding of religion. As such, Ibn Abd al-Wahhab conceptualized divine sovereignty even though he did not use the wording "God alone is the creator and ruler of the world. He alone makes the laws of nature and society, and He alone deserves worship." Ibn Abd al-Wahhab and his early followers believed that Muslims had moved away from monotheism. Innovations had spread, religious rites had become degenerate, and polytheism proliferated in the form of worshipping stones, trees, and other material objects and the application of divine attributes to humans.

For Ibn Abd al-Wahhab, this was not about just the monotheism of the singular Creator (or "deistic monotheism," as he called it), which existed even during the age of ignorance, as Ibn Taymiyya understood it, but also the monotheism of worshipping an exclusive, singular divinity (*tawḥīd al-ulūhiyya*). This meant that exaltation and worship belong only to God. While other scholars believed that veneration or praise of the Prophet (and others) is contrary to monotheism, Ibn Abd al-Wahhab went too far in his zealous quest to remove the false pretexts or excuses (*sadd al-dharāʾiʿ*) of polytheism.[42] His classical and modern opponents have accused him of shunning the Prophet. And long after his death, Wahhabis destroyed ruins in Mecca and Medina attributed to the Prophet and his companions on the pretext of protecting monotheism and removing the temptation of polytheism, in the form of worshipping the Prophet. Ibn Abd al-Wahhab believed that to treat the prophets and the *Awliyāʾ* (defenders of God)—never mind so-called saints—as if they were holy was polytheism. His contemporaries reported that the judge of Riyadh accused him of burning the book *Dalāʾil al-Khayārāt* "because its author referred to the Prophet as our master and our lord."[43] He explained to his followers that "the only way to obtain the favor of the Creator is to take vengeance against those who defile His religion." Ibn Abd al-Wahhab "also made them believe that he was the agent of God's wrath and had been sent to destroy false Muslims. At the same time, however, he warned them to restrict themselves to the true worship of the supreme Creator, to behave correctly and austerely."[44]

Ibn Abd al-Wahhab aimed for "Islamization" of the Bedouin environment in central Saudi Arabia, from which he drew his most zealous supporters. By conducting raids in the name of religion, he made plunder legitimate, enabling his Bedouin followers—for whom raiding was an important component of their livelihood—to justify their raiding as for the "inheritors" of the Earth, since God gives ownership to whom He wills. In addition, he held betrayal by cunning against the enemies of the religion to be legitimate. He laid some of the foundations for the political organization of the Bedouin under the command of the imam. Tribal bonds only started to break down later, in 1912 CE when Ibn Saʿud of the third Saudi state established fraternal settlements (*hijar*) made up of al-Ikhwān who had left their tribes to undertake jihad under the banner of Wahhabism.[45] These armies began launching operations under the slogan "The enemies of Al Saʿud are the enemies of God. Bring the enemy of God back to God's covenant and betray him."[46] These settlements facilitated the dissolution of different tribal bonds into a single doctrinal foundation.

Ibn Abd al-Wahhab listed seven issues constituting monotheism: there is wisdom behind the creation of demons and human beings; worship of God is monotheism; one who does not achieve monotheism does not worship God; there is wisdom in the sending of the messengers; the message applies to all nations; the religion of the prophets is one; and worshipping God is impossible without rejecting false gods.[47] Jihadi Salafists attach great importance to the last issue of rejecting false gods (*al-kufr bi al-ṭāghūt*), by which they mean removing regimes that do not enforce God's law and renouncing all those who do not apply God's law or who do not follow the creed of monotheism in their daily lives. The excessive use of this term is perhaps one of the most notable characteristics of jihadi Salafis' writing.

Ibn Abd al-Wahhab cites the following verses to justify his characterization of monotheism: "And I did not create the demon and mankind except that they may worship Me" (51:56); "And verily We sent forth among every community a messenger [to say]: 'Worship God and shun false deities (*al-ṭāghūt*)'" (16:36); "And your Lord has decreed that you worship none save Him, and kindness to parents" (17:23); "And worship God, and associate nothing with Him" (4:36); and "Say: 'Come, I will recite that which your Lord has made a sacred duty for you: that you associate nothing with Him." (6:151). As such, the Wahhabis see prophecy as a message borne by a man chosen by God. They believe that ascribing miracles to prophets, imploring them for help after death, or even swearing an oath by them, constitutes polytheism. They also forbid the sanctification of the tombs of the righteous and the monuments of the Prophet, including his grave, on the basis that the preservation of these sites leads to polytheism.

THE SPREAD OF IBN ABD WAHHAB'S MISSION

When trying to secure support for his mission, Ibn Abd al-Wahhab tried to form alliances with tribal leaders. His partnership with the amir of Uyayna collapsed, but his alliance with Muhammad Ibn Saʿud, the amir of Dirʿiyya, played a key role in the spread of Wahhabism. While the simplicity of his ideals suited the Najdi environment, they also gave tribal leaders a legitimate reason to raid, plunder, and "spread the word"—that is, to impose doctrine on the defeated by force. In these alliances, Ibn Abd al-Wahhab (as the sheikh) and the tribal leader (the amir who became the imam) shared power; the former was the religious authority who acknowledged the latter's political authority. When some of Ibn Abd al-Wahhab's followers, al-Ikhwān, rebelled against the third Saudi state, the Al Saʿud crushed them at the Battle of al-Sabilla (1929 CE). The tribal fighters became the recruits of the National Guard, which became a parallel army headed by a member of the ruling family. Since then, the raison d'état has dominated, and Wahhabism remained the state ideology and a major source of legitimacy until quite recently, when the total dependence of the religious establishment on the state and the consolidation of the social and political structures that developed under the rentier economy allowed Al Saʿud to dispense with it.

Wahhabism flourished during the first reign of Ibn Saʿud. Before attacking the Arab tribes, Ibn Saʿud would send a messenger to warn the tribe to accept and adhere to Ibn Abd al-Wahhab's creed (as the Qur'an itself), abandon innovations, and adhere to the precepts of the religion according to this creed's interpretation of innovation—or else they would be forced to do so by the sword. Ibn Saʿud told these tribes that heaven had placed the right to punish polytheists in his hands. His letters to tribal leaders were curt and cautionary, reminiscent of the Prophet's letters to the kings as mentioned previously, although the letters sent by the Prophet only included a warning, not an outright declaration of hostilities. The Prophet's raids were a reaction to the maneuvering of the Arabs and their declarations of war, including the conflict with the Byzantines and the Ghassanids. As reported in the classical biographies of the Prophet from the second century AH,[48] the Persians killed the messengers sent by the Prophet—which constituted a declaration of war—and sent two men to assassinate the Prophet. The Qur'anic Barāʾa chapter, which was quoted regularly by Ibn Abd al-Wahhab to justify Ibn Saʿud's raids against Arab tribes on the Arabian Peninsula and which is also heavily cited by contemporary jihadi Salafists, pertained to the Arab polytheists as it offered them the choice of Islam or the sword. Ibn Saʿud's position means that he viewed the Arabs around him as polytheists. Unlike in the Prophet's letters to Khosrow, Heraclius, and others, Ibn Saʿud considered this the natural extension of Muslims' disavowal of all obligations toward the infidels, and especially those set out in the "sword" verse.

The Wahhabis considered their Muslim contemporaries polytheists who committed graver errors than the people living in ignorance at the time of the Prophet.[49] In assuming this stance, they went further than even Ibn Abd al-Wahhab himself. From the Wahhabi perspective, "all believers in heterodox sects were polytheists, not Muslims. They held that everybody who had heard their appeal and did not join them was an infidel. Subsequently, the Wahhabis treated even Jews and Christians less harshly than non-Wahhabi Muslims."[50] In contrast, the classical (supposedly Salafi) thought of Ibn Taymiyya required that a detailed justification be given if a Muslim was to be declared an infidel. Their habit of declaring others infidels became a characteristic of the early Wahhabis that distinguished them from other Muslims and a prelude for declaring jihad against them.

The Sheikh was steadfast in his belief that the unity of God was incompatible with the practices of seeking saintly intercession and praying at graves. In his view, such practices were no different from the worship of idols practiced by individuals who lived during the age of ignorance, especially as the Arabs during this age requested intercession with God, or in the language of the Qur'an, to be brought near to God.[51] In Ibn Abd al-Wahhab's understanding of the Qur'an, the Arabs of the Peninsula prior to Islam did not worship the stone itself from which the idols are made but believed that the idols could help them intercede with God. In this sense they were not different from his contemporaries who invoked saints or supplicated for mercy or favors at graves hoping that certain human beings and things could intercede with God. This idea "took hold of Ibn Abd al-Wahhab until all he could see in life was the singular goal of returning the people to the original innocence of worshipping the one God and stopping the worship of tombs."[52]

So, he began to apply these principles in the first village with whose ruler he had taken refuge. He ordered the trees that were sacred to the people of Uyayna be cut down and an adulteress be stoned.[53] In the company of Uthman

Ibn Mu'ammar (1729–1750 CE / 1142–1163 AH), amir of Uyayna, and six hundred of his followers, Ibn Abd al-Wahhab went to demolish the tomb of Zayd Ibn al-Khattab (d. 633–634 CE / 12 AH), a companion of the Prophet who was killed there during the wars of apostasy.[54] The population of the neighboring village came to prevent it. Under the protection of the amir, Ibn Abd al-Wahhab picked up the pickax and demolished the tomb himself to demonstrate that it was merely stone and that divine wrath would not strike down those who touched it.[55] The Wahhabi Salafis and those influenced by them followed this example and became well known for their demolition of tombs, gravestones, and places of pilgrimage.

Wahhabis also prevented Levantine pilgrims from reaching Mecca and Medina and launched campaigns against the Levant that reached as far as southern Syria.[56] After the Wahhabis allowed a caravan to reach Mecca in 1807, they stipulated that no pilgrim could bring or consume anything forbidden, such as tobacco. Haydar al-Shihabi notes that pilgrims were not even allowed to bring the palanquins (*maḥmal*) traditionally used to carry new coverings for the Ka'ba.[57]

Ibn Abd al-Wahhab writes in considerable detail about more than ten different kinds of polytheism. He singles out particular aspects of popular religiosity that he observed in Arabia at that time: wearing hoops or threads to remove or ward off evil; having charms and amulets; seeking blessings from a tree or rock; swearing by anything other than God; seeking refuge from anyone other than God; seeking divine help from anyone other than God; excessively seeking guidance from the righteous; seeking blessing from graves; dealing with magic; seeking the knowledge of soothsayers and fortune tellers; reading omens from birds; and practicing astrology.[58]

There is no Sunni scholar—Ash'ari, Mu'tazilite, or otherwise—who would dispute that these practices of popular religiosity are reprehensible. Ibn Abd al-Wahhab was condemned only because he was too ready to proclaim that those who "erred" in these ways were infidels and to declare war against them. While there is orthodox scholarly consensus that engaging in some of these practices constitutes unbelief, others are universally considered innovations but do not amount to unbelief. Later on, jihadi Salafist groups became obsessed with these details and imposed their conception on others. It is also important to note that, with respect to gravestones, Ibn Taymiyya preceded Ibn Abd al-Wahhab by five centuries. The Wahhabis are aware of this and cite him: "In Damascus there were many of these monuments, and God let them be broken by [Ibn Taymiyya]'s hand.... He demolished many sites in Damascus where the people worshipped things other than God or swore oaths.... In our time [the end of the twelfth century AH], God has likewise sent one by whom He might revive the religion of Islam and pure worship of God alone after its disappearance: Sheikh Muhammad Ibn Abd al-Wahhab.... Before that, in every land and town of Najd there were idols and trees that were worshipped in place of God, oaths and sacrifices were made to them, and they exalted them more highly than God.... By means of [Ibn Taymiyya], God removed all this and established the proof against the people of his age, and all his enemies learned of tawḥīd."[59] However, the difference was that "Ibn Taymiyya preached the idea in an urban environment, and did not succeed, whereas Ibn Abd al-Wahhab preached it in a Bedouin environment and had great success."[60] Ibn Taymiyya worked in Damascus, where there were religious schools, Sufi lodges, traditions, judges, and religious endowments. Even if he had found a sultan to help him (which he did not), there was no guarantee that his thought would have spread as meaningfully and widely as Wahhabism did in Najd. As such, I propose that the spread of Wahhabism has two causes: the weakness of existing religious traditions and institutions and the readiness and ability to impose it by the sword.

The weakness of prevailing religious traditions and institutions is illustrated not only by the spread of Wahhabism but also by the spread of Twelver Shiʿism in the nineteenth century CE among the tribes of southern Iraq who were settled south of Baghdad. This weakness is also illustrated by the activities of ISIL among the newly urbanized and sedentarized rural tribal Sunni environments in Iraq and Syria. Much of ISIL's influence came from this newly urbanized tribal environment characteristic of eastern Syria, that is, the Syrian Upper Euphrates. Meanwhile, many of the recently sedentarized tribesmen of the countryside of Idlib, Homs, Hama, and Quneitra joined the Jabhat al-Nuṣra, another Salafi jihadist group fighting in Syria. Some tribes also resisted ISIL's attempts to subdue them and paid a high price.

In the 1940s CE Syrian scholar Ahmad Wasfi Zakaria (1889–1964 CE) aptly described the customs of Syrian tribes, explaining that, because they had a tenuous awareness of religion, their tribal lore was not religious. He highlighted Ibn Abd al-Wahhab's role in spreading religious consciousness in Najd by comparing

Arabs in the Najd to those in Greater Syria: "In recent centuries, ignorance of religion was common in the Arabian Peninsula except for regions such as Oman and Yemen. . . . Today, the Arabs of Najd and Qassim are less evil and ignorant of religious matters than the Arabs of the steppes of the Levant and Iraq. The Arabs of Shammar, for example, pray, while the Ruwalla do not know how to perform prayers, just like the Banu Sakhr and the Sarahan and most of the Bedouin Arabs of the Levant."[61] Zakaria wrote that their religiosity was akin to a private monotheism, a simple religion without unnecessary accretions.[62]

When a community has deeply rooted religious traditions and heritage alongside strong religious, social, and political institutions that directly engage with the masses, it is difficult to popularize a return to an austere and imagined religion, devoid of the various popular rituals and traditions that tie it to local cultures. Traditions preserved in the religious establishment, popular religiosity, and strong social structures resist ideologies like Salafism that aim to do away with them and start anew. We notice this resistance even when the existing traditions are Salafi and based on Ibn Hanbal, Ibn Taymiyya, Ibn Qayyim al-Jawziyya, and other intransigent intellectual sources. However, the Salafi mission may succeed in the context of communities with weak religious traditions. In restructuring these communities, it imitates the imagined process by which Islam was established. While Ibn Taymiyya was a scholar who worked in a cultural environment with established religious traditions and institutions and died in prison, Ibn Abd al-Wahhab, spread his call in an environment with tenuous religious traditions with his sword held high.

It is important to note that Wahhabism did not necessarily spread through religious conviction. In fact, until Ibn Abd al-Wahhab allied with Ibn Saʿud, various communities rebelled against him. At that point, the sword did its job, just as it did for members of ISIL in Mosul, Raqqa, and elsewhere. After the Kingdom of Saudi Arabia engaged in liberalization (of lifestyle) in the second decade of the twenty-first century CE and marginalized the Committee for the Propagation of Virtue and Prevention of Vice (the infamous religious police), urban Saudi Arabs gave up on this version of Salafism in droves, proving that it was imposed by the state.

Historically, spreading Islam among the Bedouin and semi-Bedouin tribes was easier due to fragile religious traditions. This took place after the religious call of Muhammad consolidated its base in Medina, and especially after the first verse of Sura al-Tawba was revealed. This Qur'an verse is directed not to the people of the book but rather the Arab polytheists. Al-Tawba states that "the Bedouins are more intense in unbelief and hypocrisy" (9:97) and gives Arabs the choice to renounce their pacts and embrace Islam or face the sword. Old reports show that those who returned to Bedouin life after they became Muslims were deemed apostates, except in certain cases, such as the Prophet's companion Dimam Ibn Thaʿlabah. When Islam spread among the Arabian Peninsula's tribal communities, it did not create institutions strong enough to displace tribal customs outside urban centers because it was difficult to establish religious institutions without a minimum level of settlement and civic life. Moreover, from the first century AH onward, Damascus, Cairo, Baghdad, and other great cities became the centers of Muslim civilization in general, including religious institutions and scholarly tradition.

The absence of old religious traditions facilitated the spread of the new mission, or the mission to renew the religion. Orientalist scholar John Lewis Burckhardt (1784–1817 CE) reported in his traveling notes, which were first published after his death in 1831, that "the Bedouins, until within a few years, had not any priests among them, neither Muslim clergy nor imams, but since their conversion to the Wahhabi faith, Muslim clergy have been introduced by a few sheikhs. . . . It is since their conversion to the Wahhabi faith (about fifteen years ago) that the Aenezes have begun an observance of the regular prayers, knowing that the Wahhabi chief is very rigid in punishing those who omit the practice."[63] According to Comte de Volney, or Constantin-François de Chasseboeuf (1757–1820 CE), "the Bedouin who live on the Turkish frontiers pretend to be Muslims for political reasons but they are so negligent of religion and their piety is so weak that they are usually considered infidels who have neither a law nor a prophet."[64]

Let us not forget that Ibn Saʿud began the hijar settlement project as an alternative to the Bedouin way of life. However, these displaced populations re-formed into new tribes, a natural development given the absence of the conditions necessary to integrate into society. Settlement, agriculture, and urbanization similarly impacted Levantine tribes.

According to Wahhabi tradition itself, Shariʿa provisions for resolving claims were applied by those who were closest to their government in settled regions. For example, one biography of Ibn Abd al-Wahhab describes his relationship with the settled people and the Bedouin as follows: When Ibn Abd al-Wahhab had declared the call, he first turned to Ibn Muʿammar, amir of Uyayna:

> And they agreed to establish this matter and the religion, to enforce the holy Shariʿa . . . and abolish all other Islamic schools of jurisprudence. Many of the notables of Uyayna and the servants of Ibn Muʿammar agreed with them, while some people were not happy with it. Ibn Abd al-Wahhab stayed a while in Uyayna. . . . The leaders and sheikhs in the rest of Najd were not happy with the spread of this religion, because it ruined all their laws and basic rules laid down by their government. . . . As for the settled people of Najd, they resorted to the Shariʿa to resolve disputes, apart from Wadi al-Dawasir and Jabal Shammar, because those people were more Bedouin than settled.[65]

We have already explained the importance of environment to the declaration of individuals as infidels and the spread of the mission through violent confrontation. Another element of the Wahhabi mission with environmental implications was that of jihad. Indeed, they believed that waging war against the enemies of Islam through raiding and plunder was a religious duty of the utmost importance; all of society could wage jihad, not just a small, organized elite. Raiding and plundering was legitimized as jihad against the infidels with the blessing of the Prophet and his companions; the lives, property, and women of the infidels were permitted, with one-fifth of the spoils going to the ruler.[66]

Life in the Najdi desert was poor. Even after the Wahhabis had assumed control, "Ibn Saʿud could not even provide Ibn Abd al-Wahhab's closest disciples with food. . . . Ibn Abd al-Wahhab acquainted his followers and adherents with the basic tenets of his teaching and inculcated the idea of the need for a jihad against 'infidels.' After the very first raids on their neighbors, the spoils were distributed 'justly' among the people of Dirʿiyya in accordance with Wahhabi doctrine: one-fifth went to Ibn Saʿud and the rest to the fighters (one share to an unmounted fighter and two shares to a mounted one)."[67] As such, while those who embraced Wahhabism were rewarded with the resources or "spoils" that came with raiding, the leaders and subjects received protection, a livelihood, and an organized society. Ibn Abd al-Wahhab was referring to this when he told Ibn Saʿud that God would enrich him with the best of the spoils.[68] Writings of the historians of the Arabian Peninsula and European explorers indicate that raiding was the main mechanism for notables to obtain wealth. For example, the Wahhabi historian Ibn Bishr estimated the tribute received by Dirʿiyya and highlighted the one-fifth shares of spoils. He wrote, "When in 1790–1791 the tribes of Mutair and Shammar were defeated, the Wahhabis obtained a great amount of spoils in the form of camels, sheep, furniture, and property. The other Bedouin were soon subject to the same fate."[69] In the fashion of raiding at the time, the victor did not look after the defeated; he took their property, including the essentials. War booty became a chief source of income for the first Saudi state; any tribe that rebelled against the rule of Al Saʿud was met with force. What is new here is the integration of the tribal principle of raiding with the principle of jihad against polytheism and innovators as well as the subjection of the warring tribes to an economy of spoils in the name of Islam.

The Saudi wars led to major demographic shifts, including vast tribal migration to Iraq and Syria.

The economy of conquest and plunder applied throughout the first Islamic mission until and after the Umayyads and Abbasids. Once raiding had been forbidden among the people in the Arabian Peninsula by Islam, the tribes began to mobilize and raid neighboring countries. The mission to spread the religion through jihad undoubtedly gave fighters a moral impetus and a sense of superiority over other societies, as illustrated by the books of conquests of al-Azdi and al-Waqidi.[70] The mission allowed not only the converted tribes to reframe raiding as jihad but also the most "backward" to despise the more "advanced" as infidels. This was the pride with which the monopolization of the true faith supplied the believer, and this was needed in order to overcome any feeling of inferiority in the fight against more advanced urban societies.

Ibn Saʿud worked to win over the tribes through the distribution of spoils. He reassured the tribes that "neither the person nor the property of anyone who accepted his rule—that is, rule by God and the Qur'an—would be touched. This decision had the desired effect in full."[71] While some amirs and sheikhs remained in command of their tribes and territory, "with the expansion of the Wahhabi state and the strengthening of the central authority, Dirʿiyya began increasingly to exchange local rulers with representatives of rival clans or members of families that in the past had had no hope of promotion."[72] This phenomenon is reminiscent of the behavior of ISIL, which appointed individuals to tribal leadership positions who would have otherwise had no hope of becoming leaders, thus ensuring blind loyalty. As Burckhardt wrote:

> The Wahabis found it necessary to change the sheikhs of almost every tribe which they subjected to their domination; well convinced that in leaving the main influence in the hands of the ruling family, the tribe would never become sincerely attached to the new supremacy. They therefore usually transferred the sheikhship to an individual of some other considerable family, who, as might be supposed, had entertained secret jealousies against the former sheikh, and was, from private motives, inclined to promote and strengthen the Wahabi interest. In general, this line of policy succeeded and was universally adopted by the Wahabis. When Mohammed Aly Pasha subjugated Hedjaz, and defeated the second Saudi dynasty he returned the long accustomed rights of the ancient families and former sheikhs, and thus created a formidable opposition to the Wahabis.[73]

The strategy of replacing tribal leadership has not only been used by the Saudi state and ISIL. Arab republics have implemented similar strategies to ensure the loyalty of tribal and clan leaders because they doubted their loyalty and feared their impact on their constituencies or their social base and needed collaborators to control it. This mechanism has nothing to do with Salafism but rather with establishing a power dynamic between ruling forces and traditional structures of societies based on a combination of clientelism and force.

Historians recount that the Saudi dynasty (before "striking oil") maintained some communitarian habits of the tribal culture of simplicity. People addressed the Saudi king informally and without any title as Ibn Saʿud (Son of Saʿud) or Akhu Noura (Brother of Noura).[74] The teacher and littérateur ʿAli al-Tantawi (1909–1999 CE) writes that when he made the pilgrimage in 1937 CE, he sat with Ibn Saʿud (of the third Saudi State) and the Damascenes accompanying him. He describes Ibn Saʿud and his companion's simplicity with admiration.[75] He also recounts that in 1926 CE an Egyptian palanquin bearing a cover for the Kaʿba arrived in Mecca, and local Bedouins began throwing stones at it as though they were casting stones at the devil,[76] crying, "An idol, an idol! They're worshiping an idol in Mina!," which nearly led to a riot. In response, Egyptian soldiers opened fire and killed several Bedouins. Then king ʿAbd al-ʿAziz arose and intervened between the two sides, shouting, "I am ʿAbd al-ʿAziz! I am ʿAbd al-ʿAziz!"[77]

Despite the large historical gap, Ibn Abd al-Wahhab successfully imitated the origins of Islam. The geographical, environmental, economic, and social circumstances of the Najd of the twelfth century AH in which he pursued his mission were not radically different from those that had prevailed during the prophet's mission: tribal customs still predominated, with small pockets of urbanization where religious custom held sway and Shariʿa was enforced.

There is a prevailing impression that Wahhabism is extreme and puritan and that it proceeded from the premise that anything new is a heretical innovation and anything unfamiliar is impermissible until a fatwa is issued permitting it. The tendency is still present in many Islamist and especially Salafi currents to immediately ask, whenever they encounter something new or foreign, "Isn't this forbidden? Is this allowed?" While the spirit of Islamic civilization and most its religious and intellectual currents is that everything is permissible unless otherwise stated, these Islamist movements assume that everything is "forbidden until proven permissible."

Contemporaries of Ibn Abd al-Wahhab wrote that the Wahhabis declared the Turks infidels because they had corrupted Islam. The Wahhabis "oppose luxury and remember that the Qur'an allowed the use of wool, not silk. They do not tolerate the eating of sweets, the drinking of coffee, and the smoking of tobacco."[78] This impression reached foreign observers in Iraq: "They fast Ramadan, shun wine, alcohol, and any other intoxicant, and even forbid the use of tobacco, setting the death penalty for those who smoke."[79] While it is true that the Wahhabis forbade tobacco and banned pilgrims from possessing it,[80] there is no evidence that Wahhabis actually put Muslims to death for tobacco.[81] French historian Edouard Driault (1864–1947 CE) must have noticed that specific groups of Muslims drank wine or took other intoxicants; otherwise, the observation would not have warranted recording, since it is well known that Islam forbids alcohol.[82] He describes the hardship of life in the Najd as follows:

> They live with great asceticism. Their food is no more than bread, usually made from barley, dates, locusts, fish, and occasionally rice and lamb, but in limited amounts. Coffee is forbidden, and they do not smoke. Their habits are simple and develop according to the circumstances of life. Complete equality is practiced among them, and there is no discrimination or use of titles to distinguish morally between people. They behave like a brotherhood towards each other and preserve their strong affection even with their leader, while they implement his will with blind obedience. . . . Their clothing and furniture are simple, they

only wear wool and cotton, and they disdain the luxurious clothing made by other nations.[83]

Driault's description of the hardship of life in Najd confirms that most of the things forbidden by the Wahhabis were not available there to start with. Importantly, rulers imposing these restrictions in historical environments were different than rulers seeking to impose similar bans in modern urban environments. Indeed, contemporary Wahhabi kings and amirs of the Saudi dynasty, who became the wealthy rulers of a large country, have themselves become much more open to worldly pleasures.

In 1796 CE, reports reached Baghdad that ʿAbd al-ʿAziz Ibn Muhammad Al Saʿud—Ibn Abdul Wahhab's son-in-law and second leader of the first Saudi project—seized al-Ahsa, al-Qatif, and al-Uqair and even reached the Gulf coast and threatened the pilgrimage route. It was rumored that he had killed two hundred of the Muslim scholars in those regions.[84] Rumors about his fighters' ferocity and violence preceded them in nearby regions and helped to generate popular hysteria. Early in the movement, ISIL enjoyed a similar reputation among locals.

On April 22, 1802, during Eid al-Ghadir, a Shiʿi celebration commemorating what Imami Shiʿism considers ʿAli Ibn Abi Talib's appointment by the Prophet Muhammad as his successor, the Wahhabis launched a surprise attack on Karbala. "Brandishing their swords, they slaughtered all those in their path, not sparing the elderly, women, and children. . . . They plundered everything in the houses, shops, and holy shrine they could lay their hands on."[85] Wahhabis exploited the fact that the majority of the city's men had assembled at Imam Ali's shrine in Najaf, leaving only 1,400 men to defend the city.[86] Although it is hard to establish the accuracy of his statements, the French consul in Basra gave a terrifying description of the Wahhabis' cruelty.[87] However, it is clear that the Wahhabis' aim was to plunder, especially because they believed they would find gifts from kings there. They also tried to dismantle the dome of the Husayn shrine in the belief that it was made of gold, until it became clear to them that it was in fact gilded copper.

ʿAbd al-ʿAziz Ibn Muhammad Al Saʿud conquered Mecca and Medina with little interference in the lives of their inhabitants. However, he did order the demolition of Turkish domed shrines and mausoleums. After Ghalib Pasha,

Mecca's amir (r. 1788–1813 CE / 1202–1228 AH), withdrew and went to Jeddah, where he fortified himself "at the beginning of Ramadan 1217 AH (December 25, 1802 CE)," 'Abd al-'Aziz Ibn Muhammad Al Sa'ud, known as Sa'ud the Great, headed for Mecca. . . . He entered without resistance and treated the inhabitants well, apart from Munib Effendi, judge of Mecca, who was removed from office and then executed for not obeying Wahhabi teaching. He was followed by twenty sheikhs who died for their creed."[88] The infamous Ta'if massacre took place more than one hundred years later in 1924 CE, during the third Saudi state's conquest of western Saudi Arabia (the Hijaz). Older generations in the Hijaz retain communal memories of atrocities, such as the capture and enslavement of women prisoners from al-Ta'if. Ibn Abd al-Wahhab's son Sheikh Abdullah received a letter from 'Abd al-'Aziz Ibn Muhammad Al Sa'ud after his conquest of Mecca in 1802 CE; in this letter, he asserted that "we are the raiding parties of the monotheists."[89] Fouad Ibrahim describes the Wahhabi invasion as follows: "The race to crush the lands of polytheism with the cavalry of the monotheists was not driven by the desire to spread peace and love, but rather a rhetoric of conquest and invasion of the Abode of Faithlessness, which incited bloodshed, the confiscation of property, the capture of women and children, the felling of trees, the sealing of wells, and the ending of all sources of life. These were the components of the image drawn by the conquests of the first Army of the Monotheists, and that was the case in al-Ta'if, Mecca, and Medina, Hail, the south, the north, and the east."[90]

After becoming guardian of the holy places, 'Abd al-'Aziz Ibn Muhammad Al Sa'ud insisted his army be granted the right to guard the pilgrims in the future. Ibrahim states that "in line with his reformist character, he banned musical accompaniment for pilgrims and also banned the decoration they carried in the procession to the Prophet's mausoleum."[91] From 1803 CE, 'Abd al-'Aziz began to block the pilgrimage routes and prevent the passage of pilgrimage caravans from the Ottoman Empire, including the Levant and Egypt. Although securing trade and transport routes and collecting taxes were the sultanate's most important functions, securing the pilgrimage routes had a special importance for the Ottomans. Each year, the caravans of pilgrims that headed for the Hijaz carried palanquins with them as well as presents to contribute to the covering of the Ka'ba, copies of the Qur'an, and goods for trade. The organization of the pilgrimage caravans took huge effort and had a festive aspect, as the caravans were normally accompanied by musicians and drummers. However, in 1806 CE, the Wahhabis stipulated that these caravans not be accompanied by any festivities, music (drums and pipes), ornaments such as the palanquin, or other celebratory displays, on the grounds that they were innovations.

While the Ottoman central government was willing to negotiate a settlement with the Saudis, their extremism at the time prevented the Wahhabis from accepting compromises that did not adhere to the strictures of their doctrine and the manifestation of adherence by others. The governors were willing to do anything to secure the pilgrimage routes and prevent their raids and took steps to placate the Saudis. For example, Kunj Yusuf Pasha, governor of Damascus (r. 1807–1810 CE / 1221–1225 AH), adhered to the religious features of Wahhabism: he closed places of entertainment and shadow-puppet theaters, banned music and late coffee shops, and forbade smoking outside the home and the shaving of beards. He set down harsh restrictions on Jews and Christians, making them wear black turbans, and he attempted to force them to convert to Islam.[92] It seems that rulers who sought to demonstrate adherence to the religion and the Sunna always imposed the so-called dhimmī rule, including a dress code (*ghiyār*). This did not last long.

Yusuf Pasha also took steps to eradicate other forms of social interaction in line with Wahhabism. For example, Louis de Corancez (1770–1832 CE) provides detailed description of the Wahhabis' rejection of and aversion to the homosexuality widespread among the Ottoman high classes.[93] He states that "sexually aberrant pashas, the wealthy, and those with high office had no shame in displaying their sexual deviation openly. When a dalliance involved a woman, it was considered a crime deserving of death, but it was permitted when it involved a male youth. . . . Among the Wahhabis, this crime was as rare as it was frequent among the Ottomans."[94] In Damascus, Yusuf Pasha punished those who engaged in this practice by having them thrown from the top of the minaret of the main mosque,[95] reminiscent of the forms of punishment used by ISIL to combat homosexuality in the twentieth century CE.

Despite his efforts, Yusuf Pasha was unable to ward off Wahhabi raids in southern Syria. Inhabitants in Damascus and Aleppo remained in a state of fear from the late eighteenth century to the early nineteenth century CE, especially after a large number of Anzah tribesmen took control of a village near Aleppo and killed its inhabitants. He compensated for his weakness by attempting to satisfy the Wahhabis with religious puritanism within Damascus and strict enforcement of the rulings on non-Muslim minorities.[96] The early Saudis mixed doctrinal fanaticism with realpolitik. They banned trade with the infidels but then resumed trading when they needed the revenue. Put differently, they boycotted foreign infidels in principle but maintained contact and sometimes even cooperated with them. They were willing to combine a position of contempt for foreigners with a determination to prove that they could be a trusted partner fit to administer a state. The French representative in Baghdad cites an example of this in the British consul in Basra's attempts to facilitate the parcel post between Basra and Aleppo by strengthening his relationship with Ibn Saʿud; Ibn Saʿud issued an order that the British consul should not be interfered with. When tribesmen robbed a messenger bearing a parcel for Aleppo, Ibn Saʿud punished the perpetrator by beheading him. He returned the parcel "stained with the blood of this unfortunate man to Monty (the British consul) to show how he kept his word."[97]

After the Saudi raids began to threaten not only pilgrimage and commercial routes but also urban centers in the Arabian Peninsula itself and in Syrian and Iraq, the Ottoman sultan ordered the governor of Egypt, Muhammad ʿAli (r. 1805–1849 CE / 1220–1265 AH), to lead a military campaign against the Saudis. The war lasted from 1811–1818 CE / 1226–1233 AH and ended with the fall of the first Saudi dynasty.

While pragmatism ultimately won out in the third Saudi state and religious authority was subordinated to political authority, it is not surprising that ISIL failed to develop a similar dynamic, whether in terms of pragmatism or adherence to international treaties and conventions. ISIL was not a state in the first place and never became a state. Even when ISIL exercised authority in the regions it controlled, it was created on the territories of sovereign states, actively opposed state logic, and challenged the international state system. In Saudi Arabia, Wahhabis evolved into a doctrine that sought integration into the state system.

Believing they were rulers and not just subjects or soldiers of the regime, the Wahhābi Ikhwān, also known as "the brothers of those who obey God," went so far as to launch raids against tribes on the other side of the northern borders (in Transjordan, Syria) and against Kuwait and Shiʿi regions, which violated Ibn Saʿud's international commitments. They criticized his friendly relations with the British (especially his son Saud's visit to London), his "tolerant" policy to the Shiʿia of Hasa, and the import of technological innovations like the telegraph. This plunged them into a bloody conflict with the third Saudi state. ʿAbd al-ʿAziz waited until he had fully occupied the Hijaz and did not need them anymore and then attacked them to make clear who ruled and who decided when to make war and peace.[98] This opposed the logic of tribal raids and that of religious fanatics who believed that political power was to serve doctrine. Furthermore, Ibn Saʿud, who established the Saudi state, did not always accept the dictates of the ʿulamaʾ: he ignored a fatwa asking him "to deny the Shiʿia of Hasa the right to worship publicly, to force them to appear before ʿulamaʾ representatives and submit to the 'religion of God and His Prophet'" and more.[99] One of the most important indications of the emergence of the Saudi state was the institutionalization of religious doctrine and its subordination to political power.

Institutionalization of the religious movement meant its subordination to the state, not the other way around. In this case, the religious establishment became a puritanical subordinate of the state—while nonetheless retaining influence because it guarded the boundaries of religion and, until recently, formed one of the most important sources of legitimacy for the ruling regime. In Saudi Arabia, the religious establishment has become not only an enforcer of outward fulfilment of religious obligation by state power but also the enforcer of and apologist for the paradigm of obedience to the ruler, condemning any attempt at rebellion as forbidden—as if obeying the ruler were one of the central precepts of Islam. It prohibited open criticism of the state and made religious welfare conditional on obedience to it. Over time, the Wahhabi religious establishment has been marginalized in Saudi Arabia, and its subordination to the ruling regime has become entrenched to such an extent that it has remained silent about major shifts away from Wahhabism. These shifts are currently being led by Crown Prince Muhammad bin Salman, particularly since the second half of 2017. It is important to note that these shifts are occurring without the religious establishment itself going through any intellectual reform. The state no longer needs prior religious reform to justify its moves, and it is unwilling to wait. The ruling regime conducts its new policies without paying attention to the "clergy," who are no more than state employees. The religious reform can come later. In fact, the reforms of Bin Salman have been accompanied by a wave of detentions targeting the most prominent Salafi political reformists.

The third Saudi state, the earliest stage of modern Saudi Arabia, used Najdi Salafism to integrate towns and provinces into a state by force or by diplomacy. It also took advantage of the breakdown of the alliance between Sharif Husayn and the British and was later supported by the British when it became the major force in the Arabian Peninsula. It would have been impossible to unite the towns and villages in a prenationalist Peninsula using secular nationalism, which in any case could not have emerged (and did not emerge) under the prevailing social and cultural conditions in Najd and its localities. Indeed, without a religious message imposed by the sword, it would have been difficult for the ruler of the village of Dirʿiyya to legitimize his ambitions to rule all of Najd, let alone the more developed Hijaz and other regions of Saudi Arabia.

When Wahhabism emerged during the Ottoman period, the inhabitants of the Arabian Peninsula were "known for their weak religious commitment and lax observance of rituals," and some of their religious traditions were considered alien to Islam.[100] As such, Wahhabism's first adversary was the prevailing popular religiosity linked to the absence of a centralized political authority. When the movement was launched, Wahhabism was subject to juristic attacks and condemnation by both Sunni and Shiʿi Muslim scholars. The force of its teachings alone was not enough for it to prevail. It had to ally itself with one of the major ambitious tribes in the Peninsula, an armed fighting force.

However, once Najdi Salafi reform was institutionalized and the rentier economy emerged due to oil wealth, the mission quickly developed into a religious establishment that coexisted with certain features of modernity. It adapted to the latest consumerist fads, far removed from puritanism and piety, while still retaining puritan and conservative Salafi ideas, practices, and (most importantly) appearances. The Wahhabi establishment's ability to fund mosques, religious seminars, and charities; host foreign students for Shariʿa and other Islamic studies; and organize the pilgrimage to Mecca significantly increased Saudi Arabia's foreign influence. At times, these same ideas were used to defy the political establishment and even became autonomous currents operating outside the establishment: a rebel Salafism calling for adherence to the "original" principles of Wahhabi Salafism and a popular Islam attracted to an unofficial Salafism that advocated rebellion against the official Salafism because it had been unfaithful to its own principles. Changing realities, including developments in communications technology and access to information, have also shaped these trends.

Most recently, the Wahhabi religious establishment's subordination to political authority has taken the extreme form of apologetics; the government has washed its hands of Wahhabi traditions, particularly with regard to the regulation of citizens' daily lives, in order to adopt a consumerist lifestyle that corresponds to the economic development of the country and the emergence of a large urban middle class that has benefited from secular education (fed by the return of more than a hundred thousand graduates from Western universities). The new rulers also have believed that the consumerist liberal lifestyle would be amenable to the West without political liberties, and that it compensates for the lack of real liberal reforms. These steps have corresponded with growing youth resentment (including young members of the ruling dynasty and its surroundings) of the imposition of religious strictures in modern daily life. Indeed, the establishment has itself proven extraordinarily flexible in accommodating the demands of the modern absolute monarchy now emerging from the rubble of dynastic power quotas and political feudalism in Saudi Arabia.

CONCLUSION

THE BEGINNING OF THIS BOOK PROVIDES AN ABSTRACT DEFINITION of Salafism as a movement whose reference sources are the Qur'an, the Sunna, and the consensus of the pious ancestors or predecessors; all inference or reasoning is based on these three sources, and any juristic and doctrinal traditions are ignored and any innovation—whether new ideas, philosophical contributions to theology, or popular beliefs and rites—are rejected. This general definition encompasses both Sunni and Shi'i juristic and doctrinal currents, religious scholars, proselytizing movements, and political movements, among others. Most importantly, it combines aspects of renewalist modernist Reformers as well as regressive Salafis who oppose reform and any textual interpretation. At the time of writing, the term *Salafi* is generally applied to regressivists. This book, which is concerned with Sunni Salafism, aims to concretize and historicize this abstract definition in order to form a richer and more useful concept.

The fact that the definition encompasses different types of Salafism raises important questions: How do renewalist modernist Reformers as well as regressive Salafis interpret the Sunna and the Qur'an? For what purpose will these interpretations be used, and how does this goal influence the interpretation? What is the definition of the innovations and new ideas that are being rejected in this return to the Prophet and his companions? Moreover, who exactly are the Salaf that are to be imitated (aside from the Prophet and his companions)? And how do these Salafisms tell their stories?

This book also distinguishes between modern and premodern Salafisms. From its inception until the beginning of the twentieth century CE, Wahhabi Salafism was thoroughly premodern—not because of its intransigent rejection of a whole range of so-called innovations, including the telegraph and girls' schooling, but because it did not emerge in the context of modernization, nor as a reaction to it. However, as an official doctrine and a conservative Salafi religious establishment, Wahhabi Salafism has adapted its approach to innovation and modernization to the raison d'état of the Saudi state.

On the other hand, although ISIL, which emerged in the context of modern states and complex interaction with the Western civilization, is well known for its masterful use of modern technology in war and propaganda, it borrowed many of the Salafist ideals of Ibn Abd al-Wahhab from the eighteenth century and leading twentieth century CE theorists of the schools of jurisprudence like Ibn Baz and Ibn al-Uthaymin alongside the ideas of jihadi ideologues. In fact, ISIL will use quotes from any jurist or scholar regardless of background to justify its actions, to the extent that the theorizations of nearly all of its "legitimizers" are taken out of context. Even though it portrays itself as the most rigid and austere of all Salafi Islamist movements, ISIL's conception of the Prophet and his companions is the least well-defined.

If jihadi Salafi takfiri organizations like ISIL identify with the Salafi juristic and doctrinal tradition, there are other currents that compete with and oppose them. Despite the fact that these movements associate themselves with the same righteous ancestors, this mutual hostility has often led them to accuse one another of being infidels and—in extreme cases—wage war against each other. The relationship between different jihadi Salafi groups has deteriorated to the extent that ISIL has turned nondoctrinal disputes with other Salafi movements into doctrinal disputes. Having branded others unbelievers, ISIL's followers are able to abandon all moral scruples in their dealings with them. In extreme cases of religious radicalism in any religion, religiosity shifts from being a stimulus for the moral sense to being an alternative to morality.

These differences cannot be explained by differing juristic traditions or disagreements over Qur'anic interpretation among Islamic jurists from the second and third centuries AH. To explain differences between Salafist movements, we must take existing social and political realities—including the struggle for leadership—into account. Indeed, without a knowledge of Ibn Hanbal's character and the way he interacted with the sociopolitical and cultural conditions of his time, it would be impossible to understand the acute discrepancy between his actual jurisprudence and what his followers have attributed to him. Similarly, it is not possible to understand Ibn Taymiyya and his internal contradictions vis-à-vis Salafism without examining his character, personal experiences, and the historical-political context, including the Mongol invasions, the Crusades, and Mamlūk rule.

Just as there is a difference between returning to the Prophet and his companions with a reformist perspective and a regressive agenda, there is a difference between how religious fundamentalism is associated with Islamic awakening and how it is associated with a return to the foundations of Islam in terms of both doctrine and law. Indeed, there is a difference between reformists' efforts to revive of the fundamentals of the religion against backwardness, which they think is caused by deviations from these fundaments, and regressivists' desire to juxtapose those fundaments or contrast them with modernity. It is important to note that no one, Muslims included, has ever experienced an abstract form of modernity. Whether in the past or the present, individuals experience modernization within specific national and societal contexts. Individuals' struggle with modernity is rooted in the contradictions and challenges they face when experiencing modernization in these specific situations.

Rather than abstract concepts, Salafism and religious fundamentalism must be understood as social phenomena directly shaped by the surrounding social, political, economic, and cultural conditions of that particular historical moment. Importantly, they must be understood in the light of their relationship with various patterns of popular, institutional, and political religiosity. Neither Salafism nor fundamentalism is a pattern of religiosity in and of itself.

For example, after Salafism became associated with Ibn Hanbal—a narrator of the stories and traditions of the Prophet and his companions—and the Hanbali school of jurisprudence,[1] Hanbalism transformed through its interaction with popular religiosity (particularly that in Baghdad), political authority, and the religious scholars who opposed the attempts of Ibn Hanbal's followers to turn him into the revered head of a jurisprudential school. Hanbalism emerged in the third and fourth centuries AH as an approach to understanding Islamic teachings; it was retroactively transformed into a school of jurisprudence and projected on Ibn Hanbal himself, whereupon Ibn Hanbal became a Hanbali. Prior to the rise of Wahhabism, the idea of returning to the Prophet and his companions was not restricted to Ibn Hanbal. Similarly, the Ahl al-Hadith were not synonymous with the Hanbalis, even in the view of Ibn Taymiyya, who decided that Ibn Hanbal had no special claim to righteous ancestors. Furthermore, Ibn Hanbal's early writings differed from his later ones, in which, according to Hanbalism, he became a true Salafist in terms of the fundamentals of jurisprudence and the fundamentals of faith and religion.

As stated previously, the general definition of *Salafism* only includes a commitment to the Qur'an and the Sunna; to reach decisions about how to apply the legal rulings of the Qur'an and the Sunna to concrete situations, individuals must rely on the words and actions of the Prophet, his companions (particularly the rightly guided caliphs), and their successors. Several criteria define the debates between a reformist, renewalist return to the Salaf on one hand and a regressive return on the other (which may take place in a modern or premodern context). The first aspect of their disagreement concerns how to interpret and apply the consensus of the Prophet and his companions when ruling on concrete situations. Specifically, renewalists and regressionists disagree over who the righteous Salaf were and, thus, whose consensus should be used, whether it is only that of the Prophet and his companions or if there are others. Second, renewalists and regressionists have different preferences for written texts and narratives, generally concerning the judgments of reason. This distinction has its origins in the early dispute between Hanbalis and Hanafis. The latter, referred to as the Ahl al-Ra'y (proponents of opinion), adopted reason as a valid basis for interpreting the Qur'anic text to deal with matters not explicitly addressed. They approach each tradition and story of the Prophet and his companions with a great deal of caution and have established strict conditions for whether a given hadith should be accepted or not; indeed, they have rejected some stories that were judged to be authentic by Hanbalis. Also called the Ahl al-Hadith (proponents of the traditions of the Prophet), Hanbalis exclusively based their legal rulings on the text and written narratives, giving the text priority in determining how to apply rulings to contemporary situations in all their complexity and preferring single reports of hadiths to application of reason.[2]

While regressive Salafism and reformist Salafism may share similar superficial similarities, they share little in terms of substance. Indeed, to call both phenomena Salafist conceals far more than it reveals. Because of the immense differences between these two phenomena, disputes over which group is truly Salafist are illusory. Both appellations are right from a historical perspective and also according to a broad definition. Restricting the use of the term *Salafism* to only one group allows us to more effectively apply it as a concept in the social sciences. Abduh—a Salafi reformist—used the term *Salafi* to emphasize a return to religious principles and the Prophet and his companions, a rejection of blind imitation (*taqlīd*), use of independent interpretation of religious texts, and purging Islamic thought of accretions viewed as having contributed to the backwardness of the Muslim community. More recently, however, reformists are rarely called Salafis.

Abduh's student Rida integrated the dual elements of Salafism and renewal to accept and adapt to the challenges of progress so as to keep the pace with "advanced nations." The partitioning of the region by French and British colonial powers, Britain's betrayal of its promises to the Arabs through the Hashemites, the insistence of the later to continue to be the protege of the British, and Atatürk's abolition of the caliphate exacerbated the struggle for territorial control and identity. Viewing this conflict as a struggle to preserve Islamic identity, Rida exhibited a growing tendency to embrace Salafism. While Rida and other reformists had previously defended Muslim identity and Islam's ability, as religion and culture, to adapt to modernity through dialogue with the modern state and colonial powers, he and especially some of his disciples shifted to actively advocating conflict with Westernization and secularization. This process served as an intellectual incubator for the emergence of dynamic types of political religiosity, like embodied in the Muslim Brotherhood. Thus, while the reformist Salafi tradition continues to impact Muslim's lives through several religious and secular influential institutions, ironically, reformist Salafism was bound to influence regressive Salafism indirectly. The process took place more than half a century later than the age of Abdu and Rida through one of its unintended offshoots, Islamist political religiosity. The emerging combination of political religiosity and Salafi religiosity is jihadi Salafism.

The link between Salafism and renewal should be viewed as not only a return to religious fundamentals with the goal of overcoming elements of backwardness but also reformists' willingness to intervene in political affairs. Involvement in politics and the public sphere was at the heart of reformist thought. Influential reformists like Abduh not only voiced political stances but also occupied positions in the Ottoman state and in Egypt's ruling establishment. Similarly, al-Afghani was ready to advise Muslim rulers and was also a political and religious propagandist. Despite being involved in politics and encouraging the formation of Muslim movements and associations, these reformists did not aim to establish Islamic political parties.

The transformation of Islam into a partisan ideology was ushered in by the Muslim Brotherhood, whose religious thought was primarily influenced by partisan activity in political mobilization and conflict with other parties and the ruling regime. As such, the Brotherhood gradually shifted away from religious reform, which led to the ideological partisan radicalization of political religiosity. As a result of the Muslim Brotherhood's interactions with the modern state and modernizing Muslim societies, this process spawned several additional types of "return." A similar reformist return took place in political Islamic movements like al-Nahda in Tunisia and the Justice and Development Parties of Morocco and Turkey.

Although the Salafi reformists returned to what they viewed as "the original, correct Islam," they neither attempted to reproduce "the original, correct Islam" nor did they promote the populist phrase "Islam is the solution" as a slogan of a political party.

Conversely, the Salafism of Ibn Abd al-Wahhab was a premodern phenomenon that sought to impose a reproduction of "the original, correct Islam" on desert tribes who, according to his understanding of monotheism, lived in a state of ignorance, a pre-Islamic state. Rather than establishing a political party, Ibn Abd al-Wahhab formed an alliance with tribal leadership to propagate his message by force. Wahhabism later became the official doctrine of the Kingdom of Saudi Arabia.

The fact that Prophet Muhammad and his companions so successfully propagated Islam and established a political entity on the Arabian Peninsula shows that it is the very antithesis of modern attempts to reproduce this experience. The Prophet and his companions imitated no one and did not try to impose a ready-made utopia on society. They openly embraced renewal and sought to preserve existing societal customs. The Sunna as it was developed and emulated in Medina in the age of the Prophet and the rightly guided caliphs illustrated vitality; rather than being applied to society, Shari'a was being created in interaction with day-to-day life. In comparison, the contemporary regressionist belief that applying the literal textual accounts of the Prophet and his companions is the only way to understand the Qur'an is evidence of intellectual rigidity and stagnation. In the first centuries of Islam, the dialogue around the Sunna was brimming with lively juristic, doctrinal, and intellectual disagreements. Conversely, viewing the apparent literal meaning of the Qur'an and the Hadith as the only possible meaning, and the practice of declaring anyone who fails to accept this meaning an infidel is evidence of a hostility to evolution that disregards modern Muslim societies' lived realities.

Ibn Hanbal was not a politician and refused to involve himself in the public sphere or the political affairs of the state. He studiously avoided worldly power and authority and took a dim view of those he considered to be "the sultan's jurisconsults." In this sense the Hanbalis of the fourth and fifth centuries AH who accepted government positions and even advocated obedience to the ruler, be they righteous or sinful, were at odds with the ethos of their master. Contemporary puritan Salafi currents similarly steer clear of politics except to advocate obedience to the ruler.

This same trajectory has been followed by official Wahhabism and numerous other puritan Salafi organizations that have emerged in Arab countries and elsewhere. These movements have taught people religious fundamentals, including prayer, fasting, and other rites, and have waged war on the innovations (*bid'a*) with which (in their view) popular religiosity is rife. They emphasize Islamic identity, enforce rigid gender segregation and strict Islamic attire, foster a negative attitude toward religious minorities and those who disagree with "correct" doctrine, insist on rejection of "imported ideas" like pan-Arabism, nationalism, patriotism, philosophy, and the social sciences, urge abstention from "imported" consumeristic habits, and so on.

At the same time, Islamic political movements have emerged that take the "original Islam" and turn it into a one-size-fits-all ideological model that can be applied to contemporary contexts. Instead of accomplishing these goals through changing people's minds and establishing committed religious communities within existing society, these movements pursue political action, regardless how varied they are in their pragmatism and their capacity to adapt to the requirements of political action, including that of party formation. In addition, while some have aimed to establish an Islamic system of rule (*niẓām ḥukm Islāmī*) through bottom-up strategies like proselytizing and political action, others have supported the idea of seizing power (by force if need be) and imposing Islamic teaching from the top down. Although these movements have divided into jihadi currents, some more pragmatic than others, all have declared that the Muslim rulers of their countries were infidels and have prepared to wage jihad against them. These developments have occurred during the crisis of the Arab dictatorships and the shaking of the hegemony of secular ideological currents prominent in the Arab world since the 1950s.

Although contemporary puritan Salafi currents like al-Jāmiyya al-Madkhaliya claim to be apolitical, they view obedience to the ruler as an unconditional obligation, which inevitably renders them political, especially in the context of social and political upheavals. Some of these movements have demonstrated a willingness to defend ruling regimes against Arab uprisings since 2011. Other political Islamic movements influenced by jihadi Salafism have declared rebellion against Muslim rulers, justifying their actions by different reading of the Salaf. It is important to note that they have applied the rulings of Ibn Taymiyya without taking historical context into account. Indeed, both Ibn Hanbal and Ibn Taymiyya placed the authority of religion above the ruler without advocating rebellion against him. Like most Muslim jurists throughout history, Ibn Hanbal refused to sanction rebellion against the ruler for fear of causing strife (*fitna*). Unlike political Islamist movements, neither Ibn Taymiyya nor Ibn Hanbal referred to his era as the new age of ignorance to justify rebellion against society and the ruler.

Ever since al-Banna, political religiosity has held that Islam exists in a state of conflict. As a youth experiencing the impact of the West on his society under British colonialization, al-Banna believed "Islam" was in confrontation with Westernization, decadence, and licentiousness. Over time, Islam, according to his understanding, came into conflict with liberalism, Arab nationalism, secularism, and then the left. The process of indoctrination and polarization has forced these movements into endless conflicts with Islam as a living civilization and with the Islam that Muslims practice and experience on a daily basis in contemporary states and societies.

Al-Banna urged his vanguard to emulate his emotional break from secular society. He consolidated the sense of community in the Brotherhood, thereby creating a mindset that influenced Qutb's belief that the believers were superior to the new ignorant society and should emotionally isolate themselves.

Encouraging feelings of alienation from one's own society is similarly reminiscent of the Wahhabi doctrine of loyalty and disavowal (*al-walā' wa al-barā'*).[3] Qutb's isolation and emotional migration (*hijra*) from Muslim society was so extreme that he refused to pray with others and urged believers to pray in their houses rather than in state mosques, as though worship itself had become a kind of political organization.

Unlike original Wahhabism, recent Salafi movements accept contemporary innovations and inventions. In this sense, these movements are fundamentally more ideological than early Wahhabism and more modern in their structure and instrumental thinking. Wahhabism was a traditional religious revivalist movement that sought to spread its understanding of religion by the force of tribal ʿaṣabiyya. Wahhabism later evolved into a religious doctrine of a state with several ideological functions. This spawned oppositional Wahhabi Salafi movements that sought to hold the Saudi state accountable for implementing the "original" Wahhabism—that is, their official declared discourse and the stated religious educational curriculum.

Modernization visibly influenced the temperaments of Islamic movements and the ideas of leaders such as Qutb. It is impossible to understand Qutb's teachings outside the context of Westernization, the impact of the modern state and its repressive apparatus, the emergence of mass society, and what Qutb viewed as the idolatrous worship of the charismatic Egyptian president Gamal Abdel Nasser. It should be remembered that in the original Islam—which Islamic movements are trying to reproduce in modern state institutions—there was no comprehensive state capable of controlling people's lives on the societal and individual levels. Inevitably, attempts to establish an Islamic system of rule in a modern state are totalitarian. However, Islam has never been, and could not have been, the ideology of a totalitarian state, whether in its earliest beginnings or under successive Islamic empires. Totalitarianism can emerge in a modern state that not only monopolizes "legitimate" violence but also aims to control all aspects of life in the state, including the economic, cultural, and ideological.

It is important to note that these movements' approach to utopia is the obverse of the conservatives' approach. Just as conservative secular thought opposes the application of revolutionary utopias and attempts to impose them in the form of sociopolitical order on society, conservative Islamic thought uses the Medinan utopia as an ideal, a moral compass to guide behavior.

Political Islamic movements oppose what they call positive law because it was created by human beings and thus interferes with divine law; some extremist political movements reject majority rule as a kind of idolatry. However, proponents of these movements approach the Shariʿa as though it were itself positive law: a set of ready-made rulings and provisions that can be directly inserted into the constitution and enforced by the state's oppressive apparatus. It is important to note that this scenario differs entirely from the way in which societies accepted Shariʿa naturally.

In addressing the age of ignorance as a condition and not a historical pre-Islamic age, there are traditions of the Prophet and his companions in *Ṣaḥīḥ al-Bukhārī,* which contains a section entitled "Acts of Disobedience Reflect Ignorant Morals and Thinking." In one story, the Prophet uses the word *ignorant* to warn some of the companions against returning to tribalism. Ibn Taymiyya also used the word *ignorant* when discussing sins. However, neither the Prophet nor notable Islamic scholars have used the term to refer to the general condition of Muslims or to declare Muslim communities or societies to be infidels. Even Qutb did not intend to declare individuals to be infidels (*takfīr al-muʿayyan*). Instead, he used the term *ignorant* to describe the state of a society as a whole. Indeed, ISIL, as the latest and most extreme of the jihadi Salafi movements, is one of the only movements to link a generalized judgment of ignorance with the act of declaring people to be infidels and thus declaring it lawful to punish them as apostates.

The interaction between more radical movements like the Qutbist current of the Muslim Brotherhood facilitated the emergence of jihadi Salafi groups that, although they draw on the same juristic and doctrinal sources as puritan Salafis, disagree with them politically. The disputes between these movements, then, are political. They revolve around the need to control the modern state and strategies for spreading the religion. In many cases this political dispute has led to doctrinal disputes, particularly over issues like declaring others infidels (*takfīr*). Even in this case, the disputing movements have drawn on the same sources to justify their positions, although each has emphasized different statements made in different contexts, on different occasions, and for different reasons. The appeal to return to the Prophet and his companions is made to justify positions on contemporary issues, making both eclectic and selective.

It is important to note that calling for a return to religion does not necessarily imply that societies were not religious before. While political Islamist movements intend to integrate the religion and state, a return to Islam as both a religion and a state is not possible. This would not be achievable within the structure of the modern state and contemporary understanding of state and religion, and Islam was never an integrated religion and state in the first place. A conjoined "religion and state" is a modern, secularized concept with its own logic, mechanisms, and institutions; the state's unification with religion would be tantamount to using religion as an ideology. Moreover, although the political power may initially be active in spreading a religion and dictating its provisions, the unity of state and religion usually means subjugating the religious establishment by the state. In some cases, religion may become a state ideology in the service of the ruling regime, as in the case of Wahhabism and Saudi Arabia.

Different Salafi currents refer to themselves as the saved sect (*al-firqa al-nājiya*), the people of the Sunna (Ahl al-Sunna), and Ahl al-Sunna wa al-Jamāʿa because they believe that they represent the entire community of Muslims rather than merely a subcommunity. However, this approach contradicts the way of thinking of the Prophet and his companions, regardless of whoever that may be. Contemporary Salafis understand the community of Muslims as an abstract idea, an international Muslim community not associated with any particular homeland or national identity. Although such a community does not exist, they consider themselves to be its perfect embodiment.

While some researchers assert that the rejection of religious innovations means adherence to Islamic culture, in reality, contemporary regressive Salafi currents that cling to an original and pristine simplicity are hostile to everything associated with Islamic culture and civilization. In their call to return to and emulate the "original Islam," they reject all achievements of the Islamic civilization since its inception as religious innovations and deviations from the righteous origins. While this approach might have made sense when Wahhabism spread among fragmented tribal communities in Najd, their efforts have been at odds with institutionalized religious traditions in more advanced countries and regions, including many urban centers in the Arabian Peninsula itself.

Before the exchanges between Wahhabi Salafism—then a prevailing and official school of jurisprudence—and radical Brotherhood figures who had taken refuge in the Arabian Peninsula itself, the Brotherhood defined itself as a movement that was simultaneously Salafi, Sufi, and political.[4] This approach has allowed the Brotherhood to effectively address a broader Muslim audience that includes Salafis, Sufis, and others. Wahhabism—which is hostile to Sufism in general—was still limited to the Peninsula and had yet to impact communities in Egypt, the Levant, and the Maghreb.

The spread of Wahhabism mirrored the emergence of a new religion because it believed the communities of the Peninsula itself to be ignorant; it justified using violence to spread its message and treated those who rejected this message as infidels that they could plunder and enslave. These practices helped the Saudis win over the tribes that benefited from the conquest economy. Given his preoccupation with the issues of monotheism and idolatry, Ibn Abd al-Wahhab was consumed with battling these communities' "idolatrous" practices, like visiting saints' graves and asking them to intercede with God on their behalf. While he did not seek to initiate a political movement, his goal of imposing his religious teachings on society required an alliance with a political power that could rule over people and country. Specifically, while he acknowledged the political leadership as an imamate, political leaders recognized his spiritual chiefdom. However, in Salafi thought, there is no connection between hereditary state power, hereditary spiritual leadership, and the latter's subordination to the former. Wahhabism pushed popular religiosity toward greater strictness and austerity without offering a political program. In this respect, it differed from the impact of Qutb, who based his thought and action on al-Mawdudi's principle of divine sovereignty. Although the term *divine sovereignty* appears nowhere in traditional Islamic writings, it was this principle that led jihadists back to Ibn Taymiyya and later Wahhabism. While Qutb linked Islamic utopia with resistance to contemporary dictatorial regimes that do not govern according to what God has revealed (*ṭāghūt*), neither Ibn Taymiyya nor Ibn Abd al-Wahhab sought to eliminate tyranny.

Ibn Abd al-Wahhab declared that he was content appealing directly to the Qur'an and the Sunna, suggesting that he supported a reformist approach that allowed any individual the freedom to understand Islam in accordance with his or her own conscience, but he viewed anyone who opposed his doctrinal teaching as hostile to the religion itself.

The main factors that have contributed to the spread of Wahhabism in the Arabian Peninsula are the absence of deep religious traditions, weakness of religious institutions in tribal communities, the reliance on force to spread their message, and the practice of rewarding tribes through plundering. Wahhabism has never adapted to modernity; instead, it has succumbed to the demands of rulers of modern states and the requirements of states intensely connected to the world economy and trade and to international relations. This can be plausibly illustrated by the Wahhabi establishment's acquiescence and even submissiveness to the reforms implemented by the Saudi crown prince since 2017 CE, carried out without any revision of its religious thought. Although Wahhabi Salafism has benefited from its partnership with the Saudi state as it has spread through the Arabian Peninsula, it has obtained these benefits only through submission to the state and its internal logic to the point that it has disengaged from some central ideas of their doctrine.

Ibn Abd al-Wahhab declared the Bedouins infidels, viewing them as nominal Muslims who needed to be taught how to perform the ritual prayer. However, he was met with opposition in urban areas and was only able to spread his teachings through force and by partnering with a powerful and politically ambitious tribe. This pattern repeated in the case of ISIL, which has more easily spread its teachings in border regions among rural tribes and clans in Iraq and Syria—although even in these communities, ISIL has resorted to brute force to advance its ideology.

Similarly, puritan Salafi ideas have more easily spread in regions that lack well-established religious culture and related traditions. Of course, this is not to say that elitist puritan Salafi movements do not arise in urbanized, developed communities. Indeed, these organizations have successfully proselytized marginalized urban and semi-urban communities harmed by modernization. Groups of this kind have been Salafis in the broadest sense of the term of preaching the "true Islam" of the sacred text and the righteous ancestors and purging the religion of idolatry innovations. They emerged in the early twentieth century CE, and in preaching pure Islam, these groups have created, in certain cases, a mode of religiosity and a cultural environment that has fostered the spread of Islamist movements and apolitical Salafi currents that have since became politically active. For example, the party al-Nour has run in parliamentary elections. In its attempts to outbid even the Muslim Brotherhood, al-Nour has fueled sectarianism and hindered any possible religious-secular understanding. It supported a military coup against Egypt's duly elected president with no hesitation and has not been heard from since the reconstitution of the dictatorship.

In these cases, puritan Salafi currents are driven by elites who spread what, in their view, is the correct religion, calling on people to perform the ritual prayers, observe Islamic rites, abandon religious innovations, and so on. In the early twentieth century CE, they began distributing copies of the Qur'an, building mosques, and founding societies that combine preaching with charity and social service provision. These societies' abstention from political action has led rulers to treat them with tolerance, thus allowing them to expand at a time when government authorities were clashing with Islamist movements. In addition, this has made it easier for them to present themselves as free from political corruption. Puritan Salafi organizations have thus been able to foster positive images of themselves and exploit the political alienation broadly felt by society. By contrast, jihadi Salafis happily declare others infidels, including any ruler who does not govern based on what God has revealed, and openly rebel against them. This is a point on which jihadi Salafis have been criticized by puritan and apolitical Salafis, whose noninvolvement in politics has served as a source of protection for them.

Since the rise of Qutb and the Qutbist current within the Muslim Brotherhood, jihadist organizations have been declaring rulers to be infidels. Because they declare others to be infidels based on acts of disobedience without taking circumstances and conditions into account, the religious establishment views jihadi organizations as Khawārij. In addition, jihadis use a broadened definition of idolatry and approve of applying the term *ignorance* to entire Muslim societies. Since these movements' interaction with Salafism, they have broadened their declaration of infidelity based on whether individuals believe only "in parts of Islam while rejecting other parts" and display their faith through action, since faith alone is not sufficient. They believe that, although the Qur'an forbids coercion of faith, this refers to inward faith and belief; coercion is permissible in relation to the external aspects of religious practice. The Qutbists go beyond the explicit meaning of the Qur'anic text and engage in the practice of hermeneutics (*ta'wīl*), which in theory they are supposed to reject. As such, while these movements accept freedom of choice in relation to inward faith and belief, they oppose freedom of choice in terms of behavior. Consequently, their opposition to any moral interpretation, religious function, and democratization represents a fundamental inconsistency in their thoughts. Not only do they engage in and justify religious coercion, but they also reject the notion of majority will if it goes against their construal of Shari'a law. Different movements, then, disagree on how to understand the religion on the one hand and how to position religion in relation to democracy on the other. In fact, the moral understanding of religion and democracy neither conflicts with Islam nor with any pattern of Islamic religiosity.

In their attempt to identify historical sources for jihadi political movements, some researchers have assumed a linear historical development from Ibn Taymiyya and Qutb to Ibn Abd al-Wahhab and ultimately to ISIL. The fact that certain movements appeal to specific texts does not demonstrate that their doctrine directly evolved from these texts. Indeed, we cannot properly understand ISIL, which was prepared to declare even al-Qaeda itself an infidel organization, without reference to the collapse of the Syrian government, the fragility of state institutions in Iraq, and the rise of sectarianism in Iraq and elsewhere. Moreover, interactions between Muslim Brotherhood members and Wahhabi Salafism after they sought refuge in Saudi Arabia during their conflict with the Nasserite regime held much greater ideological influence than any link to Ibn Taymiyya. Political religious movements are not texts generated by other texts but sociopolitical phenomena.

Hence, the disputes among modern Islamist movements such as ISIL, al-Qaeda, the Muslim Brotherhood, Anṣār al-Sunna, and others cannot be explained in terms of the differences among Muslim jurists from the third and fourth centuries AH to the time of Ibn Taymiyya. While these movements collectively appeal to the same jurists, ISIL and other jihadi groups further complicate the picture by cherry-picking fatwas and quotations from the writings of all jurists to justify their actions. These competing groups reach different conclusions and place their conclusions in the service of different aims, while religious establishments and folk religiosity has proceeded from a totally different perspective than that of political religious movements falsely branded "political Islam." Hence, these movements cannot be viewed simply as the products of jurists from the past and their writings. Rather, a proper analysis requires taking into consideration the historicity of texts and juristic doctrines and the projection of the contemporary understanding of the Salaf onto the past and then the reprojection of this imagined past onto the present. It also requires a consideration of the prevailing sociopolitical conditions, the intellectual and psychological backgrounds of involved actors, and the political struggle among the movements themselves.

Key People and Religious Associations

Abduh, Muhammad	محمد عبده	Egyptian religious reformer (1849–1905 CE).
Afghani, Jamal al-Din al-	جمال الدين الأفغاني	Islamic reformist (1838–1897 CE / 1254–1315 AH).
ahādīth al-āḥād (also known as ahādīth al-wāḥid, khabar al-āḥād, al-āḥād)	أحاديث الآحاد (ويسمّى أحاديث الواحد، خبر الآحاد، أو آحاد)	Single reports of hadiths; unsuccessive narrators' reports of sayings and deeds of the Prophet.
Ahl al-Ra'y	أهل الرأي	Proponents of opinion.
Ahl al-Sunna wa al-Hadith wa al-Athar	أهل السنّة والحديث والأثر	Followers of the Sunna, Hadith, and Narration.
Ahl al-Sunna wa al-Jamā'a	أهل السنة والجماعة	Followers of prophetic tradition and the consensus among Ahl al-Hadith.
Albani, Muhammad Nasir al-Din al-	محمد ناصر الدين الألباني	Syrian Salafi scholar known for opposing both nonviolent and violent political activism (1914–1999 CE).
Anṣār al-Sunna	أنصار السنة	Iraqi insurgent group, formed in 2003 CE after a joint operation by Iraqi and US forces, that hit Anṣār al-Islam's sites where the majority of its members were captured, killed, or fled to neighboring Iran. The group temporarily renamed itself to Anṣār al-Sunna (until 2007 CE). Anṣār al-Sunna fought against US troops and their local allies during the Iraq War and were linked with al-Zarqawi.
Anṣār al-Sunna al-Muḥammadiyya	أنصار السنّة المحمدية	Salafi association founded in 1926 CE in Egypt by Muhammad Hamid al-Fiqqi.
Baghdadi, Abu Bakr al-	أبو بكر البغدادي	Leader of the Islamic State of Iraq and the Levant (ISIL) (1971–2019 CE).
Barelvi, Sayyid Ahmad	السيد أحمد البريلوي	Indian Muslim revivalist scholar (1786–1831 CE / 1201–1246 AH).

Bukhari, Muhammad Ibn Isma'il al-	محمد بن إسماعيل البخاري	Islamic scholar who is the author of the famous hadith collection *Ṣaḥīḥ al-Bukhārī*.
Chishti	جشتية	An order or school within the Muslim Sufi tradition that was established in the tenth century CE in Chisht, Afghanistan.
Dahlawi, Shah Waliullah al-	شاه ولي الله الدهلوي	Indian Islamic scholar and theologian (1703–1762 CE / 1114–1176 AH).
Dimashqi, Ghaylan al-	غيلان الدمشقي	Leader of the Qadarī (Murj'ite) movement in Damascus who served in government positions during the Umayyad Dynasty (d. 724 CE / 106 AH).
Farra', Abu Ya'la al-	أبو يعلى الفراء	Islamic jurist of the Hanbali school (990–1066 CE / 380–458 AH).
Filastini, Abu Qatada al-	أبو قتادة الفلسطيني	Theorist of the Algerian Fighting Islamic Group and ideologue of violent jihadi Salafism (Jaysh al-Islām) (b. 1959 CE).
Fiqqi, Muhammad Hamid al-	محمد حامد الفقي	Egyptian Islamic scholar, student of Rida, who established Anṣār al-Sunna al-Muḥammadiyya in 1926 CE with the goal of spreading Ibn Taymiyya's teachings (1892–1959 CE).
Al-Gam'iyya al-Shar'iyya (or Shar'iyya Society)	الجمعية الشرعية	Egyptian Islamic Association founded in 1912 CE by al-Subki.
Ghazali, Abu Hamid al-	أبو حامد الغزالي	Theologian and jurist of Islam (1058–1111 CE / 450–505 AH).
Ghazali, Muhammad al-	محمد الغزالي	Egyptian scholar, Islamic writer, and a member of the Egyptian Muslim Brotherhood from the late 1930s CE until his expulsion in December 1953 CE (1917–1996 CE).
Ibn Abd al-Wahhab, Muhammad	محمد بن عبد الوهاب	Theologian from Najd, central Arabia, who is considered the founder of Wahhabism (1703–1792 CE / 1115–1206 AH).
Ibn al-Uthaymin, Muhammad Ibn Salih	محمد بن صالح العُثيمين	Saudi Arabian Islamic jurist (1925–2001 CE).
Ibn Badran al-Dimashqi, Abd al-Qadir	عبد القادر بن بدران الدمشقي	Hanbali fundamentalist jurist also considered to be one of the late Hanbali imams (1864–1927 CE / 1280–1346 AH).
Ibn Baz, 'Abd al-'Aziz	عبد العزيز ابن باز	Saudi Arabian Islamic jurist who served as grand mufti of Saudi Arabia (1912–1999 CE).
Ibn Dirham, al-Ja'd	الجعد بن درهم	Islamic theologian considered the first representative of the Jabrites in Islam (715–724 CE / 46–105 AH).
Ibn Hanbal, Abdullah Ibn Ahmad	عبد الله بن أحمد ابن حنبل	Jurist, son of Ahmad Ibn Hanbal (828–903 CE / 213–290 AH).
Ibn Hanbal, Ahmad	أحمد ابن حنبل	Founder of the Hanbali school of Sunni jurisprudence (780–855 CE / 164–241 AH).

Ibn Hazm, Abu Muhammad ʿAli Ibn Ahmad Ibn Saʿid	أبو محمد علي بن أحمد بن سعيد (ابن حزم)	Andalusian historian, jurist, theologian, and leading proponent and codifier of the Ẓāhirī school of Islamic thought (994–1064 CE / 384–456 AH).
Ibn Qayyim al-Jawziyya, Shams al-Din Abu Abdullah Muhammad Ibn Abi Bakr	شمس الدين أبو عبد الله محمد بن أبي بكر ابن قيّم الجوزية	Theologian and author who belonged to the Hanbali school of jurisprudence (1292–1350 CE / 691–751 AH).
Ibn Rushd, Abu al-Walid Muhammad Ibn Ahmad Ibn Muhammad	أبو الوليد محمد بن أحمد بن محمد (ابن رشد)	Andalusian Islamic philosopher (1126–1198 CE / 520–595 AH).
Ibn Safwan, al-Jahm	الجهم بن صفوان	Islamic theologian who founded the Jahmi movement (696–745 CE / 78–128 AH).
Al Saʿud, ʿAbd al-ʿAziz (Ibn Saʿud)	عبد العزيز آل سعود (ابن سعود)	Arab tribal leader and statesman who founded and ruled the Saudi Kingdom (1875–1953 CE).
Ibn Taymiyya al-Harrani, Taqi al-Din Abu al-Abbas Ahmad Ibn Abd al-Halim	ابن تيمية الحرّاني، تقي الدين أبو العباس أحمد ابن عبدالحليم	Theologian of the Hanbali school of jurisprudence (1263–1328 CE / 661–728 AH).
Ibn Thabit, Abu Hanifa al-Nuʿman	أبو حنيفة النعمان بن ثابت	Theologian and Islamist jurist who is considered the founder of the Hanafi school of Sunni jurisprudence (699–767 CE / 80–150 AH).
Al-Jamāʿa al-Salafiyya al-Muḥtasiba	الجماعة السلفية المحتسبة	Salafi group focused on apolitical action.
Jamāʿat al-Tablīgh	جماعة التبليغ	Transnational Sunni Salafi missionary movement established in 1926 CE in India.
Juwayni, Imam al-Haramayn Abu al-Maʿali Abd al-Malik Ibn Abdullah al-	إمام الحرمين أبو المعالي عبد الملك بن عبد الله الجُوَيْني	Imam and classical writer whose approach to maqāṣid has been reclaimed as part of reformism's reconstruction of Salafism (1028–1085 CE / 419–478 AH).
Kawakibi, Abd al-Rahman al-	عبد الرحمن الكواكبي	Syrian reformist and author in the second half of the nineteenth century CE who explored issues of pan-Arabism and Islamic identity and despotism and who read democracy into sacred texts and early Islam (1849–1902 CE).
Khatib, Muhibb al-Din al-	محب الدين الخطيب	Syrian Salafi writer and founder of the Salafi Bookstore in Egypt (1886–1969 CE).
Maqdisi, Abu Muhammad al-	أبو محمد المقدسي	Salafi theoretician who is one of the most important theorists of jihadi Salafism (b. 1959 CE).
Mashhur, Mustafa	مصطفى مشهور	Fifth leader (supreme guide) of the Muslim Brotherhood in Egypt (1921–2002 CE).
Mawdudi, Abu al-Aʿla al-	أبو الأعلى المودودي	Islamic scholar and activist in British India and later Pakistan who coined the term *ḥākimiyya* (God's sovereignty) (1903–1979 CE).

Muqbili, Salih Ibn Mahdi al-	صالح بن مهدي المقبلي	Yemeni Zaydi scholar (1637–1696 CE / 1047–1108 AH).
Mustafa, Shukri	شكري مصطفى	Leader and founder of al-Takfīr wa al-Hijra in Egypt (1942–1978 CE).
Mutawakkil, Jaʿfar Ibn Muhammad al-Muʿtasim billah al-	جعفر بن محمد المعتصم بالله (المتوكل)	Abbasid caliph (r. 847–861 CE / 232–246 AH) who renounced his predecessors' doctrine which mandated the belief that the Qur'an was created.
Qasimi, Jamal al-Din al-	جمال الدين القاسمي	Islamic scholar and a pioneer of the modern scientific and religious renaissance in the Levant (1866–1914 CE).
Qutb, Sayyid	سيد قطب	Islamic scholar and leading member of the Egyptian Muslim Brotherhood (1906–1966 CE).
Razi, Fakhr al-Din al-	فخر الدين الرازي	Persian Islamic scholar and pioneer of inductive logic who wrote several works of rational theology, including a work of exegesis, *The Keys to the Unknown* (1149–1210 CE / 544–605 AH).
Rida, Muhammad Rashid	رشيد رضا	Islamic scholar who further developed Abduh's reformist stance but put more emphasis on Salafism and less on commitment to the imperative of reform (1865–1935 CE).
Sanusi, Muhammad Ibn ʿAli al-	محمد بن علي السنوسي	Algerian theologian who founded the Senusi order (1787–1859 CE / 1202–1276 AH).
Shatibi, Abu Ishaq Ibrahim Ibn Musa al-	أبو اسحاق إبراهيم بن موسى الشاطبي	Classical writer whose approach to maqāṣid has been reclaimed as part of reformism's reconstruction of Salafism (1320–1388 CE / 720–790 AH).
Sindhi al-Madani, Muhammad Hayya Ibn Ibrahim al-	محمد حياة بن إبراهيم السندي المدني	Hadith scholar born in Sindh who lived and died in Medina (d. 1750 CE / 1163 AH).
Subki, Mahmoud Muhammad Khattab al-	محمود محمد خطاب السبكي	Islamic scholar who founded al-Gamʿiyya al-Sharʿiyya (the Sharʿiyya Society) in Egypt (1858–1933 CE).
Suri, Abu Musʿab al-	أبو مصعب السوري	Syrian jihadi theorist and ideologue of the Islamist jihadi stream (b. 1958 CE).
al-Takfīr wa al-Hijra	التكفير والهجرة	Islamic jihadist group, also known as Jamāʿat al-Muslimīn, that was founded by Shukri Mustafa in Egypt in the 1960s CE as an offshoot of the Muslim Brotherhood.
Utaybi, Juhayman al-	جهيمان العتيبي	Leader of al-Jamāʿa al-Salafiyya al-Muḥtasiba who shifted the group, psychologically and religiously, to messianic redemptionism (Mahdism, or believing in the return of the Mahdi) (1936–1980 CE).
Wadiʿi, Muqbil Ibn Hadi al-	مقبل بن هادي الوادعي	Yemeni scholar who founded the Dammaj school of Salafism in Yemen (1933–2001 CE).

Wahhābi Ikhwān, or Ikhwān man aṭā' Allah	إخوان الوهابية / إخوان من أطاع الله	Known as "the brothers of those who obey God," a religious and military brotherhood whose members were organized by Ibn Sa'ud in 1912 CE and left their tribes to undertake jihad under the banner of Wahhabism.
Zarqawi, Abu Mus'ab al-	أبو مصعب الزرقاوي	Al-Qaeda-affiliated leader in Iraq (1966–2006 CE).
Zawahiri, Ayman al-	أيمن الظواهري	Leader of al-Qaeda since June 2011 CE / Jamāda al-Thāni 1432 AH, succeeding Osama bin Laden following his death.

Glossary

akhbārīs	الأخباريون	Those who rely on akhbār, i.e., reported traditions.
al-amr bi al-maʿrūf wa al-nahī ʿan al-munkar	الأمر بالمعروف والنهي عن المنكر	Commanding virtue and forbidding vice.
ʿaṣabiyya	عصبية	A pre-Islamic term that became conceptualized by Ibn Khaldun in his Muqaddimah. His concept of ʿaṣabiyya (group solidarity) refers to the major driving force of the tribe to seize power from decadent rulers whose own ʿaṣabiyya has weakened due to decay caused by the luxuries of the rule itself and urban life.
asbāb al-nuzūl	أسباب النزول	Reasons for the revelation of particular verses.
ʿāṣin wa-fāsiq	عاص وفاسق	A Muslim believer in the principles of Shariʿa who deviates from the Shariʿa without being an apostate.
bayʿa	بيعة	Oath of allegiance.
bidʿa/muḥdathāt	بدعة/محدثات	Innovation.
Dār al-Islām	دار الإسلام	Abode of Islam; a juridical term for certain territories governed according to Islamic law.
Dār al-Silm	دار السلم	Abode of Peace
Dār al-Ḥarb	دار الحرب	Abode of War; a juridical term for certain territories that are not under Islamic rule.
dhimmīs	ذميون/ ذمّي	Monotheist non-Muslims living legally within an Islamic state.
farḍ ʿayn	فرض عين	Incumbent on every Muslim.
al-firqa al-nājiya	الفرقة الناجية	The saved sect.
fisq	فسق	Failure to act in the correct way.
fitna	فتنة	Chaos/strife.
fuqahāʾ, faqīh	فقهاء / فقيه	Islamic jurist(s).

al-ghayb	الغيب	Realm of the metaphysical.
al-ghulū	الغلو	Extremism.
Hadith al-iftirāq	حديث الافتراق	The hadith describing the fragmentation of Islam into multiple sects.
ḥākimiyya	حاكمية	The principle of God's sovereignty.
Hanafism	حنفية	Hanafism is a school of Islamic jurisprudence that refers to the Imam Abu Hanifa.
Hanbalism	حنبلية	Hanbalism is a school of Islamic jurisprudence that was founded by Ibn Hanbal.
ḥarām	حرام	Prohibited according to religion.
ḥudūd	حدود	Qur'anically prescribed legal sanctions.
al-iʿjāz al-ʿilmī	الإعجاز العلمي	The scientific inimitability of the Qur'an.
ijmāʿ	إجماع	Principle of consensus.
ijtihād	اجتهاد	Use of intellectual reasoning to derive rules or judgments from the basic principles of religion and religious text.
Imami Shiʿism / Twelver Shiʿism	شيعية إمامية / الشيعة الإثنا عشرية	Twelver Shiʿa, the largest branch of Shiʿi Islam, founded on the distinct beliefs that the twelve Shiʿi imams after the Prophet Muhammad are the spiritual and political successors to the Prophet.
al-iqrār bi al-janān wa al-qawl bi al-lisān wa al-ʿamal bi al-arkān	الإقرار بالجنان والقول باللسان والعمل بالأركان	Believers must be convinced in their soul, profess it with their tongue, and act according to the fundaments.
irjā'	إرجاء	Defer.
Iṣlāḥiyya/Iṣlāḥiyyūn	الإصلاحيون	Islamic reformist(s).
istiḥsān	استحسان	Rational preference.
istiʿlā'	استعلاء	Rise above, even to be arrogant.
al-jafā'	الجفاء	Harshness.
jāhili	الجاهلي	Living in a pre-Islamic stage.
jāhiliyya	جاهلية	Age of ignorance.
Jahmism/Jahmi/Jahmites	جهمية/جهمي/جهميون	A term that refers to the followers/movement of Jahm Ibn Safwan.
Jamāʿat al-Muslimīn	جماعة المسلمين	The Muslim community.
kafir/kafirūn	كافر/كافرون	Disbelievers or (individuals) who reject(s) the authority of God.
Khawārij	خوارج	A sect of Islam that emerged during the First Muslim Civil War in the crisis of leadership after the murder of the third caliph Uthman. Its teachings developed to consider faith an indivisible combination of conviction, words, and deeds. Sometimes used to refer to current extremist groups.
kufr	كفر	Infidelity, faithlessness, disbelief.
al-kufr bi al-ṭāghūt	الكفر بالطاغوت	Rejecting false gods.
madhab	مذهب	Religious legal doctrine; school of jurisprudence.

makrūh	مكروه	Reprehensible according to Islamic legal terms.
Maliki	مالكي	One of the major schools of Islamic jurisprudence, founded by Malik Ibn Anas.
maqāṣid	مقاصد	The overall objectives, intentions, or aims of the Shariʿa.
maʿṣiya	معصية	Unintentional failures and breaches; sins.
Māturīdi	الماتريدي	A school of theology established by Abu Mansur al-Maturidi (853–944 CE/238–333 AH).
Muʿaskar al-Ibāḥiyya	معسكر الإباحية	Camp of Debauchery.
Muʿaskar al-Islāmiyya	معسكر الإسلامية	Camp of Islam.
mubtadi'a/mubtadi'īn	مبتدعة/مبتدعين	Preacher(s) of the heretic innovations.
muḥdath	محدث	Eventuated or caused.
mujtahid/mujtahidūn	مجتهد/مجتهدون	Shiʿa original authorities of Islamic law.
Murj'ism/Murj'ite	مرجئة/مرجئي	Initially a neutral position on the conflict between the Khawārij and the competing supporters of the rival caliphs ʿAli and Muʿawiya. It turned into a position that rejected declaring individuals as infidels.
mutakallimūn	متكلمون	Traditions of Ashʿari theologians.
Muʿtazila/Muʿtazilite	المعتزلة	An Islamic school that believes that the Qur'an was created by God, and the interpretation of the religion and law shouldn't contradict reason and justice. They rate the Prophet's companions according to moral criteria and not according to seniority.
Naqshbandī	النقشبندية	A Sunni order of Sufism.
nawāqiḍ	نواقض	Nullifiers.
Nizārī	النزارية	The largest segment of the Ismaʿilis.
Qadarī	القدرية	Predestinationist.
qiyās	قياس	The process of deriving religious rulings by independent analogy.
sadd al-dharā'iʿ	سد الذرائع	Removal of false pretexts and excuses that may lead to sin.
al-Ṣaḥwa al-Islāmiyya	الصحوة الإسلامية	Islamic Awakening.
al-salaf al-ṣāliḥ	السلف الصالح	The righteous ancestors.
Salafiyya ʿilmiyya	السلفية العلمية	Scholarly Salafism.
Shafiʿi	شافعي	One of the major schools of Islamic jurisprudence, founded by Abu Abdullah Muhammad Ibn Idris al-Shafiʿi.
shirk	شرك	Polytheism, idolatry.
shirk al-ṭāʿa	شرك الطاعة	Polytheism-by-obedience.
shūrā	شورى	Consultation.
Suhrawardī	السهروردية	An order of Sufism established by Persian scholar Yahya Ibn Habash Suhrawardī.

tābiʿūn	تابعون	The generation of Muslims who followed the Prophet's companions.
ṭāghūt/ṭawāghīt	طاغوت/طواغيت	Irreligious tyranny, infidel tyrannical regimes.
takfīr	تكفير	The branding of an individual or a group as infidel.
takfīr al-muʿayyan	تكفير المعيّن	Specific takfīr; the branding of particular individuals and even entire groups of Muslims as being unbelievers.
takfīr al-muṭlaq	تكفير المطلق	Abstract takfīr; the categorization of positions, ideas, and actions as being un-Islamic.
tanqīḥ al-manāṭ / taḥqīq al-manāṭ	تنقيح المناط / تحقيق المناط	Theological and Shariʿa judgments / how Shariʿa judgments are implemented in practice.
taqiyya	تقية	Tactical dissimulation.
taqlīd	تقليد	Imitation.
al-taṣdīq bi al-qalb / al-iqrār bi al-lisān	التصديق بالقلب والإقرار باللسان	Internal conviction and external verbal profession (two types of faith).
tathlīth (trinitarianism)/ tarbīʿ (quaternitarianism)	تثليث/وتربيع	Trinitarianism in considering the first three caliphs as the rightly guided caliphs / Quaternitarianism in accepting the first four.
tawḥīd	توحيد	Monotheism; the singularity and unity of God.
ta'wīl	تأويل	Hermeneutics.
ʿulama'	علماء	Muslim religious scholars who have specialized knowledge of Islamic law and doctrine.
umma	أمة	Religious community.
uṣūl al-dīn	أصول الدين	fundamentals of the faith, religion.
uṣūl al-fiqh	أصول الفقه	Fundamentals of jurisprudence.
uṣūlī	أصولي	Adjective referring to the fundamentals of jurisprudence (*uṣūl al-fiqh*), namely the method or "science" guiding the development of practical legal rulings on matters of worship or daily conduct based on the fundamental principles of the Shariʿa.
al-walā' wa al-barā'	الولاء والبراء	Doctrine of "loyalty to the believers and disavowal"; enmity to the nonbelievers.
Waqf	وقف	Islamic concept of endowed land.
Yasa/Yasaq	الياسه/الياسق	Mongol's legal code
ẓāhir	ظاهر	Manifest or apparent / external.
Ẓāhirī/Ẓāhirism	ظاهريون/ظاهرية	A school of Islamic jurisprudence that accepts logic and inference to understand texts but gives tradition precedence; founded in the ninth century CE by Dawud al-Zahiri.
zanādiqa	زنادقة	Heretics.

Notes

PREFACE

1. Azmi Bishara, *The Islamic State Organization "ISIL": A General Framework and Practical Contribution to Understanding the Phenomenon* (*Tanẓīm al-Dawla al-Mukanā "Dāʿish": Iṭār ʿĀam wa Musāhama Naqdiyya fī fahm al-Ẓāhira*) (Doha: Arab Center for Research and Policy Studies, 2018).

2. *Ijtihād* literally means "making an effort." What is meant by the term in Islamic jurisprudence is creative and original interpretation of the sacred text to meet new needs, or deduction of Islamic rules from the aims of the Shariʿa and the spirit of Islam for cases that the text does not cover.

3. *Sunna* and *Hadith* refer to the sayings and deeds of the Prophet as narrated by generally recognized authorities. I capitalize *Hadith* to signify the entire corpus of the sayings of the Prophet in general and the "science" that deals with it, in contrast to when it signifies a single saying or several sayings. Either way, I will capitalize it also where it is a part of a name or title.

4. The literal translation of *muṭlaq* is "absolute," but in this case it means nonconcrete or unspecific, the right translation of which is closer to "abstract." In other words, it is not a judgment pertaining to specific individuals or groups of people.

5. *Madhab* was originally used in a narrow jurisprudential sense and later was expanded to include theological differences.

6. Ibn Taymiyya, a Syrian Hanbali jurist/theologian who lived during the catastrophic Mongol invasion of Islam's heartlands. He was famous for his uncompromising opposition to the authorities, strict advocacy of return to original Islamic tenets,

and his polemics with philosophers, mystics, and non-Sunni sects such as the Shiʿa. He was a prolific author whose works are still widely read. Ibn Hanbal is considered the founder of the Hanbali school of Sunni jurisprudence and was an influential Baghdadi narrator of Hadith, famous for his opposition to the officially sponsored Muʿtazili "rationalist" theology during his time. He was persecuted for but refused to recant his traditionalist stance, which held that religious doctrine must strictly follow a literal interpretation of the Qur'an and Hadith.

CHAPTER 1

1. The Hanbali current, named for Ibn Hanbal, first emerged in Baghdad, although Hanbali centers subsequently emerged in Palestine, Damascus, and modern Saudi Arabia (which officially recognizes the Hanbali school as the basis of Shariʿa law in the country). Unlike other Sunni schools, Hanbalism encompasses both doctrine and jurisprudence. Although the scholars of the Hanbali current occasionally disagree over how to interpret his positions, they are united in believing that the Qur'an is uncreated and that the holy texts are the primary source of law and should take priority over independent reasoning in all cases—even if their provenance was dubious, as was the case with many traditions.

2. *Athar* literally means "trace" or "impact," perhaps also "legacy" in a broader sense. In this context, the trace that the Prophet left, his legacy, is the Hadith.

3. An *athar* (pl. *āthār*) is a brief narrative recounting the deeds or opinions of the early generations of Muslims. Āthār are thus a key source for those seeking to imitate the Salaf.

4. Note that the recognition of ʿAli as an imam dates only to the late third century AH, and even then was contested. See Abd al-Qahir al-Baghdadi, *Schisms and Sects* (*Al-Farq bayn al-Firaq*) (Beirut: Dār al-Kutub al-ʿIlmiyya, 2009).

5. Muqbil Ibn Hadi al-Wadiʿi, *The Exit from Strife* (*Al-Makhraj min al-Fitna*) (Sanaa: n.p., 1982), 20.

6. Anouar Abdel-Malek, "Orientalism in Crisis," *Diogenes*, no. 44 (Winter 1963), 104–12; Bryan Turner, *Marx and the End of Orientalism* (New York: Routledge, 1978); Edward W. Said, *Orientalism* (New York: Pantheon Books, 1978).

7. For an important study on the sources of modern American fundamentalism, see Malise Ruthven, *Fundamentalism: A Very Short Introduction*, Very Short Introductions 116 (Oxford, New York: Oxford University Press, 2004).

8. The Bible Institute of Los Angeles published these ninety essays in twelve volumes between 1910 and 1915 CE. They were written to defend the Protestant denominations' perceptions of Christian religious fundamentals against contemporary intellectual trends such as liberalism, socialism, the theories of evolution and natural selection, and Catholicism.

9. Martin E. Marty and R. Scott Appleby, introduction to *Fundamentalisms and the State: Remaking Polities, Economies, and Militance*, Fundamentalism Project, vol. 3, ed. Martin E. Marty and R. Scott Appleby (Chicago: University of Chicago Press, 1993), 3.

10. In countries like Saudi Arabia or Egypt, the official religious bodies promote their own versions of pro-regime fundamentalism.

11. Patterns of mass religiosity are different than those of folk religiosity that were studied extensively. This is not the place to elaborate on mass religiosity, suffice to note that due to simultaneous atomization, conglomeration, and alienation of individuals and mass media, it is more vulnerable to the influence of modern ideological Islamism—whether political, Salafi, or other—and to that of popular preachers in the mass media—whether they are conservative, reformist, or other.

12. Muhammad Sa'id Ramadan al-Bouti, *The Salafists: A Blessed Era More than an Islamic Sect* (*Al-Salafiyya: Marḥala Zamaniyya Mubāraka Lā Madhhab Islāmī*) (Damascus: Dār al-Fikr, 1990).

13. It should be noted that Ibn Hanbal's books weren't written directly by him but by his son and followers, who recorded his sayings.

14. Ash'arism is named for Abu al-Hasan al-Ash'ari (874–936 CE/ 260-324 AH), a former Mu'tazilite who subsequently broke with that school. Al-Ash'ari adopted a middle course between Mu'tazilism and Hanbalism, maintaining that some of God's traits were incontestable while others were subject to interpretation and that while the meaning of the Qur'an was timeless and uncreated, the wording was not. Thanks to the patronage of the Seljuks, Ayyubids, and Mamlūks, Ash'arism eventually became the leading doctrinal school of the broader Ahl al-Sunna current, followed closely by the Hanbalis and the Māturīdis, a position it retains today.

15. Ja'far al-Sadiq "the truthful," was retroactively considered the sixth imam by the Twelver Shi'a. He is recognized as a significant authority by various non-Shi'i scholars: Abu Hanifa described him as the "most knowledgeable in law" of anyone he had ever seen, and although he is not mentioned in *Ṣaḥīḥ al-Bukhārī*, he does

appear in Bukhari's *Al-Adab al-Mufrad* and is cited as a source by various other collectors of prophetic traditions. The Shi'a attribute various sayings to him, some of them legal and some of them doctrinal, but many of these are disputed by Ahl al-Sunna. In this context, Ja'farism is used as another name for Twelver Shi'ism. It is founded on the distinctive beliefs that the twelve Shi'i imams after the Prophet Muhammad were innocent of sin, that they had the right to make laws, and that the twelfth imam did not die but "went into occultation" and will return for the end of times. Ja'faris also believe that 'Ali Ibn Abi Talib was explicitly named as Muhammad's successor but that the companions contravened this order after the Prophet's death, a position shared with other Shi'a. Ahl al-Sunna generally accept Ja'fari jurisprudence but reject its doctrinal positions, especially considering the imamate one of the fundaments of religion.

16. The Saudi Salafi scholar Salih al-Husayyin sees fundamentalism as a synonym for extremism and a threat to human minds, spirits, talents, and belief. He maintains that the creed of the Salaf was moderate. See Salih Ibn Abd al-Rahman al-Husayyin, *Complete Works of Shaykh Salih Ibn Abd al-Rahman al-Husayyin* (*Al-A'māl al-Kāmila li-Faḍīlat al-Shaykh Ṣāliḥ Ibn 'Abd al-Raḥmān al-Ḥuṣayyin*), ed. Raed al-Samhouri (Doha: Forum for Arab and International Relations, 2014), 568–69.

17. Ibn Taymiyya discusses this issue in precise detail in the introduction to his Dar' Ta'āruḍ al-'Aql wa al-Naql. See Taqi al-Din Abu al-Abbas Ahmad Ibn Abd al-Halim Ibn Taymiyya al-Harrani, *The Agreement of Reason and Revelation* (*Dar' Ta'āruḍ al-'Aql wa al-Naql*), ed. Muhammad Rashshad Salim, vol. 1 (Riyadh: Imam Mohammad Ibn Saud Islamic University, 1991).

18. From the singular *sira* which means "course of life" or "a biography."

19. Muhammad Abu Zahra, *History of the Islamic Schools in Politics and Doctrine and the History of Schools of Jurisprudence* (*Fiqh*) (*Tārīkh al-Madhāhib al-Islāmiyya fī al-Siyāsa wa al-'Aqā'id wa Tārīkh al-Madhāhib al-Fiqhiyya*) (Cairo: Dār al-Fikr al-'Arabi, 2009), 340–1.

20. See George Makdisi, *Hanbali Islam* (*Al-Islām al-Ḥanbalī*), trans. Saoud El-Mawla, foreword by editor Radwan al-Sayed (Beirut: Arab Network for Research and Publication, 2017), 70. Originally published in two articles: George Makdisi, "L'Islam Hanbalisant" ("Al-Islam al-Ḥanbalī"), *Revue des Études Islamiques* 43, no. 1 (1974): 45–76; George Makdisi, "L'Islam Hanbalisant" ("Al-Islam al-Ḥanbalī"), *Revue des Études Islamiques* 42, no. 2 (1975): 211–44. Compare with Wael Hallaq, *The Origins and Evolution of Islamic Law* (Cambridge: Cambridge University Press, 2005), 127–28.

21. Analyzed by George Makdisi in Makdisi, *Al-Islam al-Ḥanbalī.*

22. Taha Husayn, *The Days: Autobiography of Taha Husayn* (*Al-Ayyām*) (Cairo: Hindawi for Education and Culture, 2012), 178–9.

23. Hichem Djait, *Islamic Culture in Crisis* (*Azamat al-Thaqāfa al-Islāmiyya*) (Beirut: Dār al-Tali'ah, 2000), 77.

24. The final act of his life was meeting Prince Sa'ud Ibn 'Abd al-'Aziz. He died on his way back.

25. Al-Afghani was probably the most influential Muslim intellectual of the nineteenth century CE. Although an Iranian-born Shi'i scholar, he was more influential in Sunni regions, in which he stayed after being expelled from Istanbul in 1871 CE / 1288 AH, until he was expelled to India in 1879 CE / 1296 AH. There he met Abduh, who became one of his closest disciples, and later traveled with him to Paris in 1883, where they began to publish the magazine *Al-'Urwa al-Wuthqa*, which became a very influential organ, even though it lasted for only eighteen months. Al-Afghani had influential political roles in Afghanistan (where he was expelled in 1868 CE / 1285 AH), Iran (deported in 1892 CE / 1310 AH, after three years as advisor to the shah), and India. He died in Istanbul in 1897 CE / 1315 AH, where he was a virtual prisoner of the Sultan.

26. See Albert Hourani, *Arabic Thought in the Liberal Age 1798–1939* (Cambridge: Cambridge University Press, 2009 [1962]) 184.

27. Muhammad Abduh, "A Reply to Hanotaux's Latest Talk" ("Radd 'Alā Ḥadīth Hānōtō al-Akhīr"), *Al-Mu'ayyid* 29 (July 29, 1900 CE / Rabī' al-Awwal, 1318 AH); and Fahmi Jadaan, *The Foundations of Progress among Islamic Thinkers in the Modern Arab World* (*Usus al-Taqaddum 'Ind Mufakkirī al-Islam fi'l-'Ālam al-'Arabī al-Ḥadīth*), 2nd ed. (Beirut: Arab Enterprise for Studies and Publishing, 1981), 273.

28. Ottoman Party for Administrative Decentralization, "Communiqué of the Ottoman Party for Administrative Decentralization," *Al-UMRAN* 18, no. 725 (February 24, 1913 / Safar 28, 1331 AH), 4. The OPAD was founded in Egypt in 1912, and prominent in it were a group of Levantines residing in Egypt: Rafiq al-Azham (1867–1925 CE) (Damascus), Rida (Tripoli), Shibli al-Shamil (1850–1917 CE) (Lebanon), Iskander Ammun (1857–1920 CE) (Lebanon), Sami al-Jaridini (1881–1950 CE) (Lebanon), Haqqi al-Azm (1864–1955 CE) (Damascus), and al-Khatib (Damascus). Al-Azham was party chairman, Ammun deputy chairman, and al-Azm party secretary. Although the party was headquartered in Cairo, it had a policy of opening branches in any Ottoman town or city where ten people could be found who supported the party's key policy of decentralized government. Although membership in the party was open to all Ottomans

who believed in decentralization, it was primarily an Arab party. See Muhammad Izzat Darwaza, *On the Modern Arab Movement: History, Memoirs and Commentaries* (*Ḥawl al-Ḥaraka al-ʿArabiyya al-Ḥadītha: Tārīkh wa Mudhakkirāt wa Taʿlīqāt*), vol. 1 (Sidon, Lebanon: Matba'ah al-ʿAsriyyah, 1950), 34.

29. Taha Husayn, *Literary Life in the Arabian Peninsula* (*Al-Ḥayā al-Adabiyya fī Jazīrat al-ʿArab*) (Damascus: Maktab al-Nashir al-ʿArabi, 1935), 34–5.

30. Husayn, *Literary Life*, 37.

31. See Muhammad Rashid Rida, "The Eighth-Year Prologue" ("Fātiḥat al-Sana al-Thāmina"), *Al-Manār* 8, no. 1 (1 Muharram 1323 AH / March 7, 1905 CE): 1.

32. Henri Lauzière, "The Construction of Salafiyya: Reconsidering Salafism from the Perspective of Conceptual History," *International Journal of Middle East Studies* 42 (2010), 376. See Jamal al-Din al-Qasimi, "The Second Study on al-Muʿtazila" ("Al-Baḥth al-Thānī fī al-Muʿtazila"), *Al-Manār* 16, no. 10 (1913 CE / 1331 AH): 749.

33. Muhammad Ibn Abd al-Wahhāb, "Majmūʿat Rasāʾil fīʾl-Tawḥīd waʾl-Īmān" ("Essays on Monotheism and Faith"), edited, introduced, and explained by Ismaʿil Ibn Muhammad al-Ansari, in *Writings of Sheikh Imam Muhammad Ibn Abd al-Wahhāb* (*Muʾallafāt al-Shaykh al-Imam Muhammad Ibn ʿAbd al-Wahhāb*), prepared by ʿAbd al-ʿAziz Ibn Zayd al-Rumi, Muhammad Baltaji, and Sayyid Hijab, vol. 1, part 1 (Riyadh: Imam Mohammad Ibn Saud Islamic University, 1976), 396; see also Ahmad al-Qutban and Muhammad Tahir al-Zayn, *Imam al-Tawḥīd Muhammad Ibn Abd al-Wahhāb*, rev. ʿAbd al-ʿAziz Ibn Baz (Alexandria, Egypt: Dār al-Iman, 2001), 139; see also Abd al-Munʿim Ibrahim, *Commentary on the Book of Monotheism by Sheikh al-Islam Muhammad Ibn Abd al-Wahhāb* (*Mughnī al-Murīd: Al-Jāmiʿ li-Shurūḥ Kitāb al-Tawḥīd li-Shaykh al-Islām Muhammad Ibn ʿAbd al-Wahhāb*) (Mecca: Maktabat Nizar Mustafa al-Baz, 2000), 2421.

34. Muhammad Ibn Abd al-Wahhāb, "Fatwas and Jurisprudences" ("Fatāwā wa-Masāʾil"), in *Ibn Abd al-Wahhāb: Concise Biography and Fatwas* (*Mukhtaṣar al-Sīra wa al-Fatāwā*), ed. Salih Ibn Abd al-Rahman al-Atram and Muhammad Ibn Abd al-Razzaq al-Dawish, vol. 4 (Riyad: Ministry of Islamic Affairs, Da'wa and Irshad, 1998), 68.

35. Abd al-Qadir al-Shawi, *Salafism and Nationalism* (*Al-Salafiyya wa al-Waṭaniyya*) (Beirut: Mu'asassat al-Abhath al-ʿArabiyyah, 1985), 133.

36. Muhammad Rashid Rida, "The Pros and Cons of Europeans in the East: Despotism," ("Manāfiʿ al-Urūbbiyyīn wa-Maḍārruhum fī al-Sharq: Al-Istibdād,") *Al-Manār* 10, no. 4 (March 1907 CE / Muharram 1325 AH): 283.

37. Al-Wadiʿi founded the Dammaj school of Salafism in Yemen. Initially a Yemeni immigrant who worked in Mecca as a caretaker and doorman, al-Wadiʿi subsequently

studied at the Islamic University in Medina, embraced Wahhabi Salafism, and declared the Muslim Brotherhood and its supporters infidels. See al-Wadi'i, *Exit from Strife.*

After his deportation to Yemen in 1980 CE, he became a strident critic of Saudi Arabia. However, he was later offered medical treatment at the expense of the Saudi regime, which he praised profusely, saying that "only the wicked repay kindness with offense." See Ahmed Muhammad al-Daghshi, "The Traditional Salafiyya in Yemen: The Foundation Stage (al-Wād'iyya)" ("Al-Salafiyya al-Taqlīdiyya fī al-Yaman: Marḥalat al-Ta'sīs [al-Wādi'iyya]"), in *Wahhabism and Salafism: Ideas and Impacts* (*Al-Wahhābiyya wa al-Salafiyya: Al-Afkār wa al-Āthār*), ed. Raed al-Samhouri, revised by Muhammad Yusri Ibrahim et al, research paper presented in a symposium on Wahhabism and Salafism organized by The Forum for Arab and International Relations (Awrāq Baḥthiyya Qaddamahā al-Mushārikūn fī Mu'tamar al-Wahhābiyya wa al-Salafiyya alladhī Naẓẓamahu Muntadā al-'Alāqāt al-'Arabiyya wa al-Dawliyya), December 21–22, 2013 (Beirut: Arab Network for Studies and Publishing, 2016), 343–74.

38. See his epistle to the people of al-Majma'ah in *Personal Letters of Imam Muhammad Ibn Abdul Wahhāb* (*Al-Rasā'il al-Shakhṣiyya*), in Ibn Abd al-Wahhāb, *Writings of Sheikh Imam Muhammad Ibn Abd al-Wahhāb*, 64.

39. Uthman Ibn Abdullah Ibn Bishr, *The Glorious History of the Najd Region* (*'Unwān al-Majd fī Tārīkh Najd*), commentary by editor Abd al-Rahman Ibn Abd al-Latif Ibn Abdullah Al al-Shaykh, vol. 1, 4th ed. (Riyadh: Dār al-Malik 'Abd al-'Aziz, 1982), 37.

40. See Sulayman Ibn Abd al-Wahhāb, *The Divine Lightning in Response to Wahhabism* (*Al-Ṣawā'iq al-Ilāhiyya fī al-Radd 'alā al-Wahhābiyya*), prepared by Husayn Hilmi Ibn Sa'id Istanbuli, 3rd ed. (Istanbul: Maktabat Ishiq, 1979), which contains this important letter of less than eighty pages.

41. Ibn Abd al-Wahhāb, *Writings of Sheikh Imam Muhammad Ibn Abd al-Wahhāb*, 216.

42. See Uthman Ibn 'Abd al-'Aziz bin Mansur, *Critique of the Khawārij* (*Manhaj al-Ma'ārij li-Akhbār al-Khawārij bil-Ishrāf 'alā'l-Isrāf min Dīnihim al-Mārij, wa-Mawsūman in Shi'ta bil-Sīra al-Khārijiyya al-Muḥtawiya 'alā Kulli Ghāyila wa-Baliyya*), introduction and biography by Sulayman Ibn Salih al-Kharashi (Riyadh: Maktabat al-Rushd, 2017).

43. For further discussion of these awakenings and the scholarly work in the eighteenth century CE, see Ahmad S. Dallal, *Islam without Europe: Traditions of Reform in Eighteenth-Century Islamic Thought* (Chapel Hill: University of North Carolina Press, 2018).

44. See my discussion of Bernard Lewis approach: Azmi Bishara, *On the Arab Question: An Introduction to an Arab Democratic Manifesto* (*Fī al-Mas'ala al-'Arabiyya: Muqaddima li-Bayān Dimuqrāṭī 'Arabī*) (Beirut: Centre for Arab Unity Studies, 2007), 139–42.

45. Cf. Ahmed al-Raysuni, *Imam al-Shatibi's Theory of the Higher Objectives and Intents of Islamic Law* (*Naẓariyyat al-Maqāṣid 'Ind al-Imam al-Shāṭibī*), foreword by Taha Jabir al-Alawani, 4th ed. (Herndon, Virginia: International Institute for Islamic Thought, 1995), 47–56.

46. Henri Laoust, "Le Réformisme orthodoxe des 'Salafiya' et les caractères généraux de son orientation," ("Al-'Iṣlāḥ al-Urthudhuksī lil-Salafiyya wa Tawajuhātiha,") *Revue des Études Islamiques* 2 (1932) : 175, 178, 222; Hamilton A. R. Gibb, *Modern Trends in Islam* (Chicago: Chicago University Press, 1947), 29, 35, 133.

47. Barelvi is an Indian Muslim revivalist who is considered a scholarly authority by several Sunni Salafi reform movements that emerged in northern India.

48. Hasan Khan is the founder of the Ahl-i Ḥadīth movement.

49. Lauzière, "Construction of Salafiyya," 380.

50. Lauzière, 378, 388.

51. Lauzière, 378.

52. Frank Griffel, "What Do We Mean by 'Salafī'"? Connecting Muhammad Abduh with Egypt's Nūr Party in Islam's Contemporary Intellectual History," *Die Welt des Islams* 55, no. 2 (2015): 186–220.

53. Frank Griffel, "What Is the Task of the Intellectual (Contemporary) Historian?—A Response to Henri Lauzière's 'Reply,'" *Die Welt des Islams* 56, no. 2 (2016): 249–55.

54. Griffel, "What Do We Mean By "Salafī"?," 213.

55. Griffel, 198.

56. Albert Hourani, *Arabic Thought in the Liberal Age 1798–1939* (Cambridge: Cambridge University Press, 2009 [1962]), 149.

57. A third sense, which takes us out of the religious framework, is the neutralization of state in religious issues and the separation of religion and temporal politics, so that religion remains valid for every time and place through its organization of the relationship between man and God by means of rites, rituals, obligations (worship), and moral values. Islam can be suitable for all times and places in a secular context, which relegates it to the status of a faith in the religious sphere.

58. In Islamic theology, one of the characteristics of the Qur'an is its inimitability (*i'jāz*). What this means in practice is a subject of debate, but one popular reading is to

claim that it contains references to scientific subjects as diverse as the atomic numbers and masses of different elements, the expansion of the universe, and space travel.

59. C.f. Jadaan, *Foundations of Progress.*

60. This leads Jadaan to directly link the hadith of "the finest generations" (*khayr al-qurūn*) with the hadith describing the fragmentation of Islam into multiple sects (*hadith al-iftirāq*). See Jadaan, *Foundations of Progress*, 26–7.

61. The reference is to a council established by Umar Ibn al-Khattab on his deathbed to choose his successor as caliph.

62. Abu Ya'la al-Farra' and Muhammad Ibn al-Husayn, *History of the Hanbalites* (*Ṭabaqāt al-Ḥanābila*), vol. 1, prepared and revised by Muhammad Hamid al-Fiqqi (Beirut: Dār al-Ma'rifa, n.d.), 243–44.

63. See Abu Bakr Ahmad Ibn Muhammad al-Khallal, The Sunna (Al-Sunna), ed. Atiya Ibn Atiq al-Zahrani, part 7 (Riyadh: Dār al-Rayah, 1989), 392; Ahmad Ibn Muhammad Ibn Hani, *Issues of Imam Ahmad Ibn Ḥanbal, Narration of Ishaq Ibn Ibrahim Ibn Hani al-Nisapuri (Masā'il al-Imam 'Aḥmad Ibn Ḥanbal, Riwāyat Isḥāq Ibn Ibrāhīm Ibn Hānī' al-Naysabūrī)*, ed. Zuhayr al-Shawish, vol. 2 (Beirut: Maktaba al-Islāmiyya, [1979]), 172.

64. Although there are many different versions of this hadith, the most likely to be accurate is in al-Bukhari: "'The best of you is my generation (*qarnī*), then those who come after them, then those who come after those.' Imran said, 'I do not know whether the Prophet mentioned two or three generations after your present generation.' The Prophet added, 'There will be some people after you, who will be dishonest and will not be trustworthy and will give witness without being asked to give witness, and will vow but will not fulfill their vows, and they will grow fat (on the things of this world).'" See, Muhammad Ibn Isma'il al-Bukhari, *The Ṣaḥīḥ Collection: The Complete, Correct, Abridged Compendium of the Matters of the Prophet* (PBUH) (*Al-Jāmi' al-Ṣaḥīḥ: Wa-huwa al-Jāmi' al-Musnad al-Ṣaḥīḥ al-Mukhtaṣar min Umūr al-Rasūl Ṣalla Allah 'alayhi wa-Sallam wa-Sunanihi wa-Ayyāmihi*), prepared by Zuhayr Ibn Nasir al-Nasir, vol. 3 (Cairo: Dār Tawq al-Najah, 2001), 171.

65. Abdullah Ibn Ahmad Ibn Hanbal, *The Sunna* (*Al-Sunna*), edited and with a study by Muhammad Ibn Sa'id Ibn Salim al-Qahtani, vol. 2 (Al-Dammam: Dār Ibn al-Qayyim, 1986), 194.

66. Muslim prayers are made up of sections called *raka'āt* (prostrations). Each *rak'a* consists of reading verses of the Qur'an while standing up, then bowing down once (*yarka'*, hence the term), then prostrating twice, and repeating this two, three, or four times according to the designated prayer.

67. Al-Farra', *History of the Hanbalites,* 244.

68. Fahmi Jadaan, *The Mihna: A Study of the Dialectics of the Religious and the Political in Islam* (*Al-Miḥna: Baḥth ʿan Jadaliyyat al-Siyāsī wa al-Dīnī fī al-Islām*), 2nd ed. (Beirut: Arab Enterprise for Studies and Publishing, 2000), 276–79.

69. In the aftermath of the publication of this book in Arabic, the researcher Raed al-Samhouri dedicated a whole book to describing how Hanbali writers reproduced Ibn Hanbal to match the imagination of Hanbalism. See Raed al-Samhouri, *The Imagined Salaf: An Analytical Historical Approach to the "Salaf" of the "Mihna"* (*Ahmad Ibn Ḥanbal and the Imagined Ahmad Ibn Ḥanbal*) (*Al-Salaf al-Mutakhayyal: Muqāraba Tārīkhiyya Taḥlīliyya fī Salaf al-Miḥna* [*Aḥmad Ibn Ḥanbal wa Aḥmad Ibn Ḥanbal al-Mutakhayyal*]) (Doha: Arab Center for Research and Policy Studies, 2019).

70. Salafis do not say that the Qur'an was created; instead, they believe it was revealed in time and space and thus eventuated or caused (*muḥdath*). Abdullah Ibn Kullab, a Sunni theologian who established the Kullabi sect, considers the Qur'an itself to be eternal. As for the Ashʿarites, they think that only the words were created, while the spiritual meaning is eternal. As such, Salafis see the Qur'an as one of God's self-caused acts and not eternal, but "the species of God's words is eternal." For more, see the detailed treatment in: Jadaan, *The Mihna,* 25–55.

71. Denial of the contradiction between God, reason, and justice is well-established in classical Islamic thought, not only among the Muʿtazilis but also in the work of Salafis like Ibn Taymiyya.

72. History shows that without institutions that limit power of the rulers, principles do not supply protection from tyranny.

73. Ibn Abi Yaʿla recorded witness reports of Ibn Hanbal's miracle as follows: "Ahmad Ibn Abi Ubayd Allah said, 'I was at home on the day of the ordeal and I looked at Ahmad Ibn Hanbal when the whip was lashing his shoulders. He was wearing trousers with a cord, which was cut, and the trousers fell down. At that moment, he moved his lips and the trousers returned to the way they had been.'" See al-Farra', *History of the Hanbalites,* 85.

74. The al-Farra' citation suggests that the direct companions of Ibn Hanbal defended his miracles, unlike the Wahhabis who identified their belief with the Hanbali creed. "Ibrahim Ibn Ismaʿil Ibn Khalaf said, 'Ahmad Ibn Nasr was my friend and when he was killed during the Mihna and his head severed, I heard the head reciting the Qur'an. I went over to the head to see, and there were men and horses protecting it. When the eyes calmed down, I heard the head say: "Have the people not thought that

they will be left to say, 'We believe' and that they will not be tried?" See al-Farra', *History of the Hanbalites,* 81.

75. Abu al-Faraj Abd al-Rahman Ibn 'Ali Ibn al-Jawzi, *Virtues of the Imam Ahmad Ibn Hanbal* (*Manāqib al-Imam Aḥmad Ibn Ḥanbal*), ed. Abdullah al-Turki, 2nd ed. (Cairo: Dār Hajar, 1988), 190.

76. In Muslim folk religiosity, Illiya is the same biblical prophet. He appears also as al-Khadir in Muslim culture. But al-Khadir became much more mysterious in popular faiths, and he gets different personalities according to the local Muslim culture. In some cases, he became a new name for old local saints, including Christian ones.

77. Ibn al-Jawzi, *Virtues of the Imam,* 192.

78. Ibn al-Jawzi, 397.

79. For the religious establishment, the legalization of rebellion against the Muslim ruler as a matter of doctrine marked out the Khawārij, a sect of Islam that emerged during the First Muslim Civil War in the crisis of leadership after the murder of the third caliph Uthman. This is why some people compare current Islamist currents with the Khawārij. Abu al-Fath Muhammad Ibn Abd al-Karim Ibn Abi Bakr Ahmad ash-Shahrastani, *The Book of Religious and Philosophical Sects* (*Al-Milal wa al-Niḥal*), ed. Muhammad Sayyid Kaylani, vol. 1 (Beirut: Dār al-Ma'rifa, n.d.), 15, states, "They declare major sinners to be infidels and consider rebellion against the imam if he contravenes the Sunna as obligatory." This is contrary to some of the Murj'ite and Shi'i groups who delayed rebellion until the *qa'im* or the *mahdi* appeared.

80. Al-Mawdudi was the founder of the Jamā'at Islami on the Indian subcontinent (in 1941 CE). Although he adopted a radical rhetoric, his group was not engaged in violence. Qutb was an influential theoretician of the Muslim Brotherhood who adopted some of al-Mawdudi's trenchant rhetoric and became very influential on jihadi thought and movements.

81. Abd al-Qadir Ibn Badran al-Dimashqi, *Introduction to the Doctrine of Imam Ahmad Ibn Hanbal* (*Al-Madkhal ilā Madhhab al-Imam Aḥmad Ibn Ḥanbal*), ed. Muhammad Amin Danawi (Beirut: Dār al-Kutub al-'Ilmiyya, 1996), 28. This is the same text transmitted previously in *History of the Hanbalites* by al-Farra'.

82. Michael Cook, *Commanding Right and Forbidding Wrong in Islamic Thought* (Cambridge: Cambridge University Press, 2001), 90.

83. Cook, *Commanding Right and Forbidding Wrong,* 101.

84. Doctrine of Ibn Safwan and Ibn Dirham opposes the anthropomorphic perspective that ascribes attributes and names to God and raises the issue of necessity

and freedom in human action in moral issues and the rationality of divine punishment in this context. Salafis have usually accused Muʿtazalites and other rivals of being Jahmites.

85. Abu al-Hasan ʿAli Ibn al-Husayn al-Masʿudi, *Meadows of Gold and Mines of Gems (Murūj al-Dhahab wa Maʿādin al-Jawāhir)*, prepared and revised by Kamal Hasan Marʿi, vol. 4 (Beirut: Maktaba al-ʿAsriyya, 2005), 71.

86. Muhammad Ibn Jarir al-Tabari, *Incipient Decline*, Vol. 34 of *The History of al-Ṭabarī*, trans. Joel Kraemer (New York: State University of New York Press, 1989), 89–91.

87. Scholars often cite the Pact of Umar in this context. The Pact of Umar was supposedly an agreement between the second rightly guided caliph, Umar Ibn al-Khattab, and Christians of Syria that specifies rights and restrictions for non-Muslims living under Muslim rule. Its authenticity is dubious, and many iterations have been reproduced in each age, just like spurious hadiths. For example, the "pacts" published by Muslim historians al-Tabari and al-Baladhuri do not mention clothing, suggesting that Umar Ibn al-Khattab never gave such orders. Moreover, if the Pact of Umar was authentic, then Christians would not have built churches in Baghdad in the eighth century CE / second century AH when it was undergoing an architectural revival. Cf. discussion in Mohammad Marʿi, *Islamic State Financial and Economic Systems in Light of Abu Yusuf's "Book of Kharāj" (Al-Nuẓum al-Māliyya wa al-Iqtiṣādiyya fī al-Dawla al-Islāmiyya ʿalā Ḍaw' Kitāb al-Kharāj li-Abī Yūsuf)* (Doha: Dār al-Thaqafa, 1987), 201.

88. Ibn Taymiyya, for example, wrote in praise of these steps: "The rulers who demolished their places of worship and fulfilled God's command regarding them, such as Umar Ibn ʿAbd al-ʿAziz, Harun al-Rashid, and their like, were supported and triumphed. Those who did otherwise were defeated and cast down." See *Taqi al-Din Abu al-Abbas Ahmad Ibn Abd al-Halim Ibn Taymiyya al-Harrani, A Treatise by Ibn Taymiyya on "a Matter Concerning Churches," with a Translated Work on Islamic History, Including an Appended List of 250 Works by Ibn Taymiyya (Mas'ala fī al-Kanā'is wa maʿahu Tarjamat Shaykh al-Islām min Dhayl Tārīkh al-Islām, wa maʿahu Qā'ima bi-baʿḍ Makhṭūṭāt Shaykh al-Islām Taḥwī Akthar min Khamsīn wa-Mi'atay ʿUnwān)*, annotation by editor ʿAli Ibn ʿAbd al-ʿAziz Ibn ʿAli al-Shibl (Riyadh: Maktabat al-ʿUbaykan, 1995), 122. In this text, Ibn Taymiyya supports intolerance of Jews and Christians when Muslims are in the majority and no longer require them to work for them. In his opinion, the Muslims spared non-Muslims and their practices of worship because they were peasant farmers who produced and paid the poll tax while Muslims were engaged in jihad (118–21).

89. Al-Tabari, *History of al-Ṭabarī,* 134.

90. Wiktorowicz's categorization does not include reformists. In addition, he does not consider the variations discussed previously that arise from Salafism's interaction with the various modes of religiosity in society, since Salafism is not a socially independent mode of religiosity.

91. Quintan Wiktorowicz, "Anatomy of the Salafi Movement," *Studies in Conflict and Terrorism* 29, no. 3 (2005): 207–208.

92. We will discuss Ibn Abd al-Wahhāb's definition of this concept.

93. Abu al-A'la al-Mawdudi, *The Theory of Islam and Islam's Political, Legal, and Constitutional Guidance* (*Naẓarīyyat al-Islām wa-Hadyuhu fī al-Siyāsa wa al-Qānūn wa al-Dustūr*), trans. Jalil Hasan al-Islahi, revised by Mas'ud al-Nadwi and Muhammad Asim al-Haddad (Lahore: n.p., 1967), 152; see the chapter, "The Political Theory in Islam and Its Primary Principle" ("Al-Naẓariyya al-Siyāsiyya fī al-Islām wa-Mabda'uhu al-Asāsī"), 30–33 and 49, and the chapter on the link between *ḥākimiyya* (sovereignty) and *khilāfa* (vicegerency), "The Process of the Islamic Revolution," 97.

94. The word *ḥukm* in modern Arabic also means rule, but in the Arabic of the seventh century CE / first century AH, it meant "judgment," and *ḥakim* meant "judge," not "ruler" as in modern Arabic. These different meanings were a source of confusion that stemmed from relating the meaning of rule and system of rule to the word *ḥukm* where it is mentioned in different verses of the Qur'an.

95. This slogan was originally attributed to the Khawārij; during their schism following the decision to appoint arbitrators in the dispute between 'Ali and the Umayyads, when they chanted "There is no *ḥukm* except for God." As mentioned in the previous note, *ḥukm* then did not mean "rule" but "judgment of arbitration" (or later "of judges"). Salafis and political Islamists apply to the word in the Qur'an and ancient texts the contemporary meaning of *ḥukm,* "to rule" or "to govern." According to traditional sources, 'Ali Ibn Abi Talib described the slogan as "a true saying with a false intention." Currently it is difficult for believers to oppose the call for the "rule of God," or His sovereignty. Ultimately it is not God who rules but humans in His name.

96. Ibn Sariya was one of the Prophet's companions.

97. See Muhammad Sa'id Hawwa and Abd 'Id al-Ra'ud, "A Critical Study in the Hadith of al-Irbad Ibn Sariyah 'The Messenger of God Admonished Us . . .'" ("Dirāsa Naqdiyya fī Hadith al-'Irbāḍ Ibn Sāriya, 'Wa'aẓanā Rasūl Allah . . .'"), Sa'id Hawwa, January 31, 2012, https://bit.ly/30iYj1Z.

98. Naturally the followers of the traditions of the Prophet (Ahl al-Hadith) justify the fabrication of any hadith because the messenger of God must have predicted it since he was a prophet.

99. See Saʿid Hawwa and al-Raʿud, "A Critical Study."

100. For different narrations of this hadith, see Amir al-Hafi, "A Unifying Analysis of Discussion of the Separation of the Umma" ("Qirāʾa Tawḥīdiyya fī Ḥadīth Iftirāq al-Ummah"), *Islamiyyat al-Maʿrifa* 16, no. 63 (Winter 2011 CE / 1432 AH): 105–40. For an extensive analysis of the hadith and its origins, see Azmi Bishara, *Sectarianism without Sects* (Oxford: Oxford University Press, 2021), 113ff.

101. According to Olivier Roy (b. 1949 CE), a political scientist focused on secularization and Islam, this Salafism features a kind of neofundamentalism and deculturation: "Neofundamentalism is both a product and an agent of globalisation . . . because it embodies in itself an explicit process of deculturation. It rejects the very concept of culture, whether conceived of as arts and intellectual productions or as an integrated system of socially acquired values, beliefs, and rules of conduct, as defined by anthropology. It looks at globalisation as a good opportunity to rebuild the Muslim umma on a purely religious basis, not in the sense that religion is separated from culture and politics, but to the extent religion discards and even ignores other fields of symbolic practices. Neofundamentalism promotes the decontextualisation of religious practices. In this sense it is perfectly adapted to a basic dimension of contemporary globalisation: that of turning human behaviour into codes, and patterns of consumption and communication, delinked from any specific culture." Olivier Roy, *Globalized Islam: The Search for a New Ummah* (New York: Columbia University Press, 2004), 258.

102. Philippe-Joseph Salazar, "A Caliphate of Culture? ISIS's Rhetorical Power," *Philosophy and Rhetoric* 49, no. 3 (2016): 343–54.

103. Salazar, "Caliphate of Culture, 349.

104. Salazar, 352–53.

105. The term could be translated as "the community of Muslim believers" but is used also as a translation of "nation." The resulting confusion is used by Islamists to project the connotations of the modern translation on the old Arabic term.

106. Ibn Taymiyya, *Agreement of Reason and Revelation,* 79.

107. Ibn Taymiyya, 138.

108. See for example Shams al-Din Abu Abdullah Muhammad Ibn Abi Bakr Ibn Qayyim al-Jawziyya, *Steps of the Seekers between the Houses, Thee We Worship and*

Thee We Reclaim (*Madārij al-Sālikīn bayn Manāzil Iyyaka Na'budu wa-Iyyaka Nasta'īn*), ed. Muhammad al-Mu'tasim Billah al-Baghdadi, vol. 3 (Beirut: Dār al-Kitāb al-'Arabi, 2003), 319.

109. Abu Muhammad 'Ali Ibn Ahmad Ibn Sa'id Ibn Hazm, *Judgment on the Principles of Aḥkām* (*Al-Iḥkām fī Uṣūl al-Aḥkām*), foreword by Ihsan Abbas, part 7 (Beirut: Dār al-Afaq al-Jadidah, n.d.), 191, 53ff; see also Muhammad Abu Zahrah, *Ibn Hazm: Life and Times, Jurisprudence and Legal Opinions* (*Ibn Hazm: Ḥayātuhu wa Asruhu, Ārā'uhu wa Fiqhuhu*) (Cairo: Dār al-Fikr al-'Arabi, 1978), 40ff.

110. Abu al-Walid Muhammad Ibn Ahmad Ibn Muhammad Ibn Rushd, *Exposition of the Methods of Proof in Religious Doctrine* (*Al-Kashf 'an Manāhij al-Adilla fī 'Aqā'id al-Milla*) (Beirut: Center for Arab Unity Studies, 1998).

111. See Muhammad Abid al-Jabiri, *The Formation of Arab Reason: Critique of the Arab Reason* (*Takwīn al-'Aql al-'Arabi: Naqd al-'Aql al-'Arabi*), vol. 1, 5th ed. (Beirut: Center for Arab Unity Studies, 1991), 322–3; see also Nayila Abi Nadir, *The Heritage and Methodology between Arkoun and al-Jabiri* (*Al-Turāth wa al-Manhaj bayn Arkoun wa al-Jābiri*) (Beirut: Arab Network for Studies and Publishing, 2008), 373.

112. I agree with Abd al-Majid al-Sharafi in his debate with Sadiq Belabd, who makes contemporary exegesis conditional on knowledge of the revelation of particular verses. See Sadiq Belabd, *The Qur'an and Legislation: A New Reading of the Verse of Judgments* (*Al-Qur'an wa al-Tashrī': Qirā'a Jadīda fī Āyat al-Aḥkām*) (Beirut: Manshurat al-Halabi al-Huquqiyyah, 2004); Abd al-Majid al-Sharafi, *Islam: Between Message and History* (*Al-Islām bayn al-Risāla wa al-Tārīkh*) (Beirut: Dār al-Tali'ah, 2001), 157.

113. The sira of Ibn Ishaq (ca. 704–768 CE / 85–151 AH) comes down to us through Ibn Hisham (d. 834 CE / 218 AH).

114. See Abu Muhammad Abd al-Malik Ibn Hisham, *The Prophetic Biography of Ibn Hisham* (*Al-Sīra al-Nabawiyya li-Ibn Hishām*), annotation and indexes by Umar Abd al-Salam Tadmuri, vol. 2, 3rd ed. (Beirut: Dār al-Kitāb al-'Arabi, 1990), 150, 245.

115. And, many of these rulings and laws that do exist in the Qur'an (like the *ḥudūd* punishments) were not totally new or alien to the cultures existing then, which means that they were not specifically Islamic.

116. The Salafi Islamic jurists are against formal logic in its entirety and repeat Ibn Taymiyya's famous saying, "The intelligent have no need of it, and the dim-witted will derive no benefit from it." While they are not against the use of reason, they argue over whose reason to adopt. Hence, we find them taking the *āthār* and narration as

means to resolve disagreements, adopting their plain meaning and ignoring as far as possible any interpretation unless there is a textual, rather than rational, presumption for interpreting the text.

117. The conflict was not specifically with the Mu'tazilis, who were a broad class including Islamic jurists, judges, Ahl al-Ra'y, and the various kinds of mutakallimūn. It is these latter that Ibn Hanbal accused of Jahmism because they denied the divine attributes and the creation of the Qur'an. They included Dararites, Barghouthis, Najarites, Ahl al-Ra'y, Mu'tazilis, and others.

118. Abu Hamid al-Ghazali, *The Criterion of Distinction between Islam and Clandestine Unbelief* (*Faysal al-Tafriqa bayn al-Islām wa al-Zandaqa*), commentary and hadith annotation by editor Mahmud Biju (Damascus: n.p., 1993), 27.

119. Aziz al-Azmeh, *Muhammad Ibn 'Abd al-Wahhāb* (Beirut: Riyad al-Rayyis, 2000), 12.

CHAPTER 2

1. Taqi al-Din Abu al-Abbas Ahmad Ibn Abd al-Halim Ibn Taymiyya al-Harrani, *Book of Faith* (*Kitāb al-Īmān*), trans. Salman al-Ani and Shadia Ahmad Tel (Kuala Lumpur: Islamic Book Trust, 2009), 328.

2. There are three identifiable stages in Murj'ite thought: "rejecting criticism of the Prophet's companions; responding to the Umayyad deviation; and absorption into other groups." Muhammad Bu Hilal, *The Dialectic of Politics, Religion, and Knowledge* (*Jadal al-Siyāsa wa al-Dīn wa al-Ma'rifa*) (Beirut: Jadawil, 2011), 85.

3. Bu Hilal, *Dialectic of Politics, Religion, and Knowledge,* 87.

4. The Qur'an verses cited in support of this view are Sura al-Tawba 9:105–106. "And say (unto them, O Prophet): 'Act! And God will behold your deeds, and (so will) His Apostle, and the believers: and (in the end) you will be brought before Him who knows all that is beyond the reach of a created being's perception as well as all that can be witnessed by a creature's senses or mind, and then He will make you understand what you have been doing."

5. This was the case with al-Dimashqi, a predestinationist (Qadarī) Murj'ite. The accusations of toadyism sometimes directed at the Murj'ites are rooted in certain Murj'ite works that advocate coming to terms with the Umayyads until Judgment Day. Bu Hilal, *Dialectic of Politics, Religion, and Knowledge,* 93.

6. Bu Hilal, *Dialectic of Politics, Religion, and Knowledge,* 95–96.

7. Abu Bishr Muhammad Ibn Ahmad Ibn Hammad Ibn Sa'id Ibn Muslim al-Ansari al-Dulabi al-Razi, *Titles and Epithets* (*Al-Kunā wa al-Asmā'*), ed. Abu Qutayba Nazhar Muhammad al-Faryabi, vol. 2 (Beirut: Dār Ibn Hazm, 2000), 463.

8. They cite the following verse: "O you who believe, why do you say what you do not do? It is greatly loathsome to God that you say what you do not do" (Qur'an 61: 2–3).

9. Ibn Hani, *Masā'il al-Imam 'Aḥmad Ibn Ḥanbal*, 192.

10. Ibn Hani, 192.

11. Sarriyya (1936–1976 CE) was a Palestinian guerrilla commander who split from the PLO and joined various Islamic movements in Iraq and Egypt before founding his own Salafi militant group in Egypt in the early 1970s CE. He was arrested in 1974 CE after leading an armed attack on the Technical Military College in Cairo in an attempted coup against then-president Anwar Sadat of Egypt. He was tried by an Egyptian court and executed in 1976 CE.

12. What constitutes Dār al-Islām is a subject of some debate. One extreme says that any country where Muslims are free to practice their religion is Dār al-Islām, while the other says that only countries ruled under Shari'a by Muslims fall within Dār al-Islām.

13. Salih al-Sarriyya, "Essay on Faith" ("Wathīqat Rasā'il al-Īmān"), in Rif'at Sayyid Ahmad, *Revolutionaries* (*Al-Thā'irūn*), vol. 2 of *The Armed Prophet* (*Al-Nabiyy al-Musallaḥ*), (London: Riyad al-Rayyis, 1991), 42–43.

14. On the distinction between generalized and specific faithlessness or blasphemy, see Abu al-'Ala Ibn Rashid Ibn Abi al-'Ala al-Rashid, *A Reading of Ibn Taymiyya, Muhammad Ibn Abd al-Wahhāb and the 'Ulama' of the Reformist Call's Guidelines for Judgments of Apostasy* (*Ḍawābiṭ Takfīr al-Mu'ayyan 'Ind Shaykhay al-Islām Ibn Taymiyya wa Ibn 'Abd al-Wahhāb wa 'Ulama' al-Da'wa al-Iṣlāḥiyya: Qirā'a*), foreword and evaluation by Salih Ibn Fawzan Abdullah al-Fawzan (Riyadh: Maktabat al-Rushd Nashirun, 2004).

15. Wiktorowicz, "Anatomy of the Salafi Movement," 231.

16. Abu al-Hasan 'Ali Ibn Isma'il al-Ash'ari, *Treatises on Diverse Islamic Schools* (*Maqālāt al-Islamiyyīn wa Ikhtilāf al-Muṣallīn*), commentary by editor Nawwaf al-Jarah, 2nd ed. (Beirut: Dār Sadir, 2008), 69.

17. Al-Farra', *History of the Hanbalites*, 6.

18. Ibn Abi Ya'la, citing Abdullah Ibn Ahmad Ibn Hanbal, refers to how his father produced his musnad from "700,000 hadiths." See al-Farra', *History of the Hanbalites*, 184.

19. Muhammad Abd al-Salam Faraj, *Jihad: The Absent Commandment* (*Al-Jihad: Al-Farīḍa al-Ghā'iba*) (n.p., 1981), 10. Faraj was a leading ideologue of Jamā'at al-Jihad.

20. See Shihab al-Din Abu Abdullah Ibn Abdullah Yaqut al-Hamawi, *The Dictionary of Countries* (*Mu'jam al-Buldān*), vol. 5 (Beirut, Sader, 1977), 39.

21. See the presentation and discussion in Muhammad Amarah, *The Absent Commandment: Presentation, Dialogue, and Evaluation* (*Al-Farīḍa al-Ghā'iba: 'Arḍ wa Ḥiwār wa Taqyīm*) (Cairo: Maktabat al-Jadid, [1983]). Amarah rejects these conclusions not because he rejects Ibn Taymiyya's fatwas but because of the lack of similarity between the state of Muslims in modern Egypt and that of the Muslims under Mongol rule.

22. The full testimony of Shukri Mustafa, amir of Jamā'at al-Muslimīn (also known as al-Takfīr wa al-Hijra), before the State Security Court (1977 CE) is given in Ahmad, *The Armed Prophet*, vol. 1, *Al-Rāfiḍūn*, 86.

23. Nadir Hamami, *The Islam of the Clerics* (*Islām al-Fuqahā'*) (Beirut: Dār al-Tali'ah, 2006), 31. The claim of forcible Islamization is hotly contested by Muslim historians, citing the long-term tolerance of non-Muslim communities throughout Islamic history.

24. Ahmad, *The Armed Prophet*, vol. 2, *Al-Thā'irūn*, 33.

25. Ahmad, 34.

26. See Nasir al-Huzaymi, *Days with Juhayman: "I Was with the Salafi Muhtasiba Group"* (*Ayyam ma' Juhayman: Kuntu ma' "Al-Jamā'a al-Salafiyya al-Muḥtasiba"*) (Beirut: Arab Network for Research and Publishing, 2011), 25–26. They were also clearly influenced by Sheikh Ibn Baz and read his advice and ideas (43). This means that the boundaries between the Salafi trends were not clear and that they were not organized into movements. All of them were influenced by the same intellectual sources, be they those that chose not to get involved in politics, who are the majority, or those that were drawn to "political" action, that is, if we consider messianic redemptionism politics.

27. While expounding on hadiths cited in Ibn Abi al-'Izz's *An Explication of Tahawi's Doctrine and Faith* (*Sharḥ al-'Aqīda al-Ṭaḥāwiyya*), al-Albani took the opportunity to accuse Abu Ghuddah—whose comments on the same book he disagreed with—of being "an enemy of the creed of Ahl al-Sunna wa al-Jamā'a and a Hanafi fanatic," saying that he had "submitted a report" on him to senior Saudi officials; Abu Ghuddah had taught in several Saudi colleges. As a result, their dispute ultimately reached the highest religious body in the Kingdom, the Council of Senior Scholars. Cf. 'Ali Ibn 'Ali Ibn Muhammad Ibn Abi al-'Izz, *An Explication of Tahawi's Doctrine and Faith* (*Sharḥ*

al-'Aqīda al-Ṭaḥāwiyya), edited by a group of 'ulama', annotated by Muhammad Nasir al-Din al-Albani (Beirut: Maktaba al-Islamiyya, 2006), 26–62.

28. There are several recordings in circulation. See for example "Fatwa from Muhammad Nasir al-Din al-Albani on Palestinians' Leave from Palestine," ("Fatwa al-Shaykh al-Albānī fī mā Yakhuṣṣ Hijrat Ahl Filasṭīn minhā,") YouTube. July 18, 2013. http://bit.do/ekNSP.

29. On November 23, 2002, speaking to the Kuwaiti newspaper *Al Seyassah,* the then Saudi interior minister Nayef Ibn 'Abd al-'Aziz Al Sa'ud famously described the Brotherhood as "the source of the trouble" (*aṣl al-balā'*) and the origin of all of "our problems," alluding to 9/11 and ongoing terrorist activity in Saudi Arabia. See Al-bayan, "Nayef: 'Muslim Brotherhood' Is the Source of the Trouble" (*"Nāyif: al-Ikhwan al-Muslimun Aṣl al-Balā'"*), November 26, 2002, https://bit.ly/3C10YVD. It is clear that he wanted to absolve Wahhabi Salafism and the Kingdom itself of all responsibility by shifting it onto the Brotherhood (who had in fact worked to politicize Saudi Salafi Islam during their interaction with it). Prince Nayef claimed that Brotherhood émigrés who had sought refuge from Arab regimes' oppression in Saudi Arabia had betrayed their hosts by backing Iraq's invasion of Kuwait. Gulf authorities' hostility toward the Brotherhood reached its peak when Saudi Arabia (along with the UAE and Al-Sisi's Egypt) declared the Brotherhood a terrorist organization, contrary to the worldwide stance on the organization.

CHAPTER 3

1. According to Muhammad Abu Zahra (1898–1974 CE), the Salafis gave themselves this description in the fourth century AH. They also claimed that all their views go back to Ahmad Ibn Hanbal, "who revived the creed of the Salaf and fought anything else." See Abu Zahra, *History of the Islamic Schools,* 177.

2. Some currents within the Muslim Brotherhood, for example, have been "Salafized" but are nonetheless still anti-Salafi in terms of their practical alignment because of their historical relationship, which can basically be summarized as "Salafis oppose the Brotherhood, and vice versa, wherever both exist."

3. The Tablīghī movement was founded in 1926 CE in the Mewat province of India as a movement dedicated to renewing the faith of Muslims around the world and reorienting the religious practices of Muslims to what it believes is a more authentic form of Islam. It now boasts over 80 million adherents and is present in every country. Zacharias Pieri, "Tablīghī Jamā'at," ("Jamā'at al-Tablīgh,") in *Handbook of Islamic Sects*

and Movements, ed. Muhammad Afzal Upal and Carole M. Cusack, Brill Handbooks on Contemporary Religion (Leiden: Brill, 2021), 49–72.

4. Gibb, *Modern Trends in Islam*, 55.

5. Many radical Salafis, like al-Wadiʿi and al-Utaybi, started in the Jamāʿat al Tablīgh wa al-Daʿwa before shifting to the Salafi Group. In Syria, the leader of the Tawḥīd Brigade, Abd al-Qadir Taha (nicknamed Hajji Mariʿ), was one of the Jamāʿa's key activists before he joined the revolution and took up arms.

6. The literal meaning is patron, custodian, guardian, or the one who bears responsibility for someone.

7. Muhammad Amarah, "Why the Attack on Shaykh al-Islam?" ("Limādhā al-Hujūm ʿAlā Shaykh al-Islam?"), Arabi 21, November 10, 2016, https://bit.ly/3D99rED.

8. The book in question, *Better What Is Right Than Ancestors or Sheikhs* (*Al-ʿAlam al-Shāmikh fī Tafḍīl al-Ḥaqq ʿalāʾl-Ābāʾ waʾl-Mashāyikh*), predates Ibn Abd al-Wahhāb (al-Muqbili died in 1696 CE / 1108 AH, while Ibn Abd al-Wahhāb was born in 1703 CE / 1115 AH). It condemns the mixing of the sexes and criticizes popular religiosity in Mecca and the "heretical" celebrations held there.

9. al-Khidr Husayn's books include *Call for Reform* (*Al-Daʿwa ilā al-Iṣlāḥ*), *Perceptions of Islamic Sharia* (*Madārik al-Sharīʿa al-Islāmiyya*), *Freedom in Islam* (*Al-Ḥurriyya fī al-Islām*), *Revocation of "Islam and the Origins of Rule"* (*Naqd Kitāb al-Islām wa-Uṣūl al-Ḥukm*), *Revocation of "Jahiliyya Poetry"* (*Naqd Kitāb fī al-Shiʿr al-Jāhilī*), *Life Ponderings* (*Khawāṭir al-Ḥayā*, a poetry anthology), *The Eloquence of the Qurʾan* (*Balāghat al-Qurʾan*), *The Great Happiness* (*Al-Saʿāda al-ʿUẓmā*), and *Tunisia and al-Zitouna University* (*Tūnis wa Jāmiʿ al-Zaytūniyya*). See Khayr al-Din al-Zirkali, *Al-Aʿlām: Biographical Dictionary of Famous Arab Men and Women, Arabists and Orientalists* (*Al-Aʿlām: Qāmūs Tarājim li-Ashhar al-Rijāl min al-ʿArab wa al-Mustaʿribīn wa al-Mustashriqīn*), vol. 6, 15th ed. (Beirut: Dār al-ʿIlm lil-Malayin, 2002), 113.

10. Some researchers do not consider the Sharʿiyya Society to be Salafi, but I do not agree with this categorization. While certainly neither Wahhabi nor Hanbali, the Sharʿiyya Society interacted with popular mass religiosity and propagated the general principles of Salafism.

11. Mahmoud Muhammad Khattab al-Subki's books include *Pure Religion or Guiding Creation to the Religion of Truth* (*Al-Dīn al-Khāliṣ aw Irshād al-Khalq ilā al-Dīn al-Ḥaq*) in six parts, *The Masterpiece of Sight and Insight in Expounding the Way of Marching with the Funeral Procession to Graves* (*Tuḥfat al-Abṣār wa al-Baṣāʾir: Fī Bayān Kayfiyyat al-Sayr maʿ al-Janāza ilā al-Maqābir*), *The Splendid Letter: Fatwas on Forbid-*

ding Some Types of Innovations (*Al-Risāla al-Badīʿa*), *The Purpose of Clarity: An Essay on the Evidence for Fasting and Breaking Fast* (*Ghāyat al-Tibyān Limā Bihi Thubūt al-Ṣiyām wa al-Ifṭār*), *Interpretations of Sunan Abu Dawud: Parts of It* (*Sharḥ Sunan Abi Dawood*), and *Case Pleading, Documents, and Legal Suits* (*Faṣl al-Qaḍiyya fī al-Murāfaʿāt wa-Ṣuwar al-Tawthīqāt wa al-Daʿāwā al-Sharʿiyya*). See al-Zirkali, *Al-Aʿlām*, vol. 7, p. 186.

12. This information comes from old pamphlets published by Egypt's Sharʿiyya Society that I collected on research trips to Cairo. Reports cited by Morroe Berger (1917-1981 CE) suggest that the Society had millions of members at one point; however, by the mid-1960s CE, its membership had dwindled to only 2,800. Berger drew his information from official sources at the Ministry of Social Affairs and the directory published by the American University in Cairo. See Isis Istiphan, *Directory of Social Agencies in Cairo* (Cairo: American University in Cairo, Social Research Center, 1956), 185; and Morroe Berger, *Islam in Egypt Today: Social and Political Aspects of Popular Religion*, Princeton Studies on the Near East (Cambridge: Cambridge University Press, 1970), 90–106.

13. Mahmud Muhammad Khattab al-Subki, *Satisfying Beings with the Statement of the Doctrine of the Salaf and the Successors on the Similarities and the Rebuttal against Atheist and Anthropomorphist Claims and What They Believe to Be Slander* (*Itḥāf al-Kāʾināt bi-Bayān Madhhab al-Salaf wa al-Khalaf fī al-Mutashābihāt wa-Radd Shubah al-Mulḥida wa al-Mujassima wa mā Yaʿtaqidūnahu min al-Muftarayāt*), edited by Yusuf Amin Khattab, 2nd ed. (Cairo: n.p., 1974), 5, 11. In true Salafi style, the author is titled "Possessor of Excellence and Guidance, Grand Professor and Magnificent Imam, Champion of the Sunna, Crusher of Innovation, the late Mahmud Muhammad Khattab al-Subki."

14. Richard Gauvain, *Salafi Ritual Purity: In the Presence of God* (London: Routledge, 2017 [2013]), 37–38.

15. Gauvain, *Salafi Ritual Purity*, 38–39.

16. Gauvain, 39, n41, 286–87.

17. Emmanuel Sivan, *Radical Islam: Medieval Theology and Modern Politics*, enlarged. ed. (New Haven: Yale University Press, 1990).

18. For Qutb, the age of ignorance "is based on rebellion against Allah's sovereignty on earth (*ḥākimiyya*). It transfers to man one of the greatest attributes of Allah, namely sovereignty, and makes some men lords over others. . . . The result of this rebellion against the authority of Allah is the oppression of His servants. Thus, the humiliation of the common man under communist systems and the exploitation of individuals

and nations due to greed for wealth and imperialism . . . are but a corollary of rebellion against Allah's authority." He continues, "We are also surrounded by age of ignorance today, which is of the same nature as it was during the first period of Islam, perhaps a little deeper. Our whole set of environment, people's beliefs and ideas, habits and art, rules and laws is the age of ignorance, even to the extent that what we consider to be Islamic culture, Islamic sources, Islamic philosophy, and Islamic thought are also constructs of the age of ignorance." See Sayyid Qutb, *Milestones*, ed. A. B. al-Mehri (Birmingham: Maktabah Booksellers and Publishers, 2006), 27, 34. See also al-Mawdudi, *Theory of Islam*, 23: "If you examine human society from this perspective, you become certain that the true spring of evil and corruption is 'man's acting as God over man' whether directly or by an intermediary."

19. National Commission on Terrorist Attacks upon the United States, *The 9/11 Commission Report: Final Report of the National Commission on Terrorist Attacks upon the United States* (New York: Norton, [2004]), 362.

20. Theoretically, and outside of the current sociological context, we can add a fourth feature: the phenomenon of individual extremism *in general*—including extreme positions and political or violent behavior—which is a feature of the secular formation of individual modern subjectivity. Modernization is distinguished by the individual asserting and affirming his subjectivity through extremism.

21. François Burgat, *Islamism in the Shadow of al-Qaeda* (*L'islamisme à l'heure d'al-Qaida*), trans. Patrick Hutchinson (Austin: University of Texas Press, 2008), 18.

22. Note the contrast between the relatively moderate influence of Muhammad al-Ghazali, a traditional Brotherhood scholar who broke with Qutb, and the influence of Qutbites like Muhammad Qutb and Muhammad Surur on Wahhabi youth.

23. Ibrahim al-Bayumi Ghanim, *The Political Thought of Imam Hasan al-Banna* (*Al-Fikr al-Islāmī li al-Imam Hasan al-Bannā*), Al-Dirasat al-Hadariyyah (Cairo: Dār al-Tawzi' wal-Nashr al-Islamiyyah, 1992), 136.

24. The origin of the idea of the new jahiliyya is found in Rida, who used the word *jāhiliyyatunā* (our age of ignorance) in passing. Qutb and his brother Muhammad turned the new age of ignorance into a concept in his book *Jāhiliyyat al-Qarn al-'Ishrīn*.

25. At the heart of Qutb's thought is a rejection of Nasserist charismatic control and an attempt to overcome authoritarian political and ideological marginalization by spiritually rising above it (organizationally or as a brotherhood of believers). However, Qutb gives ideological expression to this idea in inverted form after his ordeal in prison. Prior to imprisonment, Qutb was involved in the national struggle and showed

a distinctly romantic and modernist bent in his appreciation of Qur'anic aesthetics; his words reflect something like a nascent socialism and express a keen sense of class injustice. All of this is recorded in his autobiography, *A Child from the Village* (*Ṭifl min al-Qarya*), which he dedicated to Taha Husayn.

26. See Taqi al-Din Abu al-Abbas Ahmad Ibn Abd al-Halim Ibn Taymiyya al-Harrani, *Following the Straight Path to Contravene the Companions of Hell* (*Iqtidā' al-Ṣirāt al-Mustaqīm li-Mukhālafāt Aṣḥāb al-Jaḥīm*), ed. Nasir Abd al-Karim al-'Aql, vol. 1, 7th ed. (Beirut: Dār 'Alam al-Kutub, 1999), 72–73. As noted previously, Rida made similar comments, even entitling a section of al-Bukhari's *Ṣaḥīḥ al-Bukhārī*, the chapter on sins that reflect ignorance. See also Yusuf al-Qaradawi, "A Final Word on Sayyid Qutb" ("Kalima Akhīra ḥawl Sayyid Quṭb"), Yusuf al-Qaradawi, September 17, 2004, https://bit.ly/39uxml9.

27. Muqbil Ibn Hadi al-Wadi'i, *Religious Polemic against Sophistry and Ignorance* (*Ghārat al-Ashriṭa 'alā Ahl al-Jahl wa al-Safsaṭa*), vol. 2 (Cairo: Dār al-Haramayn, 1998), 473–34.

28. Hasan Isma'il al-Hudaybi, *Preachers, Not Judges: Research in the Islamic Faith and Methods of Proselytization, The Book of Invitation* (*Du'āt Lā Quḍāt: Abḥāth fī al-'Aqīda al-Islāmiyya wa Manhaj al-Da'wa ilā Allah, Kitāb al-Da'wa*) (Cairo: Dār al-Tiba'a wal-Nashr al-Islamiyya, 1977), 76–77.

29. Taha Husayn summarized this in 1938. Taha Husayn, *The Future of Culture in Egypt* (*Mustaqbal al-Thaqāfa fī Miṣr*) (Cairo: Matba'at wa-Maktabat al-Ma'arif, n.d.), 45.

30. Ghanim, *Political Thought of Imam Hasan al-Banna*, 68.

31. Hasan al-Banna, *Collection of Epistles of the Martyr Imam Hasan al-Banna* (*Majmū'at Rasā'il al-Imam al-Shahīd Ḥasan al-Bannā*) (Alexandria, Egypt: Dār al-Da'wa, 2002), 167.

32. Khalil al-Anani has also noted this in his description of how the Brotherhood was constructed as an identity movement. See Khalil al-Anani, *Inside the Muslim Brotherhood: Religion, Identity and Politics* (Oxford: Oxford University Press, 2016), 56–60.

33. Modern and secular, Arab nationalism competed with and triumphed over Islamists' claim for authenticity for decades. Conversely, the ethnicization of local identities by connecting them to archeological entities like the Pharaonic and Phoenician never had a chance for success anywhere in the Arab world. It is clear that modernist enlightened challengers to Salafism must be forged in the Muslim Arab cultural context and not in alienation to it.

34. Djait, *Islamic Culture in Crisis*, 10.

35. In the last decade, the internal elections inside the Muslim Brotherhood in different countries displayed a high level of internal democracy with no equivalent in any secular, Nationalist, or leftist party in the region.

36. Ishaq Musa al-Husayni, *The Muslim Brotherhood: The Largest Modern Muslim Movement* (*Al-Ikhwan al-Muslimun: Kubrā al-Ḥarakāt al-Islāmiyya al-Ḥadītha*) (Beirut: Dār Beirut lil-Tiba'a wal-Nashr, 1952).

37. On this subject, see Muhammad Jamal Barout, *New Yathrib: Contemporary Islamic Movements* (*Yathrib al-Jadīda: Al-Ḥarakāt al-Islamiyya al-Rāhina*) (Beirut: Riyad al-Rayyis, 1994), 95–124.

38. We have already shown that the term *fundamentalist* has a different meaning than the traditional use of the word.

39. Ghanim, *Political Thought of Imam Hasan al-Banna,* 154.

40. Ghanim, 162.

41. Hasan al-Banna, *Memoirs of the Call and the Preacher* (*Mudhakkirāt al-Da'wa wa al-Dā'iya*) (Cairo: Dār al-Tawzi' wal-Nashr al-Islamiyyah, 2001), 57.

42. Al-Banna, *Memoirs of the Call and the Preacher,* 58–59. See Darwaza, *Modern Arab Movement,* 34.

43. Al-Banna, *Collection of Epistles*, 165.

44. More specifically, the doctrine concerns loyalty to the believers and enmity to the nonbelievers.

45. The full title is *Matters of Jāhiliyya on Which the Prophet of God (PBUH) Opposed Unlettered and Lettered Jāhilī People* (*Masā'il al-Jāhiliyya allatī Khālaf fīhā Rasūl Allah Ṣallā Allah 'alayhi wa-Sallam Ahl al-Jāhiliyya min al-Ummiyyīn wa'l-Kitābiyyīn*). The original is less than twenty pages long. A 1907 CE edition with commentary by the Iraqi scholar Muhammad Shukri al-Alusi (1802–1854 CE / 1217–1270 AH) runs to more than 150 pages in small print. Many other editions have followed, including a 1924 Salafi Library print with commentary by al-Khatib.

46. Sayyid Qutb, *In the Shade of the Qur'an* (*Fī Ẓilāl al-Qur'an*), vol. 3, 32nd ed. (Cairo: Dār al-Shurouk, 2003), 1816.

47. See Malik Bennabi, *Vocation de l'Islam* (Paris: ANEP, 2006), 32.

48. I am referring here to the fact that although Ibn Abd al-Wahhāb was a traditional Hanbali, he did not take his Salafism from the deserts of Najd or from its Hanbalis. Uyayna (Ibn Abd al-Wahhāb's native village), then Huraymila, then al-Dir'iyya (the stronghold of Muhammad Ibn Sa'ud Ibn Muqrin) were mud-brick villages. They had

Shari'a judges, learned men, and a certain level of order. They were not primitive Bedouin settlements. Ibn Abd al-Wahhāb studied Islamic jurisprudence under his father Abd al-Wahhāb Ibn Sulayman, a traditional Hanbali judge and not Salafi. He then met in the village of al-Majma'ah Sheikh Abdullah Ibn Ibrahim al-Sayf, who introduced him to al-Sindhi. See Ibn Bishr, *Glorious History of the Najd Region,* 33–36.

49. I don't use the translation *brotherhood* here to avoid confusing the Wahhabi "brothers of those who obey God" (*Ikhwān man aṭā' Allah*) with the Muslim Brotherhood.

50. Ahmad Ra'if, *The Black Gateway: Pages from the History of the Muslim Brotherhood* (*Al-Bawwāba al-Sawdā': Ṣafaḥāt min Tārīkh al-Ikhwan al-Muslimin*), 3rd ed. (Cairo: Al-Zahra' lil-'Ilm al-'Arabi, 1986), 385–97.

51. Ra'if, *Black Gateway*, 422–23.

52. Ra'if, 398–400, 509.

53. Ra'if, 354–55.

54. Muhammad Sa'id Hawwa, *God's Soldiers: Culture and Ethics* (*Jund Allah: Thaqāfatan wa-Akhlāqan*), 2nd ed. (Cairo: Dār al-Tiba'a al-Haditha, 1977), 19–20.

55. Mustafa Mashhur, *Questions on the Path* (*Tasā'ulāt 'alā al-Ṭarīq*) (Algiers: Dār al-Irshad, 1989), 88–90.

56. Al-Hudaybi, *Preachers, Not Judges,* 6, 45–47, 204–8.

57. See, for example, the report of Abu Anas al-Shami and his recording of the Battle of Fallujah in Maysarah al-Gharib, ed., "The Battle of al-Ahzab under Siege," ("Ma'rakat al-Aḥzāb taḥt al-iṣār"), AQI Media Bureau, https://bit.ly/30bUDXt.

58. Isaiah Berlin, "The Apotheosis of the Romantic Will: The Revolt against the Myth of an Ideal World," in *Crooked Timber of Humanity: Chapters in the History of Ideas* (London: John Murray, 1990), 211–12.

59. F. A. Voigt, *Unto Caesar* (London: Constable, [1939]), 49. This important and little-known book reviews the quasi-salvationist religious elements in Nazi ideology. I became interested in the book when studying the thinking of secular religions while preparing to write my *Religion and Secularism in Historical Context.*

60. Taqi al-Din Abu al-Abbas Ahmad Ibn Abd al-Halim Ibn Taymiyya al-Harrani, *The Correctness of the Principles of the People of Medina* [the Maliki School] (*Ṣiḥḥat Uṣūl Madhhab Ahl al-Madīna*), ed. Ahmad Hijazi al-Saqa (Cairo: Maktabat al-Thaqafah al-Diniyyah, 1998), 28.

61. Muhammad Ibn Salih Ibn al-Uthaymin, *Sunni Lectures on the Doctrine of Ibn Taymiyya, Sheikh of Islam* (*Al-Muhāḍarāt al-Sunniyya fī Sharḥ al-'Aqīda al-Wāsiṭiyya li-Shaykh al-Islām Ibn Taymiyya*), with commentary by editors 'Abd al-'Aziz Ibn Baz

and Abu Muhammad Ashraf Abd al-Maqsud Ibn Abd al-Rahman (Riyadh: Maktabat al-Tabariyyah, n.d.).

62. Abu al-Khayr Muhammad Ibn Abd al-Rahman al-Sakhawi, *Gems in the History of the Holy City of Medina* (*Al-Tuḥfa al-Laṭīfa fī Tārīkh al-Madīna al-Sharīfa*), ed. Muhammad Hamid al-Fiqqi, foreword by Taha Husayn (Cairo: Dār al-Thaqafah, 1979).

63. Taqi al-Din Abu al-Abbas Ahmad Ibn Abd al-Halim Ibn Taymiyya al-Harrani, The Collection of the Shaykh al-Islam's Fatwas (Majmūʿ al-Fatāwā), ed. Abd al-Rahman Ibn Muhammad Ibn Qasim, vol. 28 (Medina: King Fahd Complex for the Printing of the Holy Qur'an, 1995), 61.

64. It seems that the caliph Uthman Ibn Affan first used this expression. Unlike under the Prophet and the rightly guided caliphs, when obedience rested on faith and not on worldly interests, during his reign, the early Muslims became aware of the meaning of the temporal state and the interests it guaranteed. Burhan Ghalioun explains this as meaning that the state compels what people do not obey by the emotional force of faith. Here we propose a different interpretation. See Burhan Ghalioun, *Criticism of Politics: State and Religion* (*Naqd al-Siyāsa: Al-Dawla wa al-Dīn*), 4th ed. (Beirut: Al-Markaz al-Thaqafi al-ʿArabi, 2007), 73.

CHAPTER 4

1. Muhammad Qutb wrote *Twentieth-Century Jahiliyya* two centuries after him. In addition, the age of ignorance is also central to Sayyid Qutb's commentary *In the Shade of the Qur'an* and his *Milestones*.

2. Naturally this does not include ignorant rulers. However, Saudi Muslim scholars have developed this concept into a paradigm that prohibits criticism of the ruler and makes obedience to God, the Prophet, the imams, and rulers the means to a happy society. This is explained by Ibn Baz in his many writings and in his interpretation of the Qur'anic Sura al-Nisa' 4:59, "O you who believe, obey God, and obey the Messenger and those in authority among you."

3. Muhammad Ibn Abd al-Wahhāb, "Four Letters" ("Arbaʿ Rasā'il"), in Taqi al-Din Abu al-Abbas Ahmad Ibn Abd al-Halim Ibn Taymiyya al-Harrani and Muhammad Ibn Abd al-Wahhāb, *Writings on Monotheism* (*Majmūʿat al-Tawḥīd*) (Riyadh: Maktabat Riyadh al-Ḥadīthah, n.d.), 275–76.

4. Ibn Khaldun, *The Muqaddimah: An Introduction to History*, trans. Franz Rosenthal, edited and abridged by N. J. Dawood, introduction by Bruce B. Lawrence (Princeton: Princeton University Press, 2015), 126–28.

5. Ayman al-Yassini, *Religion and State in the Kingdom of Saudi Arabia* (Boulder: Westview, 1985), 41.

6. Abd al-Rahman Ibn Muhammad Ibn Qasim, ed., *The Glistening Pearls of Najdi Responsa* (*Al-Durar al-Saniyya fī al-Ajwiba al-Najdiyya*), vol. 16, 6th ed. (n.p., 1996), 348. This is neither an objective source for the conversation between the two men nor that of an eyewitness. It is framed to bolster the image of the relationship. See also Ibn Bishr, *Glorious History of the Najd Region,* 42.

7. The Kingdom of Saudi Arabia as a united entity was declared in 1932 CE, but the real state-building process (i.e., of state institutions) began in 1953 CE. Until then ʿAbd al-ʿAziz ruled "personally and informally." He acted as a patriarch who "administered the country as a gigantic personal household." Al-Yassini, *Religion and State,* 59.

8. History books use the word *state*: the first Saudi state (1744–1818 CE / 1157–1233 AH), the second Saudi state (1818–1891 CE / 1233–1234 AH), and the third Saudi state (1902 CE–present), while I prefer to use the term *reign* because it wasn't a state yet. According to my understanding, *state* applies only to the third dynasty, under Ibn Saʿud.

9. Natana J. DeLong-Bas, *Wahhabi Islam: From Revival and Reform to Global Jihad* (London: I. B. Tauris, 2007), 34–35.

10. Gibb, *Modern Trends in Islam,* 27.

11. al-Sindhi al-Madani was a Hadith scholar born in Sindh who lived and died in Medina. His works include *Explaining Persuasion and Intimidation for al-Munthiri: An Introduction to Doctrine, Al-Mubīn's Masterpiece* (*Sharḥ al-Targhīb wal-Tarhīb li'l-Mundhirī, Muqaddima fī'l-ʿAqā'id, Tuḥfat al-Muhibbīn*) (commentary on the Al-Arbaʿīn hadiths of al-Nawawi), and *Explaining al-Atā'iyya's Wisdoms* (*Sharḥ al-Ḥikam al-ʿAtā'iyya*). See al-Zirkali, *Al-Aʿlām,* vol. 6, 111.

12. John Voll, "Muḥammad Ḥayyā al-Sindī and Muḥammad Ibn ʿAbd al-Wahhāb: An Analysis of an Intellectual Group in Eighteenth-Century Madīna," *Bulletin of the School of Oriental and African Studies* 38, no. 1 (1975), 32.

13. Al-Dahlawi was a Hanafi faqīh and Hadith scholar from Delhi in India. His books include *The Big Victory in the Origins of Interpretation* (*Al-Fawz al-Kabīr fī Uṣūl al-Tafsīr*), *The Eloquent Case for God* (*Hujjat Allah al-Bāligha*), *Eliminating Mystery over the Succession of the Caliphs* (*Izālat al-Khafā' ʿan Khilāfat al-Khulafā'*), *Fairness in the Causes of Dispute* (*Al-Inṣāf fī Asbāb al-Khilāf*), *Necklaces in the Rulings of Diligence and Tradition* (*ʿIqd al-Jayyid fī Ahkām al-Ijtihād wa al-Taqlīd*), and *The Blossoming Seeds in Sufism and Wisdom* (*Al-Budūr al-Bāzigha fī'l-Tasawwuf wa'l-Ḥikmah*). See al-Zirkali,

Al-A'lām, vol. 1, 149. *The Big Victory in the Origins of Interpretation* (*Al-Fawz al-Kabīr fī Uṣūl al-Tafsīr*).

14. Voll, "Muḥammad Ḥayyā al-Sindī and Muḥammad Ibn 'Abd al-Wahhāb," 32–39.

15. Voll, 35.

16. Voll, 38.

17. DeLong-Bas, *Wahhabi Islam*, 21.

18. Dallal, *Islam without Europe*, 57–58.

19. Dallal, 58.

20. Haydar Ahmad al-Shihabi, *Lebanon in the Era of Prince Bashir the Second* (*Lubnān fī 'Ahd al-Amir Bashīr al-Thāni*), vol. 3 of *Lebanon in the Era of the Shihabi Princes: The Second and Third Parts of The Fine Deception in the Akhbār of the Ancestors* (*Lubnān fī 'Ahd al-Umarā' al-Shihābiyyin: Wa huwa al-Juz' al-Thāni wa al-Thālith min Kitāb al-Ghurar al-Ḥisān fī Akhbār Abnā' al-Zamān*), foreword and commentary by editors Asad Rustum and Fouad Afram al-Bustani, Majmū'at al-Duktūr Asad Rustum 2–4, 2nd ed. (Beirut: Maktabah al-Bulisiyyah, 1984), 569.

21. Several factors helped Wahhabism reemerge in the beginning of twentieth century CE, including the decline of the Ottoman Empire, the rise of a British influence in the Arab region which ended up supporting the Saudis against their former ally the Hashimites, and the discovery of oil in Arabia. Dallal notes that "European influence not only shaped 20th century CE Wahhabism and allowed it to reemerge despite its limited popular appeal, but it also aborted the rich, non-Wahhabi traditions of the 18th and early 19th centuries CE that had previously been alternatives to Wahhabi ideology" (Dallal, *Islam without Europe*, 6–7).

22. Interestingly, in their attacks on Arab nationalism and its stance against Ottoman rule, Islamist movements overlook the fact that Wahhabis were the first to wage war on the Ottoman sultan. In 1803, when Wahhabi Saudis were in control of Mecca, pilgrims were forced to pay a tax of eight piastres and Turks had to pay twice that amount. Both Salafis and traditional nationalist historians overlook this, instead focusing on Wahhabism as a reformist precursor of Arab nationalism in view of its hostility to the Ottomans. These accounts miss the character of Wahhabi Salafism as the oldest Muslim separatist tendency that developed before Turkish and Arab nationalism evolved into political movements. Wahhabism led a prolonged rebellion against the sultanate and at various periods appropriated the guarding of pilgrimage routes and the title "guardian of the sanctuary from the caliphate."

23. Louis de Corancez, *The Wahhabis: A History of What History Neglected* (*Al-Wahhābiyyun: Tārīkh ma Ahmalahu al-Tārīkh*), trans. a group of researchers (Beirut: Riyad al-Rayyis, 2003), 62. It is worth noting that this book, or its foreword at least, was written in 1808.

24. de Corancez, *The Wahhabis,* 68.

25. de Corancez, 69–70.

26. "Because of its historical record and recent militant manifestation, Hanbalism has been claimed as a 'radical' trend in Sunni Islam; a Sunni counterpart to the Shiʿi radicalism which culminated in the Iranian revolution . . . modern 'fundamentalist' Islam, and especially Khomeinism, represent radical departures from the mainstream of Islamic political thought. To that end, I have to show that the Hanbali tradition does not constitute an ancestry to modern radical Islam in challenging the legitimacy of the de facto separation of government from religion." Sami Zubaida, *Islam, the People and the State: Political Ideas and Movements in the Middle East* (London: I. B. Tauris, 2009 [1989]), 8.

27. "We have shown that Wahabism, at least in its manifestation in the Brotherhood movement, can be classified with the modern 'fundamentalists' in its insistence on the unity of religion and the state in Islam. But in one crucial respect it is different from the radical ideologies which developed and thrived among the urban poor and 'traditional' middle classes of Egypt (Muslim Brothers) or the equivalent groups in connection with sectors of the clergy in Iran. Islam and Islamic authority for the Ikhwan was clearly conceived in terms of a tribal model, and Ibn Saʿud was for them a chieftain with a religious charisma. It is a much simpler and more direct kind of politics than that are assumed by the modern 'fundamentalist' ideologies, especially those of Khomeini and Shara'ati." Zubaida, *Islam, the People and the State,* 12.

28. Abdelwahab Meddeb, *The Malady of Political Islam* (*Awhām al-Islām al-Siyāsī*), trans. Abdelwahab Meddeb and Mohammed Bennis (Beirut: Dār al-Nahar, 2002). In particular, see the second section on the origins of fundamentalism, 59–114. The book is an attempt to understand how Wahhabism led to 9/11.

29. Meddeb does not believe Ibn Hanbal merits being called an Islamic jurist. I agree with this estimation that reiterates the characterization of Ibn Hanbal by jurisprudents of the other schools of jurisprudence as early as the tenth century CE; the Hanbalis themselves maintained that he was an Islamic jurist, going so far as to harass the famous historian al-Tabari and prevent his burial outside his home because he had

described Ibn Hanbal as a hadith scholar and not a jurist. 'Izz al-Din Ibn al-Athir, *The Second Abbasid Age (The Age of Turkish Influence) from the Caliphate of al-Muʿtasim until 321 and the Caliphate of al-Qāhir Billāh (218–321 AH)*, part 6 of *The Complete History of Ibn al-Athir (Al-Kāmil fī al-Tārīkh)*, ed. Omar Abd al-Salam Tadmuri (Beirut: Dār al-Kitāb al-ʿArabi, 1997), 677–78.

30. DeLong-Bas rejects this assessment. She contends, in response to Stephen Schwartz, that Ibn Abd al-Wahhāb was an Islamic jurist and scholar in the context of his historical period. See DeLong-Bas, *Wahhabi Islam*, 5. See also Stephen Schwartz, *The Two Faces of Islam: The House of Saʿud from Tradition to Terror* (New York: Doubleday, 2002), 133.

31. Karen DeYoung, "Saudi Prince Denies Kushner Is 'in His Pocket,'" *Washington Post*, March 22, 2018, http://bit.do/ekSy3.

32. Gauvain, *Salafi Ritual Purity*, 9.

33. Gauvain, 10.

34. Madawi al-Rasheed, "Banning Politics: The Wahhabi Religious Rhetoric in Saudi Arabia" ("Ḥaẓr al-Siyāsa: Al-Khiṭāb al-Dīnī al-Wahhābī fī al-ʿArabiyya al-Saʿūdiyya,"), in Abdellah Hammoudi, Denis Bauchard, and Rémy Leveau, *Is Democracy Compatible with Islam? (Hal Tatawāfaq al-Dīmuqrātiyya maʿ al-Islām?)*, ed. Judith Cahen, trans. Riyadh Suma (Beirut: Dār al-Farabi, 2009), 242–43.

35. Al-Masʿudi, *Meadows of Gold*, 137.

36. Qutb, *Milestones*, 30–34, 49–50, 55.

37. Ahmad Mustafa Abu Hakimah, ed., *The Shining Meteor: A Biography of Muhammad Ibn Abd al-Wahhāb (Kitāb Lamʿ al-Shihāb fī Sīrat Muhammad Ibn Abd al-Wahhāb)*, 27–28, http://bit.do/ekSB6. Alternatively, DeLong-Bas contends that Ibn Abd al-Wahhāb was a preacher who used argument and dialogue rather than violence. She says that there is no evidence that he advocated jihad after the publication of his book *Al-Tawḥīd (The Book of Monotheism)*. See DeLong-Bas, *Wahhabi Islam*, 23. She also argues that Ibn Abd al-Wahhāb imposed restrictions on violence against the faithless, only declaring those who openly and spiritually rejected the call to monotheism infidels. She argues that his followers greatly expanded the interpretation of faithlessness and the use of violence—a tendency he tried to moderate through his book on jihad. See DeLong-Bas, *Wahhabi Islam*, 224.

38. The *Ṣiḥaḥ* are two collections of hadith by Muhammad al-Bukhari and Muslim Ibn al-Hajjaj that are generally acknowledged as truthful resources.

39. *Zakat* means yearly individual donation for charitable causes.

40. Muhammad Ibn Abd al-Wahhāb, *Summarized Biography of the Prophet* (*Mukhtaṣar Sīrat al-Rasūl*) (Riyadh: Ministry of Islamic Affairs, Awqaf, Dawah, and Guidance, 1998), 42–43.

41. Ibn Abd al-Wahhāb, *Summarized Biography of the Prophet*, 43.

42. In Shari'a, removing the means (*sadd al-dharā'i'*) includes prohibiting practices or acts that are not in themselves sinful or wrong but which may lead to things that are. In this case the argument is that praising the Prophet is a step toward worshipping him.

43. Al-Yassini, *Religion and State*, 24.

44. de Corancez, *The Wahhabis*, 17.

45. Ibn Abd al-Wahhāb had already, long before, classified Dir'iyya as a "land of hijra" and the whole of Najd as an Islamic emirate. For him hijra was the basis of jihad. See Ibn Qasim, ed., *Glistening Pearls*, vol. 8, 238–41 (quoted from Abdullah Ibn Mas'ud), as well as the response of Sheikh Sulayman Ibn Sahman that Najd was *dār hijrah* (474–78).

46. Fu'ad Ibrahim, *Jihadi-Salafism in Saudi Arabia* (*Al-Salafiyya al-Jihādiyya fī al-Sa'ūdiyya*) (Beirut: Dār al-Saqi, 2009), 27.

47. Ibn Abd al-Wahhāb, *The Book of Monotheism, a Right for Slaves* (*Kitāb al-Tawḥīd alladhī huwa Ḥaqq Allah 'alā al-'Abīd*) (Riyadh: Imam Mohammad Ibn Saud Islamic University, 2001), 9–11.

48. Relying on the classical biographies of the Prophet as sources and chronicles for the aforementioned events does not stem from a supposition that they are scientific historiographies but rather sources about those events for pious believers.

49. Alexei Vassiliev, *The History of Saudi Arabia* (*Tārīkh al-'Arabiyya al-Sa'ūdiyya*), trans. Khayri al-Damin and Jalal al-Mashitah (Beirut: Dār al-Farabi, 2011), 91–92.

50. Vassiliev, *History of Saudi Arabia*, 93.

51. "Surely to God belongs pure religion. And those who take besides Him patrons, [say]: 'We only worship them so that they may bring us near to God'. God will indeed judge between them concerning that about which they differ. Truly God does not guide one who is a liar, a disbeliever" (Al-Zumar 39:3).

52. 'Ali al-Wardi, *From the Beginning of the Ottoman Era to the Mid-Nineteenth Century* (*Lamahāt Ijtimā'iyya min Tārīkh al-'Irāq al-Ḥadīth*). Vol. 1 of *Social Glimpses of Modern Iraqi History* (*Min Bidāyat al-'Ahd al-'Uthmānī ḥattā Muntaṣaf al-Qarn al-Tāsi' 'Ashar*) (London: Al-Warraq lil-Nashr, 2007), 195.

53. Vassiliev, *History of Saudi Arabia*, 98. DeLong-Bas also narrates how Ibn Abd al-Wahhāb personally cut down the tree from which people sought blessings and clashed

with the inhabitants of Uyayna as a result. In her detailed explanation of the stoning of the adulteress, DeLong-Bas wrote that Ibn Abd al-Wahhāb had no choice, since she had confessed and insisted on her public confession of adultery, despite Ibn Abd al-Wahhāb's efforts to dissuade her. See DeLong-Bas, *Wahhabi Islam*, 25–27.

54. Wars were declared by the caliph Abu Bakr against the Arab tribes who stopped paying zakat (tribute) after the death of Prophet Muhammad, and against those who reverted to their old beliefs and were considered renegades or apostates.

55. Al-Wardi, *From the Beginning of the Ottoman Era*, 195–96; Vassiliev, *History of Saudi Arabia*, 97.

56. Abd al-Raziq Ibn al-Hasan Ibn Ibrahim al-Baytar, *Exemplary Persons of the Thirteenth Century* (*Ḥilyat al-Bashar fī Tārīkh al-Qarn al-Thālith ʿAshar*), commentary by editor Muhammad Bahjah al-Baytar, vol. 3, 2nd ed. (Beirut: Dār Sadir, 1993), 1600.

57. Al-Shihabi, *The French Campaign in Egypt and the Early Rule of Amir Bashir II* (*Al-Ḥamla al-Faransāwiyya ʿalā Miṣr wa-Awāʾil Ḥukm al-Amir Bashīr al-Thāni*), vol. 2, part 2, of *Lebanon in the Era of the Shihabi Princes*, 524.

58. Collected by Aziz al-Azmeh along with other texts in al-Azmeh, *Muhammad Ibn ʿAbd al-Wahhāb*, 77–90. I refer to the original text: Ibn Abd al-Wahhāb, *The Book of Monotheism*, where the following issues are found in various places: declaring those who wear bracelets and threads to ward off evil, which is deemed lesser polytheism, one of the greatest sins (27–8); forbidding of amulets (against the evil eye) and charms (apart from the evil eye and fever) and beads (29–30); forbidding the seeking of blessings from trees or stones, which is a tradition and practice taken from the people of the book, especially Christians; "the practice of the people of the book is condemned like the practice of the polytheists." (34); seeking help from other than God (41); to seek relief from other than God is "major polytheism" (43); the "intercession" of the Prophet on Judgment Day is not for the polytheist (53); "knowledge that the first polytheism on Earth was the doubt of the righteous" (57); "knowledge of the prohibition of statues and the rule to remove them" (58); killing magicians because they are faithless and should not be given the chance to repent (73); "belief and faith in soothsayers and fortune tellers constitutes faithlessness" (77); "seeing omens in the flight of birds" (83); "an oath sworn by anything other than God" (110); "idolaters are particularly egregious [infidels], and the people who will be tortured most [in Hell]" (139); people are warned "against exaggerated descriptions of the Prophet or exaggerated praise of him" (146).

59. Abdullah Ibn Saʿdi al-Ghamidi al-ʿAbdali, ed., *The Monotheists' Faith Doctrine and Rejoinder to the Error of Heretics* (*ʿAqīdat al-Muwaḥḥidīn wa al-Radd ʿalā Ḍalāl al-*

Mubtadi'īn), foreword by 'Abd al-'Aziz Ibn Abdullah Ibn Baz (Al-Ta'if: Dār al-Tarafayn, 1999), 279–80.

60. Ibn Sa'di al-Ghamidi al-'Abdali, *Monotheists' Faith Doctrine*, 279–80.

61. Ahmad Wasfi Zakaria, *Damascene Clans and Tribes* (*'Ashā'ir al-Shām*), 10th ed. (Damascus: Dār al-Fikr; Beirut: Dār al-Fikr al-Mu'āṣir,[1946] 2009), 299.

62. Zakaria, *Damascene Clans*, 300.

63. John Lewis Burckhardt, *Notes on the Bedouins and Wahábys: Collected during His Travels in the East*, vol. 1, (London: Henry Colburn and Richard Bentley, 1831), 99–102; Vassiliev, *The History of Saudi Arabia*, 85.

64. Vassiliev, *The History of Saudi Arabia*, 85.

65. Abu Hakimah, ed., *The Shining Meteor*, 32–3.

66. See also al-Wardi, *From the Beginning of the Ottoman Era*, 198.

67. Vassiliev, *The History of Saudi Arabia*, 100.

68. See also: Ibrahim, *Jihadi-Salafism in Saudi Arabia*, p. 12.

69. Vassiliev, *The History of Saudi Arabia*, 134–5.

70. See Abu Isma'il Muhammad Ibn Abdullah al-Azdi, *The Islamic Conquests of the Levant* (*Futūḥ al-Shām*), ed. Isam Mustafa 'Aqlah and Yusuf Ahmad Banī Yasin, foreword by 'Abd al-'Aziz al-Duri (Amman: Mu'asassat Hamadah lil-Dirasat al-Jami'iyya, Dār al-Yazarawī al-'Ilmiyya, 2011), 201–2. See also the dialogue in al-Waqidi between Wardan and Khalid Ibn al-Walid on the eve of the Battle of Ajnadayn, when Wardan met with Khalid and said to him, "O Khalid, tell me what you want, and draw me near to you. If you ask for something from us, we will not stint in giving it to you as a sign of friendship, because we are not weaker than you. We know that you were in a land of drought and starvation and were dying of hunger. Be content with a little from us and be on your way." See Abu Abdullah Muhammad Ibn Omar al-Waqidi, *The Islamic Conquest of the Levant* (*Futūḥ al-Shām*), prepared and revised by Abd al-Latif Abd al-Rahman, vol. 1, 2nd ed. (Beirut: Dār al-Kutub al-'Ilmiyya, 205), 59.

71. de Corancez, *The Wahhabis*, 33.

72. Vassiliev, The History of Saudi Arabia, 149.

73. Burckhardt, *Notes on the Bedouins and Wahábys*, 287–8; Vassiliev, *The History of Saudi Arabia*, 149.

74. In Arabic, it is common to refer to others by reference to their relatives.

75. 'Ali al-Tantawi, *Memories* (*Dhikrayāt*), 3rd ed., vol. 3 (Mecca: Dār al-Manarah lil-Nashr wal-Tawzi', 2000), 138. In fact, this was a common custom among the tribes. Even the Prophet himself was addressed by his contemporaries by his first name until

the divine command was revealed to the companions that they should stop addressing him as they did each other. The Bedouin, however, continued to address him with "O Muhammad."

76. One of the rites of the pilgrimage (*Hajj*) in Mecca, during which pilgrims throw seven stones at the devil.

77. Al-Tantawi, *Memories*, 147–48. That was the final year for the Egyptian maḥmal.

78. Edouard Driault, "Introduction" ("Al-Muqaddima"), in "Report of the French Consul in Baghdad Jean Raymond 1806," "Taqrīr al-Qunsul al-Faransī fī Baghdād Jean Raymond bi-Tārīkh 1806: Mabḥath fī Usūl al-Wahhābiyya wa fī Nash'at Quwwatihim wa fī al-Nufudh alladhī Yatamatta'ūna bihi," trans. Huda Muawwad, in *Wahhabism in the Reports of the French Consulate in Baghdad (1806 AD / 1221 AH–1808 AD / 1224 AH) with a Study on the Wahhabi Movement by Dr. 'Ali al-Wardi (Al-Wahhābiyya bi-Taqārīr al-Qunsuliyya al-Faransiyya fī Baghdād (1806 AD / 1221 AH–1808 AD / 1224 AH) ma' Dirāsa 'an al-Ḥaraka al-Wahhābiyya lil-Duktūr 'Ali al-Wardī)*, introduction by editor Hashim Naji, trans. Huda Muawwad and Khalid Abd al-Latif Hasan (London: Al-Warraq lil-Nashr, 2015), 56.

79. de Corancez, *The Wahhabis*, 67.

80. Al-Shihabi, *The French Campaign in Egypt and the Early Rule of Amir Bashir II (Al-Ḥamla al-Faransāwiyya 'alā Miṣr wa-Awā'il Ḥukm al-Amir Bashīr al-Thāni)*, vol. 2, part 2, of *Lebanon in the Era of the Shihabi Princes*, 524.

81. See the denial of statements of this kind, particularly issues where fatwas from Ibn Abd al-Wahhāb were not issued stipulating the punishments to be applied, contrary to what is commonly claimed, in Sulayman Ibn Salih al-Kharashi, *The Deceitful Memoirs of the British Spy Hempher to Distort the Call of Sheikh Muhammad Ibn Abd al-Wahhāb and the First Saudi State (Ukdhūbat Mudhakkarāt al-Jasūs al-Briṭāni Humfir: Wa Bayān Haqīqat man Kadhhabaha li-Tashwīh Da'wat al-Shaykh Muhammad Ibn Abd al-Wahhāb wa al-Dawla al-Sa'ūdiyya al-Ūlā)* (Riyadh: Dār al-'Al wal-Sahb lil-Nashr wal-Tawzi', 2010), 34.

82. As for smoking, the obsession of ISIL over preventing it in the areas it ruled in Syria and Iraq cannot be understood without a recognition that imitating the Wahhabi traditions, that were forsaken in the Saudi Kingdom itself, is for them a goal in itself.

83. "Report of the French Consul in Baghdad Jean Louis Rousseau 1809 CE / 1224 AH" (*"Taqrir al-Qunsul al-Faransi fī Baghdad Jean Louis Rousseau 1809 CE / 1224 AH"*), trans. Khalid Abd al-Latif Hasan, in *Wahhabism in the Reports of the French Consulate in Baghdad*, 114.

84. Al-Wardi, *From the Beginning of the Ottoman Era*, 200.

85. Al-Wardi, 205–6.

86. de Corancez, *The Wahhabis*, 26.

87. "*Taqrir al-Qunsul al-Faransi fī Baghdad Jean Raymond bi-Tārīkh 1806*," 118.

88. de Corancez, *The Wahhabis*, 88.

89. Ibrahim, *Jihadi-Salafism in Saudi Arabia*, 219.

90. Ibrahim, *Jihadi-Salafism in Saudi Arabia*, 194.

91. Ibrahim, 139.

92. Ibrahim al-'Awrah, *History of Sulayman Pasha al-Adil's Rule: Including the History of Palestine, Lebanon and Its Cities, the Alawite, and the Levant* (*Tārīkh Wilāyat Sulaymān Bāshā al-'Ādil: Yashtamilu 'alā Tārīkh Filasṭīn wa-Lubnān wa-Mudunihi wa-Bilād al-'Alawiyyīn wa al-Shām*), commentary and contributions by Qustantin Pasha al-Mukhlisi (Sidon, Lebanon: Maṭba'at Dir al-Mukhlis, 1936), 94; Al-Shihabi, *The French Campaign in Egypt and the Early Rule of Amir Bashir II* (*Al-Ḥamla al-Faransāwiyya 'alā Miṣr wa-Awā'il Ḥukm al-Amir Bashīr al-Thāni*), vol. 2, part 2, of *Lebanon in the Era of the Shihabi Princes*, 523–26. Cf. Mikha'il Mashaqqah, *Selected Replies to the Suggestion of Dear Friends* (*Muntakhabāt min al-Jawāb 'alā Iqtirāḥ al-Aḥbāb*), foreword and indexes by editor Asad Rustum and Subhi Abu Shaqra, Majmū'at al-Duktur Asad Rustum 8, 2nd ed. (Beirut: Maktabah al-Bulisiyyah, 1985), 41–42. Abd al-Raziq Ibn al-Hasan Ibn Ibrahim al-Baytar, a Damascene Sunni influenced by Wahhabism and historian of the notables of Damascus in the nineteenth century CE, praised Yusuf Pasha's policy and stated that he "trod the path of justice in judgments. He upheld the Shari'a and Sunna and did away with innovations and evil things. He let fallen women repent and found them husbands. . . . Word of his justice spread abroad, but the local people found it hard to give up their familiar ways." See al-Baytar, *Exemplary Persons of the Thirteenth Century*, 1600. Kurd 'Ali, however, saw him as a tyrant, infamous for "oppressing people." See Muhammad Kurd 'Ali, *Description of Syria* (*Khiṭaṭ al-Shām*), vol. 6, 3rd ed. (Beirut: Maktabat al-Nuri, 1983), 27.

93. It is difficult to define sexual intercourse between males in that age as homosexuality because it is retroactively impossible to distinguish between sexual practices due to deprivation (like in prisons) and the "really" homosexual trends that became, in the circumstance, indirectly tolerated without being legitimized.

94. The translation kept the original expressions of the author. Perhaps this was because of extreme jealousy over women, a similar reason found at the time of the Mamlūks. Homosexual affairs were common even among the religious scholars and judges. An opponent of Ibn Taymiyya, Sadr al-Din al-Wakil had a reputation for such

practices, which are rooted in the Abbasid period. Al-Jahiz wrote about slave boys and eunuchs, and in a tradition about Ibn Hanbal, it is said that he refused to allow pubescent boys to attend his meetings. Ibn Taymiyya wrote a great deal on the subject, blaming the Sufis for it, and Ibn Qayyim has a book entitled, *The Satisfactory Response to Those Who Asked Regarding the Curing Medicine* (*Al-Jawāb al-Kāfi li-man Sa'ala 'an al-Dawā' al-Shāfi*), which deals with homosexuality.

95. de Corancez, *The Wahhabis*, 178.

96. de Corancez, 178–80.

97. de Corancez, 34.

98. On this conflict, see Madawi al-Rasheed, *A History of Saudi Arabia* (New York: Cambridge University Press, 2002), 62–71.

99. Al-Yassini, *Religion and State*, 49.

100. Al-Rasheed, "Banning Politics," 225–26.

CONCLUSION

1. The association between Salafism and Hanbalism was a mistaken one, given that the movement to return to the sayings and traditions of the Prophet and his companions was not restricted to Ibn Hanbal alone.

2. One aspect of this growing complexity was the burgeoning corpus of stories and traditions of the Prophet and his companions, especially given the emergence of the phenomenon of hadith forgery in popular and institutional (official) religiosity alike.

3. The doctrine of *al-walā' wa al-barā'* states that one should love, or hate, others solely on the basis of whether or not they profess Islam, and that no Muslim should bear any allegiance to a non-Muslim in any capacity.

4. In al-Banna's speech during the 1939 Fifth Conference of the Muslim Brotherhood, which marked the tenth anniversary of the movement, he stated that the idea of the Muslim Brothers included "all categories of reform in al-umma" and defined the movement as a Salafiyya message, a Sunni way, a Sufi truth, a political organization, an athletic group, a cultural-educational union, an economic company, and a social idea. See al-Banna, *Collection of Epistles*, 170–71.

Bibliography

ARABIC BOOKS

Abi Nadir, Nayila. *The Heritage and Methodology between Arkoun and al-Jabiri* (*Al-Turāth wa al-Manhaj bayn Arkoun wa al-Jābiri*). Beirut: Arab Network for Studies and Publishing, 2008.

Abu Hakimah, Ahmad Mustafa, ed. *The Shining Meteor: A Biography of Muhammad Ibn Abd al-Wahhab* (*Kitāb Lam' al-Shihāb fī Sīrat Muhammad Ibn Abd al-Wahhāb*). http://bit.do/ekSB6.

Abu Zahrah, Muhammad. *History of the Islamic Schools in Politics and Doctrine and the History of Schools of Jurisprudence* (*Fiqh*) (*Tārīkh al-Madhāhib al-Islāmiyya fī al-Siyāsa wa al-'Aqā'id wa Tārīkh al-Madhāhib al-Fiqhiyya*). Cairo: Dār al-Fikr al-'Arabi, 2009.

———. *Ibn Hazm: Life and Times, Jurisprudence and Legal Opinions* (*Ibn Hazm: Ḥayātuhu wa Asruhu, Ārā'uhu wa Fiqhuhu*). Cairo: Dār al-Fikr al-'Arabi, 1978.

Ahmad, Rif'at Sayyid. *The Armed Prophet* (*Al-Nabiyy al-Musallaḥ*). 2 vols. London: Riyad al-Rayyis, 1991.

'Ali, Muhammad Kurd. *Description of Syria* (*Khiṭaṭ al-Shām*). Vol. 6. 3rd ed. Beirut: Maktabat al-Nuri, 1983.

Amarah, Muhammad. *The Absent Commandment: Presentation, Dialogue, and Evaluation* (*Al-Farīḍa al-Ghā'iba: 'Arḍ wa Ḥiwār wa Taqyīm*). Cairo: Maktabat al-Jadid, [1983].

Ash'ari, Abu al-Hasan 'Ali Ibn Isma'il al-. *Treatises on Diverse Islamic Schools* (*Maqālāt al-Islamiyyīn wa Ikhtilāf al-Muṣallīn*). Commentary by editor Nawwaf al-Jarah. 2nd ed. Beirut: Dār Sadir, 2008.

Atram, Salih Ibn Abd al-Rahman al-, and Muhammad Ibn Abd al-Razzaq al-Dawish, eds. *Ibn Abd al-Wahhab: Concise Biography and Fatwas* (*Mukhtaṣar al-Sīra wa al-Fatāwā*). Vol. 4. Riyad: Ministry of Islamic Affairs, Da'wa and Irshad, 1998.

ʿAwrah, Ibrahim al-. *History of Sulayman Pasha al-Adil's Rule: Including the History of Palestine, Lebanon and Its Cities, the Alawite, and the Levant* (*Tārīkh Wilāyat Sulaymān Bāshā al-ʿĀdil: Yashtamilu ʿalā Tārīkh Filasṭīn wa-Lubnān wa-Mudunihi wa-Bilād al-ʿAlawiyyīn wa al-Shām*). Commentary and contributions by Qustantin Pasha al-Mukhlisi. Sidon, Lebanon: Maṭbaʿat Dir al-Mukhlis, 1936.

Azdi, Abu Ismaʿil Muhammad Ibn Abdullah al-. *The Islamic Conquests of the Levant* (*Futūḥ al-Shām*). Edited by Isam Mustafa ʿAqlah and Yusuf Ahmad Banī Yasin. Foreword by ʿAbd al-ʿAziz al-Duri. Amman: Mu'asassat Hamadah lil-Dirasat al-Jāmiyya, Dār al-Yazarawī al-ʿIlmiyya, 2011.

Azmeh, Aziz al-. *Muhammad Ibn ʿAbd al-Wahhab.* Beirut: Riyad al-Rayyis, 2000.

Baghdadi, Abd al-Qahir al-. *Schisms and Sects* (*Al-Farq bayn al-Firaq*). Beirut: Dār al-Kutub al-ʿIlmiyya, 2009.

Banna, Hasan al-. *Collection of Epistles of the Martyr Imam Hasan al-Banna* (*Majmūʿat Rasāʾil al-Imam al-Shahīd Ḥasan al-Bannā*). Alexandria, Egypt: Dār al-Daʿwa, 2002.

———. *Memoirs of the Call and the Preacher* (*Mudhakkirāt al-Daʿwa wa al-Dāʿiya*). Cairo: Dār al-Tawziʿ wal-Nashr al-Islamiyyah, 2001.

Barout, Muhammad Jamal. *New Yathrib: Contemporary Islamic Movements* (*Yathrib al-Jadīda: Al-Ḥarakāt al-Islamiyya al-Rāhina*). Beirut: Riyad al-Rayyis, 1994.

Baytar, Abd al-Raziq Ibn al-Hasan Ibn Ibrahim al-. *Exemplary Persons of the Thirteenth Century* (*Ḥilyat al-Bashar fī Tārīkh al-Qarn al-Thālith ʿAshar*). Commentary by editor Muhammad Bahjah al-Baytar. Vol. 3. 2nd ed. Beirut: Dār Sadir, 1993.

Bouti, Muhammad Saʿid Ramadan al-. *The Salafists: A Blessed Era More Than an Islamic Madhab* (*Al-Salafiyya: Marḥala Zamaniyya Mubāraka Lā Madhhab Islāmī*). Damascus: Dār al-Fikr, 1990.

Belabd, Sadiq. *The Qur'an and Legislation: A New Reading of the Verse of Judgments* (*Al-Qur'an wa al-Tashrīʿ: Qirāʾa Jadīda fī Āyat al-Aḥkām*). Beirut: Manshurat al-Halabi al-Huquqiyyah, 2004.

Bishara, Azmi. *The Islamic State Organization "ISIL": A General Framework and Practical Contribution to Understanding the Phenomenon* (*Tanẓīm al-Dawla al-Mukanā "Dāʿish": Iṭār ʿĀam wa Musāhama Naqdiyya fī fahm al-Ẓāhira*). Doha: Arab Center for Research and Policy Studies, 2018.

———. *On the Arab Question: An Introduction to an Arab Democratic Manifesto* (*Fī al-Mas'ala al-'Arabiyya: Muqaddima li-Bayān Dimuqrāṭī 'Arabī*). Beirut: Centre for Arab Unity Studies, 2007.

Bu Hilal, Muhammad. *The Dialectic of Politics, Religion, and Knowledge* (*Jadal al-Siyāsa wa al-Dīn wa al-Ma'rifa*). Beirut: Jadawil, 2011.

Bukhari, Muhammad Ibn Isma'il al-. *The Ṣaḥīḥ Collection: The Complete, Correct, Abridged Compendium of the Matters of the Prophet (PBUH)* (*Al-Jāmi' al-Ṣaḥīḥ: Wahuwa al-Jāmi' al-Musnad al-Ṣaḥīḥ al-Mukhtaṣar min Umūr Rasūl Allah Ṣalla Allah 'alayhi wa-Sallam wa-Sunanihi wa-Ayyāmihi*). Prepared by Zuhayr Ibn Nasir al-Nasir. Vol. 3. Cairo: Dār Tawq al-Najah, 2001.

de Corancez, Louis. *The Wahhabis: A History of What History Neglected* (*Al-Wahhābiyyun: Tārīkh ma Ahmalahu al-Tārīkh*). Translated by a group of researchers. Beirut: Riyad al-Rayyis, 2003.

Darwaza, Muhammad Izzat. *On the Modern Arab Movement: History, Memoirs, and Commentaries* (*Ḥawl al-Ḥaraka al-'Arabiyya al-Ḥadītha: Tārīkh wa Mudhakkirāt wa Ta'līqāt*). Vol. 1. Sidon, Lebanon: Matba'ah al-'Asriyyah, 1950.

Djait, Hichem. *Islamic Culture in Crisis* (*Azmat al-Thaqāfa al-Islāmiyya*). Beirut: Dār al-Tali'ah, 2000.

Dulabi al-Razi, Abu Bishr Muhammad Ibn Ahmad Ibn Hammad Ibn Sa'id Ibn Muslim al-Ansari al-. *Titles and Epithets* (*Al-Kunā wa al-Asmā'*). Edited by Abu Qutayba Nazhar Muhammad al-Faryabi. Vol. 2. Beirut: Dār Ibn Hazm, 2000.

Faraj, Muhammad Abd al-Salam. *Jihad: The Absent Commandment* (*Al-Jihad: Al-Farīḍa al-Ghā'iba*). N.p., 1981.

Farra', Abu Ya'la al-, and Muhammad Ibn al-Husayn. *History of the Hanbalites* (*Ṭabaqāt al-Ḥanābila*). Vol. 1, prepared and revised by Muhammad Hamid al-Fiqqi. Beirut: Dār al-Ma'rifa, n.d.

Ghalioun, Burhan. *Criticism of Politics: State and Religion* (*Naqd al-Siyāsa: Al-Dawla wa al-Dīn*). 4th ed. Beirut: Al-Markaz al-Thaqafi al-'Arabi, 2007.

Ghanim, Ibrahim al-Bayumi. *The Political Thought of Imam Hasan al-Banna* (*Al-Fikr al-Islāmī li al-Imam Hasan al-Bannā*). Al-Dirasat al-Hadariyyah. Cairo: Dār al-Tawzi' wal-Nashr al-Islāmiyyah, 1992.

Ghazali, Abu Hamid al-. *The Criterion of Distinction between Islam and Clandestine Unbelief* (*Faysal al-Tafriqa bayn al-Islām wa al-Zandaqa*). Commentary and hadith annotation by editor Mahmud Biju. Damascus: n.p., 1993.

Hamami, Nadir. *The Islam of the Clerics* (*Islām al-Fuqahā'*). Beirut: Dār al-Tali'ah, 2006.

Hammoudi, Abdellah, Denis Bauchard, and Rémy Leveau. *Is Democracy Compatible with Islam?* (*Hal Tatawāfaq al-Dīmuqrātiyya ma' al-Islām?*). Edited by Judith Cahen. Translated by Riyadh Suma. Beirut: Dār al-Farabi, 2009.

Hawwa, Muhammad Sa'id. *God's Soldiers: Culture and Ethics* (*Jund Allah: Thaqāfatan wa-Akhlāqan*). 2nd ed. Cairo: Dār al-Tiba'a al-Haditha, 1977.

Hudaybi, Hasan Isma'il al-. *Preachers, Not Judges, Research in the Islamic Faith and Methods of Proselytization, The Book of Invitation* (*Du'āt Lā Quḍāt: Abḥāth fī al-'Aqīda al-Islāmiyya wa Manhaj al-Da'wa ilā Allah, Kitāb al-Da'wa*). Cairo: Dār al-Tiba'a wal-Nashr al-Islāmiyya, 1977.

Husayn, Taha. *The Days: Autobiography of Taha Husayn* (*Al-Ayyām*). Cairo: Hindawi for Education and Culture, 2012.

———. *The Future of Culture in Egypt* (*Mustaqbal al-Thaqāfa fī Miṣr*). Cairo: Matba'at wa-Maktabat al-Ma'arif, n.d.

———. *Literary Life in the Arabian Peninsula* (*Al-Ḥayā al-Adabiyya fī Jazīrat al-'Arab*). Damascus: Maktab al-Nashir al-'Arabi, 1935.

Husayni, Ishaq Musa al-. *The Muslim Brotherhood: The Largest Modern Muslim Movement* (*Al-Ikhwan al-Muslimun: Kubrā al-Ḥarakāt al-Islāmiyya al-Ḥadītha*). Beirut: Dār Beirut lil-Tiba'a wal-Nashr, 1952.

Husayyin, Salih Ibn Abd al-Rahman al-. *Complete Works of Shaykh Salih Ibn Abd al-Rahman al-Husayyin* (*Al-A'māl al-Kāmila li-Faḍīlat al-Shaykh Ṣāliḥ Ibn 'Abd al-Raḥmān al-Ḥuṣayyin*). Edited by Raed al-Samhouri. Doha: Forum for Arab and International Relations, 2014.

Huzaymi, Nasir al-. *Days with Juhayman: "I Was with the Salafi Muhtasiba Group"* (*Ayyām ma' Juhaymān: Kuntu ma' "al-Jamā'a al-Salafiyya al-Muḥtasiba"*). Beirut: Arab Network for Research and Publishing, 2011.

Ibn Abd al-Wahhab, Muhammad. *The Book of Monotheism, a Right for Slaves* (*Kitāb al-Tawḥīd alladhī huwa Ḥaqq Allah 'alā al-'Abīd*). Riyadh: Imam Mohammad Ibn Saud Islamic University, 2001.

———. *Summarized Biography of the Prophet* (*Mukhtaṣar Sīrat al-Rasūl*). Riyadh: Ministry of Islamic Affairs, Awqaf, Dawah, and Guidance, 1998 [1991].

———. *Writings of Sheikh Imam Muhammad Ibn Abd al-Wahhab* (*Mu'allafāt al-Shaykh al-Imam Muhammad Ibn 'Abd al-Wahhāb*). Prepared by 'Abd al-'Aziz Ibn Zayd al-Rumi, Muhammad Baltaji, and Sayyid Hijab. 13 vols. Riyadh: Imam Mohammad Ibn Saud Islamic University, 1976.

Ibn Abd al-Wahhab, Sulayman. *The Divine Lightning in Response to Wahhabism* (*Al-Ṣawā'iq al-Ilāhiyya fī al-Radd 'alā al-Wahhābiyya*). Prepared by Husayn Hilmi Ibn Sa'id Istanbuli. 3rd ed. Istanbul: Maktabat Ishiq, 1979.

Ibn Abi al-'Izz, 'Ali Ibn 'Ali Ibn Muhammad. *An Explication of Tahawi's Doctrine and Faith* (*Sharḥ al-'Aqīda al-Ṭaḥāwiyya*). Edited by a group of 'ulama'. Annotated by Muhammad Nasir al-Din al-Albani. Beirut: Al-Maktab al-Islāmī, 2006.

Ibn al-Athir, 'Izz al-Din. *The Second Abbasid Age* (*The Age of Turkish Influence*) *from the Caliphate of al-Mu'tasim until 321 and the Caliphate of al-Qāhir Billāh* (*218–321 AH*) (*Al-'Aṣr al-'Abbāsī al-Thānī* (*'Aṣr al-Nufūdh al-Turkī*) *min Khilāfat al-Mu'taṣim ḥattā Sanat 321 min Khilāfat al-Qāhir Billāh* (*min Sanat 218–Ilā Sanat 321 Hijriyya*). Part 6 of *The Complete History of Ibn al-Athir* (*Al-Kāmil fī al-Tārīkh*). Edited by Omar Abd al-Salam Tadmuri. Beirut: Dār al-Kitāb al-'Arabi, 1997.

Ibn al-Jawzi, Abu al-Faraj Abd al-Rahman Ibn 'Ali. *Virtues of the Imam Ahmad Ibn Hanbal* (*Manāqib al-Imam Aḥmad Ibn Ḥanbal*). Edited by Abdullah al-Turki. 2nd ed. Cairo: Dār Hajar, 1988.

Ibn al-Uthaymin, Muhammad Ibn Salih. *Sunni Lectures on the Doctrine of Ibn Taymiyya, Sheikh of Islam* (*Al-Muḥāḍarāt al-Sunniyya fī Sharḥ al-'Aqīda al-Wāsiṭiyya li-Shaykh al-Islām Ibn Taymiyya*). With commentary by editors 'Abd al-'Aziz Ibn Baz and Abu Muhammad Ashraf Abd al-Maqsud Ibn Abd al-Rahman. Riyadh: Maktabat al-Tabariyyah, n.d.

Ibn Badran al-Dimashqi, Abd al-Qadir. *Introduction to the Doctrine of Imam Ahmad Ibn Hanbal* (*Al-Madkhal ilā Madhhab al-Imam Aḥmad Ibn Ḥanbal*). Edited by Muhammad Amin Danawi. Beirut: Dār al-Kutub al-'Ilmiyyah, 1996.

Ibn Bishr, Uthman Ibn Abdullah. *The Glorious History of the Najd Region* (*'Unwān al-Majd fī Tārīkh Najd*). Commentary by editor Abd al-Rahman Ibn Abd al-Latif Ibn Abdullah Al al-Shaykh. Vol. 1. 4th ed. Riyadh: Dār al-Malik 'Abd al-'Aziz, 1982.

Ibn Hanbal, Abdullah Ibn Ahmad. *The Sunna* (*Al-Sunna*). Edited and with a study by Muhammad Ibn Sa'id Ibn Salim al-Qahtani. Vol. 2. Al-Dammam: Dār Ibn al-Qayyim, 1986.

Ibn Hani, Ahmad Ibn Muhammad. *Issues of Imam Ahmad Ibn Hanbal, Narration of Ishaq Ibn Ibrahim Ibn Hani al-Nisapuri* (*Masā'il al-Imam Aḥmad Ibn Ḥanbal, Riwāyat Isḥāq Ibn Ibrāhīm Ibn Hānī' al-Naysabūrī*). Edited by Zuhayr al-Shawis. Vol. 2. Beirut: Maktaba al-Islāmiyya, 1979.

Ibn Hazm, Abu Muhammad 'Ali Ibn Ahmad Ibn Sa'id. *Judgment on the Principles of Aḥkām* (*Al-Iḥkām fī Uṣūl al-Aḥkām*). Foreword by Ihsan Abbas. Part 7. Beirut: Dār al-'Afaq al-Jadidah, n.d.

Ibn Hisham, Abu Muhammad Abd al-Malik. *The Prophetic Biography of Ibn Hisham* (*Al-Sīra al-Nabawiyya li-Ibn Hishām*). Annotation and indexes by Umar Abd al-Salam Tadmuri. Vol. 2. 3rd ed. Beirut: Dār al-Kitāb al-ʿArabi, 1990.

Ibn Mansur, Uthman Ibn ʿAbd al-ʿAziz. *Critique of the Khawārij* (*Manhaj al-Maʿārij li-Akhbār al-Khawārij*). Introduction and biography by Sulayman Ibn Salih al-Kharashi. Riyadh: Maktabat al-Rushd, 2017.

Ibn Qasim, Abd al-Rahman Ibn Muhammad, ed. *The Glistening Pearls of Najdi Responsa* (*Al-Durar al-Saniyya fī al-Ajwiba al-Najdiyya*). 6th ed. 16 vols. N.p., 1996.

Ibn Qayyim al-Jawziyyah, Shams al-Din Abu Abdullah Muhammad Ibn Abi Bakr. *Steps of the Seekers between the Houses, Thee We Worship and Thee We Reclaim* (*Madārij al-Sālikīn bayn Manāzil Iyyaka Naʿbudu wa-Iyyaka Nastaʿīn*). Edited by Muhammad al-Muʿtasim Billah al-Baghdadi. Vol. 3. Beirut: Dār al-Kitāb al-ʿArabi, 2003.

Ibn Rushd, Abu al-Walid Muhammad Ibn Ahmad Ibn Muhammad. *Exposition of the Methods of Proof in Religious Doctrine* (*Al-Kashf ʿan Manāhij al-Adilla fī ʿAqāʾid al-Milla*). Beirut: Center for Arab Unity Studies, 1998.

Ibn Saʿdi al-Ghamidi al-ʿAbdali, Abdullah. *The Monotheists' Faith Doctrine and Rejoinder to the Error of Heretics* (*ʿAqīdat al-Muwaḥḥidīn wa al-Radd ʿalā Ḍalāl al-Mubtadiʾīn*). Foreword by ʿAbd al-ʿAziz Ibn Abdullah Ibn Baz. Al-Taʾif: Dār al-Tarafayn, 1999.

Ibn Taymiyya al-Harrani, Taqi al-Din Abu al-Abbas Ahmad Ibn Abd al-Halim. Book of Faith (Kitāb al-Īmān). Translated by Salman al-Ani and Shadia Ahmad Tel. Kuala Lumpur: Islamic Book Trust, 2009.

———. *The Agreement of Reason and Revelation* (*Darʾ Taʿāruḍ al-ʿAql wa al-Naql*). Edited by Muhammad Rashad Salim. Vol. 1. Riyadh: Imam Mohammad Ibn Saud Islamic University, 1991.

———. *The Collection of the Shaykh al-Islam's Fatwas* (*Majmūʿ al-Fatāwā*). Edited by Abd al-Rahman Ibn Muhammad Ibn Qasim. Vol. 28. Medina: King Fahd Complex for the Printing of the Holy Qur'an, 1995.

———. *The Correctness of the Principles of the People of Medina* (*Ṣiḥḥat Uṣūl Madhhab Ahl al-Madīna*). Edited by Ahmad Hijazi al-Saqa. Cairo: Maktabat al-Thaqafah al-Diniyyah, 1998.

———. *Following the Straight Path to Contravene the Companions of Hell* (*Iqtidāʾ al-Ṣirāt al-Mustaqīm li-Mukhālafāt Aṣḥāb al-Jaḥīm*). Edited by Nasir Abd al-Karim al-ʿAql. Vol. 1. 7th ed. Beirut: Dār ʿAlam al-Kutub, 1999.

———. *A Treatise by Ibn Taymiyya on "a Matter Concerning Churches," with a Translated Work on Islamic History, Including an Appended List of 250 Works by Ibn Taymiyya* (*Masʾala fī al-Kanāʾis wa maʿahu Tarjamat Shaykh al-Islām min Dhayl Tārīkh *al-Islām, wa ma'ahu Qā'ima bi-ba'ḍ Makhṭūṭāt Shaykh al-Islām Taḥwī Akthar min Khamsīn wa-Mi'atay 'Unwān*). Annotation by editor 'Ali Ibn 'Abd al-'Aziz Ibn 'Ali al-Shibl. Riyadh: Makatabat al-'Ubaykan, 1995.

Ibn Taymiyya al-Harrani, Taqi al-Din Abu al-Abbas Ahmad Ibn Abd al-Halim and Muhammad Ibn Abd al-Wahhab. *Writings on Monotheism* (*Majmū'at al-Tawḥīd*). Riyadh: Maktabat Riyadh al-Hadithah, n.d.

Ibrahim, Abd al-Mun'im. *Commentary on the Book of Monotheism by Sheikh al-Islam Muhammad Ibn Abd al-Wahhab* (*Mughnī al-Murīd: Al-Jāmi' li-Shurūḥ Kitāb al-Tawḥīd li-Shaykh al-Islām Muhammad Ibn 'Abd al-Wahhāb*). Mecca: Maktabat Nizar Mustafa al-Baz, 2000.

Ibrahim, Fu'ad. *Jihadi-Salafism in Saudi Arabia* (*Al-Salafiyya al-Jihādiyya fī al-Sa'ūdiyya*). Beirut: Dār al-Saqi, 2009.

Jabiri, Muhammad Abid al-. *The Formation of Arab Reason: Critique of the Arab Reason* (*Takwīn al-'Aql al-'Arabi: Naqd al-'Aql al-'Arabi*). Vol. 1. 5th ed. Beirut: Center for Arab Unity Studies, 1991.

Jadaan, Fahmi. *The Foundations of Progress among Islamic Thinkers in the Modern Arab World* (*Usus al-Taqaddum 'Ind Mufakkirī al-Islām fī al-'Ālam al-'Arabī al-Ḥadīth*). 2nd ed. Beirut: Arab Enterprise for Studies and Publishing, 1981.

———. *The Mihna: A Study of the Dialectics of the Religious and the Political in Islam* (*Al-Miḥna: Baḥth 'an Jadaliyyat al-Siyāsī wa al-Dīnī fī al-Islām*). 2nd ed. Beirut: Arab Enterprise for Studies and Publishing, 2000.

Khallal, Abu Bakr Ahmad Ibn Muhammad al-. *The Sunna* (*Al-Sunna*). Edited by Atiyah Ibn Atiq al-Zahrani. Part 7. Riyadh: Dār al-Rayah, 1989.

Kharashi, Sulayman Ibn Salih al-. *The Deceitful Memoirs of the British Spy Hempher to Distort the Call of Sheikh Muhammad Ibn Abd al-Wahhab and the First Saudi State* (*Ukdhūbat Mudhakkarāt al-Jasūs al-Briṭāni Humfir: Wa Bayān Haqīqat man Kadhhabaha li-Tashwīh Da'wat al-Shaykh Muhammad Ibn Abd al-Wahhāb wa al-Dawla al-Sa'ūdiyya al-Ūlā*). Riyadh: Dār al-'Al wal-Sahb lil-Nashr wal-Tawzi', 2010.

Makdisi, George. *Hanbali Islam* (*Al-Islām al-Ḥanbalī*). Translated by Saoud El-Mawla. Foreword by editor Radwan al-Sayed. Beirut: Arab Network for Research and Publication, 2017.

Mar'i, Mohammad. *Islamic State Financial and Economic Systems in Light of Abu Yusuf's "Book of Kharāj"* (*Al-Nuẓum al-Māliyya wa al-Iqtiṣādiyya fī al-Dawla al-Islāmiyya 'alā Ḍaw' Kitāb al-Kharāj li-Abī Yūsuf*). Doha: Dār al-Thaqafa, 1987.

Mashaqqah, Mikha'il. *Selected Replies to the Suggestion of Dear Friends* (*Muntakhabāt min al-Jawāb 'alā Iqtirāḥ al-Aḥbāb*). Foreword and indexes by editor Asad Rustum and Subhi Abu Shaqra. Collection of Dr. Asad Rustum, 8 (Majmū'at al-Duktur Asad Rustum 8). 2nd ed. Beirut: Maktabah al-Bulisiyyah, 1985.

Mashhur, Mustafa. *Questions on the Path* (*Tasā'ulāt 'alā al-Ṭarīq*). Algiers: Dār al-Irshad, 1989.

Mas'udi, Abu al-Hasan 'Ali Ibn al-Husayn al-. *Meadows of Gold and Mines of Gems* (*Murūj al-Dhahab wa Ma'ādin al-Jawāhir*). Prepared and revised by Kamal Hasan Mara'i. Vol. 4. Beirut: Maktabah al-'Asriyyah, 2005.

Mawdudi, Abu al-A'la al-. *The Theory of Islam and Islam's Political, Legal, and Constitutional Guidance* (*Naẓarīyyat al-Islām wa-Hadyuhu fī al-Siyāsa wa al-Qānūn wa al-Dustūr*). Translated by Jalil Hasan al-Islahi. Revised by Mas'ud al-Nadwi and Muhammad Asim al-Haddad. Lahore: n.p., 1967.

Meddeb, Abdelwahab. *The Malady of Political Islam* (*Awhām al-Islām al-Siyāsī*). Translated by Abdelwahab Meddeb and Mohammed Bennis. Beirut: Dār al-Nahar, 2002.

Naji, Hashim, ed. *Wahhabism in the Reports of the French Consulate in Baghdad (1806 AD / 1221 AH–1808 AD / 1224 AH) with a Study on the Wahhabi Movement by Dr. 'Ali al-Wardi* (*Al-Wahhābiyya bi-Taqārīr al-Qunsuliyya al-Faransiyya fī Baghdād (1806AD / 1221 AH–1808 AD / 1224 AH) ma' Dirāsa 'an al-Ḥaraka al-Wahhābiyya lil-Duktūr 'Ali al-Wardī*). Introduction by Hashim Naji. Translated by Huda Muawwad and Khalid Abd al-Latif Hasan. London: Al-Warraq lil-Nashr, 2015.

Qutb, Sayyid. *In the Shade of the Qur'an* (*Fī Ẓilāl al-Qur'an*). Vol. 3. 32nd ed. Cairo: Dār al-Shurouk, 2003.

Qutban, Ahmad al-, and Muhammad Tahir al-Zayn. *Imam al-Tawḥīd Muḥammad Ibn Abd al-Wahhāb*. Revised by 'Abd al-'Aziz Ibn Baz. Alexandria, Egypt: Dār al-Iman, 2001.

Ra'if, Ahmad. *The Black Gateway: Pages from the History of the Muslim Brotherhood* (*Al-Bawwāba al-Sawdā': Ṣafaḥāt min Tārīkh al-Ikhwan al-Muslimin*). 3rd ed. Cairo: Al-Zahra' lil-'Ilam al-'Arabi, 1986.

Rashid, Abu al-'Ala Ibn Rashid Ibn Abi al-'Ala al-. *A Reading of Ibn Taymiyya, Muhammad Ibn Abd al-Wahhab and the 'Ulama' of the Reformist Call's Guidelines for Judgments of Apostasy* (*Ḍawābiṭ Takfīr al-Mu'ayyan 'Ind Shaykhay al-Islām Ibn Taymiyya wa Ibn 'Abd al-Wahhāb wa 'Ulama' al-Da'wa al-Iṣlāḥiyya: Qirā'a*). Foreword and evaluation by Salih Ibn Fawzan Abdullah al-Fawzan. Riyadh: Maktabat al-Rushd Nashirun, 2004.

Raysuni, Ahmed al-. *Imam al-Shatibi's Theory of the Higher Objectives and Intents of Islamic Law* (*Naẓariyyat al-Maqāṣid 'Ind al-Imam al-Shāṭibī*). Foreword by Taha Jabir al-Alawani. 4th ed. Herndon, Virginia: International Institute for Islamic Thought, 1995.

Sakhawi, Abu al-Khayr Muhammad Ibn Abd al-Rahman al-. *Gems in the History of the Holy City of Medina* (*Al-Tuḥfa al-Laṭīfa fī Tārīkh al-Madīna al-Sharīfa*). Edited by Muhammad Hamid al-Fiqqi. Foreword by Taha Husayn. Cairo: Dār al-Thaqafah, 1979.

Samhouri, Raed al-. *The Imagined Salaf: An Analytical Historical Approach to the "Salaf" of the 'Mihna'"* (*Ahmad Ibn Hanbal and the Imagined Ahmad Ibn Hanbal*) (*Al-Salaf al-Mutakhayyal: Muqāraba Tārīkhiyya Taḥlīliyya fī Salaf al-Miḥna* [*Aḥmad Ibn Ḥanbal wa Aḥmad Ibn Ḥanbal al-Mutakhayyal*]). Doha: Arab Center for Research and Policy Studies, 2019.

Samhouri, Raed al-, ed. *Wahhabism and Salafism: Ideas and Impacts* (*Al-Wahhābiyya wa al-Salafiyya: al-Afkār wa al-Āthār*). Research paper, presented in a symposium on Wahhabism and Salafism organized by The Forum for Arab and International Relations (Awrāq Baḥthiyya Qaddamahā al-Mushārikūn fī Mu'tamar al-Wahhābiyya wa al-Salafiyya alladhī Naẓẓamahu Muntadā al-'Alāqāt al-'Arabiyya wa al-Dawliyya), December 21–22, 2013. Beirut: Arab Network for Studies and Publishing, 2016.

Shahrastani, Abu al-Fath Muhammad Ibn Abd al-Karim Ibn Abi Bakr Ahmad al-. *The Book of Religious and Philosophical Sects* (*Al-Milal wa al-Niḥal*). Edited by Muhammad Sayyid Kaylani. Vol. 1. Beirut: Dār al-Ma'rifah, n.d.

Sharafi, Abd al-Majid al-. *Islam: Between Message and History* (*Al-Islām bayn al-Risāla wa al-Tārīkh*). Beirut: Dār al-Tali'ah, 2001.

Shawi, Abd al-Qadir al-. *Salafism and Nationalism* (*Al-Salafiyya wa al-Waṭaniyya*). Beirut: Mu'asassat al-Abhath al-'Arabiyyah, 1985.

Shihabi, Haydar Ahmad al-. *Lebanon in the Era of the Shihabi Princes: The Second and Third Parts of The Fine Deception in the Akhbār of the Ancestors* (*Lubnān fī 'Ahd al-Umarā' al-Shihābiyyin: Wa huwa al-Juz' al-Thāni wa al-Thālith min Kitāb al-Ghurar al-Ḥisān fī Akhbār Abnā' al-Zamān*). Foreword and commentary by editors Asad Rustum and Fouad Afram al-Bustani. Collection of Dr. Asad Rustum 2–4. (Majmū'at al-Duktūr Asad Rustum 2–4). 3 vols. 2nd ed. Beirut: Maktabah al-Bulisiyyah, 1984.

Subki, Mahmoud Muhammad Khattab al-. *Satisfying Beings with the Statement of the Doctrine of the Salaf and the Successors on the Similarities and the Rebuttal against Atheist and Anthropomorphist Claims and What They Believe to Be Slander* (*Itḥāf al-Kā'ināt bi-Bayān Madhhab al-Salaf wa al-Khalaf fī al-Mutashābihāt wa-Radd

Shubah al-Mulḥida wa al-Mujassima wa mā Ya'taqidūnahu min al-Muftarayāt). Edited by Yusuf Amin Khattab. 2nd ed. Cairo: n.p., 1974.

Vassiliev, Alexei. *The History of Saudi Arabia* (*Tārīkh al-'Arabiyya al-Sa'ūdiyya*). Translated by Khayri al-Damin and Jalal al-Mashitah. Beirut: Dār al-Farabi, 2011.

Wadi'i, Muqbil Ibn Hadi al-. *The Exit from Strife* (*Al-Makhraj min al-Fitna*). Sanaa: n.p., 1982.

———. *Religious Polemic against Sophistry and Ignorance* (*Ghārat al-Ashriṭa 'alā Ahl al-Jahl wa al-Safsaṭa*). Vol. 2. Cairo: Dār al-Haramayn, 1998.

Waqidi, Abu Abdullah Muhammad Ibn Omar al-. *The Islamic Conquest of the Levant* (*Futūḥ al-Shām*). Prepared and revised by Abd al-Latif Abd al-Rahman. Vol. 1. 2nd ed. Beirut: Dār al-Kutub al-'Ilmiyya, 2005.

Wardi, 'Ali al-. *From the Beginning of the Ottoman Era to the Mid-Nineteenth Century* (*Min Bidāyat al-'Ahd al-'Uthmānī ḥattā Muntaṣaf al-Qarn al-Tāsi' 'Ashar*). Vol. 1 of *Social Glimpses of Modern Iraqi History* (*Lamahāt Ijtimā'iyya min Tārīkh al-'Irāq al-Ḥadīth*). London: Al-Warraq lil-Nashr, 2007.

Yaqut al-Hamawi, Shihab al-Din Abu Abdullah Ibn Abdullah. *The Dictionary of Countries* (*Mu'jam al-Buldān*). Vol. 5. Beirut: Sader, 1977.

Zakaria, Ahmad Wasfi. *Damascene Clans and Tribes* (*'Ashā'ir al-Shām*). 10th ed. Damascus: Dār al-Fikr; Beirut: Dār al-Fikr al-Mu'āṣir, 2009.

Zirkali, Khayr al-Din al-. *Al-A'lām: Biographical Dictionary of Famous Arab Men and Women, Arabists and Orientalists* (*Al-A'lām: Qāmūs Tarājim li-Ashhar al-Rijāl min al-'Arab wa al-Musta'ribīn wa al-Mustashriqīn*). 8 vols. 15th ed. Beirut: Dār al-'Iilm lil-Malāyin, 2002.

NON-ARABIC BOOKS

Anani, Khalil al-. *Inside the Muslim Brotherhood: Religion, Identity and Politics.* Oxford: Oxford University Press, 2016.

Bennabi, Malik. *Vocation de l'Islam.* Paris: ANEP, 2006.

Berger, Morroe. *Islam in Egypt Today: Social and Political Aspects of Popular Religion.* Princeton Studies on the Near East. Cambridge: Cambridge University Press, 1970.

Berlin, Isaiah. *Crooked Timber of Humanity: Chapters in the History of Ideas.* London: John Murray, 1990.

Bishara, Azmi. *Sectarianism without Sects.* Oxford: Oxford University Press, 2021.

Burckhardt, John Lewis. *Notes on the Bedouins and Wahábys: Collected during His Travels in the East.* Vol. 1. London: Henry Colburn and Richard Bentley, 1831.

Burgat, François. *Islamism in the Shadow of al-Qaeda*. Translated by Patrick Hutchinson. Austin: University of Texas Press, 2008.

Cook, Michael. *Commanding Right and Forbidding Wrong in Islamic Thought*. Cambridge: Cambridge University Press, 2001.

Dallal, Ahmad S. *Islam without Europe: Traditions of Reform in Eighteenth-Century Islamic Thought*. Chapel Hill: University of North Carolina Press, 2018.

DeLong-Bas, Natana J. *Wahhabi Islam: From Revival and Reform to Global Jihad*. London: I. B. Tauris, 2007.

Gauvain, Richard. *Salafi Ritual Purity: In the Presence of God*. London: Routledge, 2017 [2013].

Gibb, Hamilton A. R. *Modern Trends in Islam*. Chicago: Chicago University Press, 1947.

Hallaq, Wael. *The Origins and Evolution of Islamic Law*. Cambridge: Cambridge University Press, 2005.

Hourani, Albert. *Arabic Thought in the Liberal Age 1798–1939*. Cambridge: Cambridge University Press, 2009 [1962].

Ibn Khaldun. *The Muqaddimah: An Introduction to History*. Translated by Franz Rosenthal. Edited and abridged by N. J. Dawood. Introduction by Bruce B. Lawrence. Princeton: Princeton University Press, 2015.

Istiphan, Isis. *Directory of Social Agencies in Cairo*. Cairo: American University at Cairo, Social Research Center, 1956.

Marty, Martin E., and R. Scott Appleby, eds. *Fundamentalisms and the State: Remaking Polities, Economies, and Militance*. Fundamentalism Project, vol. 3. Chicago: University of Chicago Press, 1993.

Qutb, Sayyid. *Milestones*. Edited by B. al-Mehri. Birmingham: Maktabah Booksellers and Publishers, 2006.

Rasheed, Madawi al-. *A History of Saudi Arabia*. New York: Cambridge University Press, 2002.

Roy, Olivier. *Globalized Islam: The Search for a New Ummah*. New York: Columbia University Press, 2004.

Ruthven, Malise. *Fundamentalism: A Very Short Introduction*. Very Short Introductions 116. Oxford: Oxford University Press, 2004.

Said, Edward W. *Orientalism*. New York: Pantheon Books, 1978.

Schwartz, Stephen. *The Two Faces of Islam: The House of Sa'ud from Tradition to Terror*. New York: Doubleday, 2002.

Sivan, Emmanuel. *Radical Islam: Medieval Theology and Modern Politics*. Enlarged ed. New Haven: Yale University Press, 1990.

Tabari, Muhammad Ibn Jarir al-. *Incipient Decline*. Vol. 34 of *The History of al-Ṭabarī*. Translated by Joel Kraemer. New York: State University of New York Press, 1989.

Turner, Bryan. *Marx and the End of Orientalism*. New York: Routledge, 1978.

Upal, Muhammad Afzal, and Carole M. Cusack, eds. *Handbook of Islamic Sects and Movements*. Brill Handbooks on Contemporary Religion. Leiden: Brill, 2021.

Voigt, F. A. *Unto Caesar*. London: Constable, [1939].

Yassini, Ayman al-. *Religion and State in the Kingdom of Saudi Arabia*. Boulder: Westview, 1985.

Zubaida, Sami. *Islam, the People and the State: Political Ideas and Movements in the Middle East*. London: I. B. Tauris, 2009 [1989].

ARABIC ARTICLES

Abduh, Muhammad. "A Reply to Hanotaux's Latest Talk" ("Radd 'Alā Ḥadīth Hānōtō al-Akhīr"). *Al-Mu'ayyid* 29 (July 29, 1900 CE / Rabī' al-Awwal, 1318 AH).

Hafi, Amir al-. "A Unifying Analysis of Discussion of the Separation of the Ummah" ("Qirā'a Tawḥīdiyya fī Ḥadīth Iftirāq al-Umma"). *Islamiyyat al-Ma'rifa* 16, no. 63 (2011 CE / 1432 AH): 105–40.

Ottoman Party for Administrative Decentralization. "Communiqué of the Ottoman Party for Administrative Decentralization." *Al-UMRAN* 18, no. 725 (February 24, 1913 CE / Safar 28, 1331 AH).

Qasimi, Jamal al-Din al-. "The Second Study on al-Mu'tazilas" ("Al-Baḥth al-Thānī fī al-Mu'tazila"). *Al-Manār* 16, no. 10 (1913 CE / 1331 AH).

Rashid Rida, Muhammad. "The Eighth-Year Prologue" ("Fātiḥat al-Sana al-Thāmina"). *Al-Manār* 8, no. 1 (March 7, 1905 CE / 1 Muharram 1323 AH).

———. "The Pros and Cons of Europeans in the East: Despotism." ("Manāfi' al-Urūbbiyyīn wa-Maḍārruhum fī al-Sharq: Al-Istibdād.") *Al-Manār* 10, no. 4 (March 1907 CE / Muharram 1325 AH).

NON-ARABIC ARTICLES

Abdel-Malek, Anouar. "Orientalism in Crisis." *Diogenes*, no. 44 (Winter 1963): 104–12.

DeYoung, Karen. "Saudi Prince Denies Kushner Is 'in His Pocket.'" *Washington Post*. March 22, 2018. http://bit.do/ekSy3.

Griffel, Frank. "What Do We Mean by 'Salafī'? Connecting Muhammad Abduh with Egypt's Nūr Party in Islam's Contemporary Intellectual History." *Die Welt des Islams* 55, no. 2 (2015).

———. "What Is the Task of the Intellectual (Contemporary) Historian?—A Response to Henri Lauzière's 'Reply.'" *Die Welt des Islams* 56, no. 2 (2016): 249–55.

Laoust, Henri. "Le Réformisme orthodoxe des 'Salafiya' et les caractères généraux de son orientation." *Revue des Études Islamiques* 2 (1932).

Lauzière, Henri. "The Construction of Salafiyya: Reconsidering Salafism from the Perspective of Conceptual History." *International Journal of Middle East Studies* 42 (2010): 369–389.

Makdisi, George. "L'Islam Hanbalisant." *Revue des Études Islamiques* 43, no. 1 (1974): 45–76.

———. "L'Islam Hanbalisant." *Revue des Études Islamiques* 42, no. 2 (1975): 211–44.

Salazar, Philippe-Joseph. "A Caliphate of Culture? ISIS's Rhetorical Power." *Philosophy and Rhetoric* 49, no. 3 (2016): 343–54.

Voll, John. "Muḥammad Ḥayyā al-Sindī and Muḥammad Ibn Abd al-Wahhāb: An Analysis of an Intellectual Group in Eighteenth-Century Madīna." *Bulletin of the School of Oriental and African Studies* 38, no. 1 (1975): 32–39.

Wiktorowicz, Quintan. "Anatomy of the Salafi Movement." *Studies in Conflict and Terrorism* 29, no. 3 (2005): 207–39.

REPORTS

National Commission on Terrorist Attacks upon the United States. *The 9/11 Commission Report: Final Report of the National Commission on Terrorist Attacks upon the United States*. New York: Norton, [2004].

WEBSITES

al-Albani, Muhammad Nasir al-Din. "Fatwa from Muhammad Nasir al-Din al-Albani on Palestinians' Leave from Palestine" ("Fatwa al-Shaykh al-Albānī fī mā Yakhuṣṣ Hijrat Ahl Filasṭīn Minhā"). July 18, 2013. YouTube video. http://bit.do/ekNSP.

Albayan, "Nayef: 'Muslim Brotherhood' Is the Source of the Trouble" ("*Nāyif: al-Ikhwan al-Muslimun Aṣl al-Balā*"). November 26, 2002. https://bit.ly/3C1oYVD.

Amarah, Muhammad. "Why the Attack on Shaykh al-Islam?" ("Limādhā al-Hujūm 'Alā Shaykh al-Islam?"). Arabi 21, November 10, 2016. https://bit.ly/3D99rED.

Gharib, Maysarah al-, ed. "The Battle of al-Ahzab under Siege" ("Maʿrakat al-Aḥzāb taḥt al-Ḥiṣār"). AQI Media Bureau, n.d. https://bit.ly/30bUDXt.

Hawwa, Muhammad Saʿid, and Abd ʿId al-Raʿud. "A Critical Study in the Hadith of Al-Irbad Ibn Sariyah 'The Messenger of God Admonished Us . . .'" ("Dirāsa Naqdiyya fī Hadith al-ʿIrbāḍ Ibn Sāriya, 'Wa'aẓanā Rasūl Allah . . ."). Saʿid Hawwa, January 31, 2012. https://bit.ly/30iYj1Z.

Qaradawi, Yusuf al-. "A Final Word on Sayyid Qutb" ("Kalima Akhīra ḥawl Sayyid Quṭb"). Yusuf al-Qaradawi, September 17, 2004. https://bit.ly/39uxml9.

Index

Abbasids, 31–32, 34–35, 37, 69
Abd al-Raziq, ʿAli: *Islam and the Foundations of Government*, 66
Abdel-Malek, Anouar, 4
Abduh, Muhammad, viii, 10–12, 21–23, 65, 138, 151
Abu Ghuddah, Abd al-Fattah, 60–61
Afghani, Jamal al-Din al-, viii, 11–12, 21, 83, 139, 165n25
Afghanistan, 53, 165n25
aḥādīth al-āḥād, 28
ahl al-ahwāʾ al-ḍālla, 3
Ahl al-Athar, 2, 7
Ahl al-Hadith, x, 2–3, 7–9, 46, 54
Ahl al-Raʾy, 8, 32, 43, 54
Ahl al-Sunna, 3, 88, 144, 163n14, 164n15
Ahl al-Sunna wa al-Hadith wa al-Athar, 38, 54, 151
Ahl al-Sunna wa al-Jamāʿa, x, 2–3, 7, 16, 61, 101, 144, 151, 178n27. See also Jamāʿa
Ahsaʾi, Ibn Fayruz al-, 19
akhbār/akhbārīs, 6, 8–9, 54
al-Ahsa, 127
al-ʿāmma, 45
al-amr bi al-maʿrūf wa al-nahī ʿan al-munkar, 30
al-Ashʿari. *See* Ashʿari/Ashʿarism/Ashʿarites
al-Azhar, 10
Albani, Muhammad Nasir al-Din al-, 60–61, 108–9, 178n27
al-dār al-murakkaba, 54
al-Dirʿiyya, 184n48
Aleppo, 130
al-firqa al-nājiya, 144, 157
al-Gamʿiyya al-Sharʿiyya. *See* Sharʿiyya Society
al-ghayb, 96, 157
al-ghulū, 13
Al-Hilāl (journal), 22
al-iʿjāz al-ʿilmī, 24, 158. *See also* Qurʾan/Qurʾanic

al-Ikhwān, 85, 116–17
al-iqrār bi al-lisān, 48
al-jafā', 13
al-Jamā'a al-Islāmiyya al-Muqātila (Algerian Fighting Islamic Group), 60
al-Jāmi Salafism, 33. *See also* Salafism
al-Jāmiyya al-Madkhaliya, 141
al-Khadir, 32
al-khāssa, 45
al-Majma'ah, 167n38, 185n48
al-Maktaba al-Salafiyya. *See* Salafi Bookstore (Al-Maktaba al-Salafiyya)
al-Ma'mun, 31, 49
Al-Manār (reformist journal), 11, 22, 65, 81
Al-Muqtabas (journal), 22
Al-Muqtaṭaf (journal), 22
al-Mu'tasim, 31
al-Nahda, 24–25, 139. *See also* renaissance
Al-Nour party, 68–69
Al-Qaeda, 1, 16, 51, 69
al-Qatif, 127
al-Qazwini, Ahmad Ibn Faris, 21
Al-Ṣaḥwa al-Islāmiyya, 108
al-salaf al-ṣāliḥ, 2–3, 14
Al Sa'ud, 'Abd al-'Aziz Ibn Sa'ud, 12, 17, 63, 101, 125
Al Sa'ud (House of Sa'ud), 60. *See also* Saudi Arabia
al-shirk bi al-ulūhiyya, 36
al-siyāsa al-shar'iyya, 93
al-Ta'if, 46, 54
al-takfīr al-muṭlaq, ix, 30
al-Takfīr wa al-Hijra, 70–71, 87, 154, 178n22
al-taṣdīq bi al-qalb, 48
al-Uqair, 127
al-Wahhāb. *See* Wahhabism
al-walā' wa al-barā', 83, 142, 160, 196n3
al-Wathiq, 31
amīr al-mu'minīn, 29
amīr al-umarā', 93
Anṣār, 27
Anṣār al-Sunna, 16
Anṣār al-Sunna al-Muḥammadiyya, 22, 65, 67–68
Anzah, 129
apostasy, 48–53, 56–57; of Muslim rulers, 56
Arab Cold War, 37
Arabian Peninsula: birthplace of Islam in the, 38; Islamic awakening in the, 12, 25, 63; Qutbism in the, 37; Salafism of the, 10, 53, 80; Wahhabism in the, 30, 145–46. *See also* Saudi Arabia
Arab radical left, 56. *See also* Arabs
Arabs: dictatorships of the, 141; intellectual and literary life of the, 13; liberation of, 56; revival of the Islam of, 12–13, 64; secular ideological currents in the world of the, 141; urban life of the, 84, 86, 121, 127. *See also* Arab radical left; Bedouin
'aṣabiyya, 97, 157; tribal, 142
asbāb al-nuzūl, 45
Aṣḥāb al-Āthār, 2. *See also* āthār/atharī/atharīs; Athariyyūn
Aṣḥāb al-Ḥadith, 33
Aṣḥāb al-Shūrā, 27

Ash'ari/Ash'arism/Ash'arites, 7, 49; doctrinal rigidity of the, 16; positions of the, 67; theology of the, 9, 23, 42, 46; traditionalist, 23. *See also* al-Ash'ari
'āṣin wa-fāsiq, 50
aṣl al-balā', 179n29
Asqalani, Ibn Hajr al-, 67
Associations Law, 66
āthār/atharī/atharīs, 9, 29; interpretation as, 46. See also Athariyyūn
Athariyyūn, 2. See also *āthār/atharī/atharīs*
Azharis, 67

Badr, 27
Baghdad, 21, 34, 122
Baghdadi, Abd al-Qahir al-, 3
Baghdadi, Abu Bakr al-, 3, 14, 16, 59
balāgh, 47
Banna, Hasan al-, 73–84, 141; *Memoirs of the Mission and the Missionary*, 81
Banu Qurayza, 19
Banu Sakhr, 121
Banu Tamim, 18, 113
Baqillani, 23
Barā'a, 117. *See also* Qur'an/Qur'anic
barbarians, 39; violence of, 89
Barelvi, Sayyid Ahmad, 21, 100, 152, 168n47
Basra, 18, 127, 130
Batti, Uthman al-, 9
Battle of Ajnadayn, 193n70
Battle of al-Sabilla (1929), 117
Battle of Fallujah (April 2004, November/December 2004), 53, 185n57
bay'a, 59, 157
Baytar, Abd al-Raziq Ibn al-Hasan Ibn Ibrahim al-, 195n92
Bedouin, 18, 101, 109, 112–16, 120–25, 146, 185n48, 194n75. *See also* Arabs
benefit: to Arabophone culture of Orientalists, 4; of the conquest economy, 145; of secular education, 133; to Wahhabi Salafism from its partnership with the Saudi state, 146
Bennabi, Malik, 85
bid'a, ix, 1, 8, 10, 38, 140, 157. *See also* heresy; *muḥdathāt*
bin Salman, Muhammad, 107, 131
Bouti, Muhammad Sa'id Ramadan al-, 7
Bukhārī, Muhammad Ibn Isma'il al-: *Ṣaḥīḥ al-Bukhārī* (*al-Jāmi' al-Ṣaḥīḥ*), 110, 143, 152, 163n15, 169n64, 183n26, 191n38
Burckhardt, John Lewis, 122

Cairo, 13, 21, 82, 122
caliphs: Abbasid, 31, 34–35, 37; abolition of the, 11; first, 14; restoration of the, 11; rightly guided, 8, 28, 37–38; rival, 48; Umayyad, 35, 37, 49
charisma: of Arab leaders, 79, 142; and extremism, 72; in folk imagination, 32; religious, 189n27
China, 77
Chishtis, 64, 152. *See also* Sufism
Christianity, 5; of Baghdad, 172n87; Byzantine, 85; fundamentalism in, 5, 163n8; ignorance of monasticism as the error of, 111; intolerance toward,

Christianity (*continued*)
172n88; missionaries of, 73, 81; modernization and, 85; old local saints of, 171n76; as people of the book, 192n58; persecution by caliphs of, 35–36; of Syria, 172n87; Wahhabism and, 103–4, 118, 129; Westernization and, 82. *See also* Protestantism; religion
colonialism, 15, 56, 84; and world trade, 85
Communism/Communists, 5, 7, 78–80, 181n18; Arab nationalism and, 107; fraternal world of movements of, 76. *See also* Marx, Karl; socialism/socialists
companions, 2–3, 8, 26–29, 44–45, 59, 67. *See also* Prophet
consciousness: of decline from a virtuous origin, 20; extreme form of inverted, 19; ideology of regressive, 15; Marxist sense of false, 19; religious, 6, 120
constitution, 92, 143; of Syria, 12. *See also* Shariʿa
Constitution of Medina, 15. *See also* Prophet
consumerism, 132–33; extreme forms of, 5; habits of, 140
Cook, Michael, 33–34
corruption: of Islam, 20, 91, 96, 126; lifestyles of, 61; political, 68, 147; of rulers, ix; of time, 26; true spring of evil and, 182n18
Creator, 30–31; divine sovereignty of God as the, 115; Ibn Abd al-Wahhab on the, 115; responsibility for one's actions in front of one's, 104
creedal disagreements, 46–47. *See also* Islam
Crusaders (Firanja), 56, 69, 136

Dāʿish (ISIL). *See* Islamic State of Iraq and the Levant (ISIL)
Dallal, Ahmad, 100
Damascus, 21, 101, 120, 122, 129–30, 152; Hanbali center in, 162n1; history of the notables of, 195n92
Dār al-Ḥarb, 52, 54–56, 157
Dār al-Islām, 52, 54, 157
Dār al-Manār, 65
Dār al-Silm, 55, 61, 157
dār hijrah, 191n45
Darwinism, 5
daʿwa, 68
DeLong-Bas, Natana, 100, 190n30
democracy/democratic: advocacy of, 11; as idolatry, 58; liberal, 41; as the modern form of consultation (*shūrā*), 15–16, 55; nonreformist Salafi rejection of, 38, 42; principles of, 16; Salafi organizations abiding by elected institutions of, 69. *See also* proponents of democracy
despotism, 15, 153
dhimmīs, 35, 65, 109, 129, 157
Dimashqi, Ghaylan al-, 31, 152
dīn wa dawla, 87
divorce, 44, 105
Driault, Edouard, 126–27

Egypt, 12–13, 37, 63–69, 145; Arab renaissance in, 22; government of, 68; as an infidel state, 56; modernization of, 81
Egyptian Islamist jihadi organizations, 50, 55
Eid al-Ghadir, 127
Enlightenment/enlightenment, 4, 22, 78, 103
exegesis: of al-Banna, 81; allegorical, 45, 51, 67; interpretive, 45; Qur'anic, 91, 175n112; work of rational theology as a work of, 16, 154. *See also* Qur'an/Qur'anic

faḍl, 28
faqīh, 53, 157; Hanafi, 187n13
Farabi, Abu Nasr al-, 22
Faraj, Muhammad Abd al-Salam, 33, 55; *Jihad: The Absent Commandment* (*Al-Jihad: Al-Farīḍa al-Ghā'iba*), 55–56, 111
farḍ 'ayn, 55, 157
Farra', Abu Ya'la al-: *History of the Hanbalis* (*Ṭabaqāt al-Ḥanābila*), 27–29, 54
Fassi, Allal al-, 10–11, 15
Fatimid, 17; Shi'i Isma'ili, 112
fatwa, 31, 44, 47, 53, 126, 131, 148; of al-Albani, 61; of al-Wadi'i, 74; of Ibn Abd al-Wahhāb, 194n81; Ibn Taymiyya's Mardin, 54–56, 109, 178n21
Filastini, Abu Qatada al-, 60
fiqh, 28, 36, 43, 160. *See also* jurisprudent/jurisprudential; *uṣūl al-fiqh*
Fiqqi, Muhammad Hamid al-, 22, 68, 151–52
Firanja, 56
fisq, 50, 157
fitna, 69, 141, 157
folk religiosity, 5, 10, 26–36, 87, 163n11; condescending attitude of Salafism to, 102; of good neighborliness, 65; Muslim, 171n76; religious establishments and, 148. *See also* religion
France, 10
Franks, 56
freedom: authoritarian rule and, 109; of choice, 148; of conscience, 37; religious, 56–57, 145–46; of thought, 82; values of progress and, 10
fundamentalism, ix, 4–6, 164n16; Christian, 163n8; classic Islamic, 105; purist Islamist, 22, 59; religious, 59, 99, 106, 136; Wahhabism and Islamic, 106, 189n28. See also *uṣūlī*
fuqahā', 31, 157
furqa, 37

Gauvain, Richard, 67–68
Ghalib Pasha, 127
Ghazali, Abu Hamid al-, 16–17, 20, 45–46; *Al-Mustaṣfā*, 44
Ghazali, Muhammad al-: *Islam Slandered among Communists and Capitalists*, 80; *Thus We Know*, 80
ghiyār, 129
Gibb, Hamilton, 21, 64
globalization, 39; al-Qaeda as a product of, 70

God: and the infidel, 50; as judge, 49, 58; knowledge of, 45; punishment by, 57; sovereignty of, 36, 51. *See also* religion
Good Islamic Ethics Society, 65
Griffel, Frank, 22–23
Grotius, Hugo, 31

Hadith/ḥadith/ḥadiths, viii, 3, 8, 27, 37, 47, 67, 88, 137, 151, 158, 161n3; collection of, 110, 114; literal meaning of, 140, 162n6; religious judgments from the, 6; revival of studies of the, 100; Salafi reliance on the, 53–54, 60–61; scholars of the, 35, 37; "sciences" of the, 9; spurious, 53; of Tawus, 50. *See also* Islam
ḥākimiyya, 36, 74, 79, 154, 158, 173n93, 181n18
ḥākimiyyat Allah, 51
Halabi, Abu Tayy al-, 112
Hama, 120
Hanafis, 48, 99–100, 137, 178n27; Sunni, 21; Syrian, 60–61. *See also* Hanafism
Hanafism, 9, 153, 158; condemnation of, 28. *See also* Hanafis
Hanbalis, 46, 92, 100, 137, 140; early, 34; later Salafi, 28; Najdi (Wahhabi), 30, 32; as social actors, 30. *See also* Hanbalism
Hanbalism, 2, 7–9, 18–19, 33, 64, 136, 158; juristic-theological amalgam of imagined, 13; in Morocco, 21; revival of, 63; school of Sunni jurisprudence of, 28, 136–37, 162n1; as a theological doctrine, 28; and Wahhabism, 99–100, 105; writings of, 29. *See also* Hanbalis; Ibn Hanbal; Salafism; Wahhabism
ḥarām, 10, 158
Hashimites, 188n21
Hawwa, Sa'id, 55, 87
Haytami, Ibn Hijr al-, 67
hearken, 20
heresy, 12, 14; heretical movements, 68; innovations of, 66–67; killing of theologians condemned for, 52. See also *bid'a*
hijar, 116, 122
Hijaz, 13, 114, 128, 131–32
hijra, 27, 61, 142, 191n45
Himsi, Abd al-Rahman Ibn Amr al-Sullami al-, 37
history: "archeological" investigations of, 3; era of intellectual decadence in Islamic, 59; of ideas, 2, 7; memory and, 2; Muslim, viii
Hobbes, Thomas, 38
homosexuality, 129, 195n93, 196n94
Homs, 36, 120
Hourani, Albert, 22–23
Hudaybi, Hasan al-, 75; *Preachers, Not Judges*, 74, 88, 111
ḥudūd, 29, 158, 175n115
ḥukm, 36, 140, 173nn94–95
Huraymila, 18, 184n48
Husayn, Muhammad al-Khidr, 66, 180n9
Husayni, Ishaq Musa al-: *The Greatest of the Modern Islamic Movements*, 79
Husayyin, Salih al-, 164n16

Hysayn, Taha, 10, 12–13; Works: *Gems in the History of the Holy City of Medina*, 92; *On Jahili Poetry*, 66; *On Pre-Islamic Poetry*, 66

ʿibādāt, 46
Ibn ʿAbd al-ʿAziz, Umar, 35, 172n88
Ibn Abd al-Wahhab, Muhammad, ix–x, 12–14, 17–19, 44, 53, 63, 152, 190n30; concept of divine sovereignty of, 115; concept of "nullifiers" of Islam of, 53; fundamentalism of, 79–85; ideology of, 85, 95–126; literal meaning of the work of, 47; mission of, 117–33; Salafism of, 36, 60, 135; *Works: Matters of Jahiliyya*, 84
Ibn Abi Talib, ʿAli, 3, 27–28, 48
Ibn Abi Talib, Jaʿfar Ibn Muhammad Ibn ʿAli, 7, 27–28, 127, 164n15, 173n95
Ibn Abi Waqqāṣ, Saʿd, 27
Ibn Affan, Uthman, 27–28
Ibn al-Awwam, Zubayr, 27
Ibn al-Hanafiyya, Hasan Ibn Muhammad, 49
Ibn Ali, Husayn, 26
Ibn al-Jawzi, Abu al-Faraj Abd al-Rahman Ibn ʿAli, 32
Ibn al-Khattab, Umar, 27–28, 169n61, 172n87
Ibn al-Zubayr, Talha, 27
Ibn Anas, Malik, 32, 159
Ibn Aʿtaʾ, Wasil, 31
Ibn Awf, Abd al-Rahman, 27
Ibn Badran al-Dimashqi, Abd al-Qadir, 31, 33
Ibn Baz, ʿAbd al-ʿAziz, 68, 109, 135, 152, 178n26
Ibn Dirham, al-Jaʿd, 31
Ibn Hanbal, Abdullah Ibn Ahmad, 28, 152, 177n18
Ibn Hanbal, Ahmad, x, 7–9, 28, 30–34, 42, 47, 50–54, 63, 66, 69, 73, 79–80, 85, 105–6, 121, 136–37, 140–41, 152–53, 158, 162n1, 162n6, 163n13, 170n69, 176n117, 179n1, 190n29, 196n1, 196n94
Ibn Hani: *Issues of Imam Ahmad Ibn Hanbal, Narration of Ishaq Ibn Ibrahim Ibn Hani al-Nisapuri* (*Masāʾil al-Imam Aḥmad Ibn Ḥanbal, Riwāyat Isḥāq Ibn Ibrāhīm Ibn Hāniʾ al-Naysabūrī*), 50
Ibn Hazm, Abu Muhammad ʿAli Ibn Ahmad Saʿid, 43–45
Ibn Jahsh, Abdullah, 45
Ibn Muhammad, Abdullah, 78
Ibn Qayyim al-Jawziyya, Shams al-Din Abu Abdullah Muhammad Ibn Abi Bakr, 12, 18, 47, 53, 69, 153, 196n94; new editions of, 65; Salafi traditions based on, 121
Ibn Rushd, Abu al-Walid Muhammad Ibn Ahmad Ibn Muhammad, 17, 44, 153; Works: *Al-Ḍarūrī fī Uṣūl al-Fiqh*, 44; *Exposition of the Methods of Proof*, 44
Ibn Safwan, al-Jahm, 31, 153
Ibn Sariya, al-Irbad, 37
Ibn Saʿud. *See* Al Saʿud, ʿAbd al-ʿAziz Ibn Saʿud

Ibn Sina, Abu ʿAli al-Husayn Ibn Abdullah, 22
Ibn Sulayman, Abd al-Wahhab, 18
Ibn Taymiyya al-Harrani, Taqi al-Din Abu al-Abbas Ahmad Ibn Abd al-Halim, 7, 12, 16–18, 36, 42–*47*, *51*–56, 63, 66–69, 79–80, 85, 153; new editions of, 65; political theory of, 91–93; positioning the ideal in the past in, 91–92; and Wahhabism, 99–100; Works: *Averting the Conflict between Reason and Revelation*, 65; *The Way of the Prophetic Sunna*, 65
Ibn Thabit, Abu Hanifa al-Nuʿman, 9, 32, 54
Ibn Thaʿlaba, Abdullah Ibn Zayd, 45
Ibn Ubayd, Amr, 31
identity: defense of Muslim, 10, 73, 138; fundamentalist, 5; ideological religiosity and, 70, 90; Islamic, 15, 76, 138, 140, 153; modernization as a process of elimination of Muslim, 41, 83; national, 144
ideology: Marxist, 7; modernist secular, 7; regressive, 25; and religiosity, 70, 90; violence in the name of, 40
Idlib, 120
idolatry, 10, 12, 27, 38, 102, 145–47, 159; democracy as a form of, 58; majority rule as a kind of, 143; and monotheism, 91, 145; purging Islam from, 146. See also *shirk*
iʿjāz. See *al-iʿjāz al-ʿilmī*
ijmāʿ, 8, 158
ijmāʿ al-salaf al-ṣāliḥ, 37
ijtihād, viii, 6–9, 14, 18, 20, 44, 158
ʿilm al-kalām, 36
Ilyas, 32
imams, 3, 8; Bedouin without Muslim clergy or, 122; fitness to be, 27; Hadith establishes criteria for a state to be ruled by, 54; late Hanbali, 152; Muhammad Ibn Saʿud and his heirs recognized as, 98
India, 21; British in, 36, 99, 111; Sunni Salafi reform movements in, 153, 168n47; Sufism in, 64
Internet, 39–40
Iraq, 13, 30, 64, 108, 126, 130; American occupation of, 71, 81; ISIL in regions of, 71, 102, 120, 146; sectarian conflict in, 40, 51, 89, 148; tribal migration to, 124; Twelver Shiʿism in the tribes of southern, 120
irjāʾ, 28, 158
Iṣlāḥ/Iṣlāḥiyya/Iṣlāḥiyyūn, viii, 60, 82, 158
Islam: early, 67; in Egypt, 75–76; era of, 54; extremist, 38–39, 77; formation and expansion of, 57; globalization of, 39; Islams and, 5; of jihadi Salafis, 58–59; orthodox, 48, 139; political, 105; pure, 41; revival of, 12–13, 41, 64, 105–11; traditions of, 41, 105–6. *See also* creedal disagreements; Hadith/ḥadith/ḥadiths; Islamic civilization; Islamist movements; Prophet; prophetic; Qurʾan/Qurʾanic; Reformists; religion; Salafism; Shiʿism; Sufism; Sunna; Sunni; theology; Wahhabism

Islamic civilization, viii, 2, 41–42, 122; history of, 106. *See also* Islam
Islamic Da'wa Society, 65
Islamic Guidance Society, 64, 66
Islamic historiography, 20
Islamic just war theory, 52
Islamic modernism, 22
Islamic State of Iraq and the Levant (ISIL), vii, 1–2, 16, 19–20, 39–41, 47, 120; declaration of infidels by, 52–53; destruction of culture, civilization, and history of, 39; doctrinal issues of Sunnism of, 59; monopolization of doctrinal truth of, 53; religious officials of, 51; as a social phenomenon, 60
Islamic University of Medina, 33
Islamist movements, 1–5, 36, 78–88; extremist, 38–39, 77; interpretation of religion and religiosity of, 58; jihadi, 56–60; justification of armed rebellion against Muslim rulers of, 33, 188n22; as modern movements, 78–88; peaceful proselytism of, 55. *See also* Islam; jihadi movements; political Islamic movements
Isma'ilis/Ismailia, 3, 82; masses of the, 51. *See also* Nizārī Isma'ilis
istiḥsān, 43, 158

Jabhat al-Nuṣra, 47, 120
Jabiri, Muhammad al-, 44–45
Jadaan, Fahmi, 24
jāhilī/jāhiliyya, 33, 54 84, 95, 158; two different meanings of, 105–11
Jahmism, 35, 42, 45–46, 52, 158
Jamā'a, 2. *See also* Ahl al-Sunna wa al-Jamā'a
Jamā'a al-Salafiyya al-Muḥtasiba (JSM), 60, 108, 153–54
jamā'a min al-Muslimīn, 58
Jamā'at al-Jihād, 55, 178n19
Jamā'at al-Muslimīn, 58, 158
Jamā'at al-Tabligh, 108, 153, 179n3
Jama'at al Tablīgh wa al-Da'wa, 3, 64–65
Jāmi, Muhammad Aman al-, 33
Jam'iyyat Man' al-Muharramāt, 82
Japan, 77
Jaysh al-Islām, 60, 152
Jaza'iri, Tahir al-, 21
Jeddah, 128
Jerusalem, 61, 112
jihad, ix, 29, 73–74, 98, 141, 172n88; al-Qaeda as a military and ideological center for, 70; classical rulings on, 30; in early Islam, 57; establishment of the caliphate by, 40; histories of, 69; justification for eschewing moral standards when waging, 53; program for, 91; violence in the name of, 33, 53; volunteering for, 71, 102; Wahhabi, 116, 118, 123–24. *See also* jihadi movements; violence
jihadi movements, 19, 41, 56–60; authoritarian, 74; histories of, 69; Islamist, 78; Salafi, 13, 25. *See also* jihad; Islamist movements
Judaism, 5, 129. *See also* religion
Judgment Day, 14, 28–29, 49, 58, 176n5

judgments: of arbitration, 173n95; of Islamic texts, 14; pertaining to individuals or groups of people, 161n4; of reason, 137; Shariʿa, 160
jurisprudent/jurisprudential, 6–7, 9, 12, 18, 67–69, 80, 92–98, 135–37, 145, 158; codification of Islamic, 77; four traditional schools of, 67, 101, 105; Hanbali school of Sunni, 28, 92; Hanifa's school of Sunni, 28; particular school of, 113, 123; rational, 55; writings of, 16. See also *fiqh*; madhab; *uṣūl al-fiqh*
juristic-theological, 9, 13
Juwayni, Abu al-Maʿali Abd al-Malik Ibn Abdullah al-, 20, 45, 153

Kaʿba, 32
kāfir/kāfirs/kāfirūn, 50
Karbala, 127
katātīb, 35
Kawakibi, Abd al-Rahman al-, viii, 15
Khalid, Muhammad: *Thus We Begin, 80*
Khan, Genghis, 56
Khan, Siddiq Hasan, 21
Kharāj, 36, 49, 101
Khatib, Muhibb al-Din al-, 21–22, 82, 165n28, 184n45
Khawārij, 48–50, 53; Ibadi, 53; Wahhabis branded as, 101
khayr al-qurūn, 169n60
khilāfa, 173n93
Khmer Rouge, 90
khurūj, 49
Khuzaʿi, Ahmad Ibn Nasr al-, 31–*32*
Kingdom, The. *See* Saudi Arabia
kufr, 29, 38, 42, 48, 158
Kunj Yusuf Pasha, 101, 129, 195n92
Kutub as-Siyar, 8

Laost, Henri, 21
Lauzière, Henri, 21
Lebanon, 24, 81
Levant, 12–*13, 30, 63, 101*–2, 119, 121, 128, 145
liberalism, 5, 10, 79–80, 141, 163n8
Luther, Martin, 105

madhab, ix, 9, 12, 14, 23, 158, 161n5; Hanafi, 54, 102; mujtahid within the, 9, 105. *See also* jurisprudent/jurisprudential; madhabs/madhāhib
madhabs/madhāhib, 7; partisan, 13; rejection of the, 23. *See also* madhab
Madkhalism, 68
Mafātīh al-Ghayb, 16
Maghreb, 21, 145
Mahdism, 60, 97, 154
maḥmal, 119, 194n77
Maliki, 9, 47, 53, 100, 159; Ashʿari, 65
Mamlūks, 54, 56, 136, 163n14
Manar School, 69
manjanīq, 54
maqāṣid, 15, 20, 153–54, 159. *See also* Shariʿa
Maqdisi, Abu Muhammad al-, 51, 60
Mardin, 54–56, 109
Marwazi, Ahmad Ibn Shabbawayh al-, 34
Marx, Karl, 7. *See also* Marxism
Marxism, 7, 40, 79. *See also* Communism/Communists; Marx, Karl
masā'il, 47

Mashhur, Mustafa, 87–88
maʿṣiya, 50
Massignon, Louis, 21
Masʿudi, Abu al-Hasan ʿAli Ibn al-Husayn al-, 35
Māturīdi: rationalist school of the, 49; theology of the, 9, 23, 46, 159
Mawdudi, Abu al-Aʿla al-, 33, 44, 69, 111
Mecca, 27, 32, 46, 63; emigration of the Prophet to Medina from, 61; Grand Mosque in, 60
Meddeb, Abdelwahab, 105–6, 189n29
Medina, 27, 41, 63; emigration of the Prophet from Mecca to, 61; "ideal society" of, 92
Middle Eastern studies, 1, 3, 10
minhum barāʾ, 67
miracles, 32; folk religiosity and, 10; of Ibn Hanbal, 170nn73–74; of Jesus, 5; of the prophets, 116
modernity, viii, 4, 14, 22, 85–86, 104, 136; Arab, 77; aversion to, 83; capitalism and, 90; and colonialism, 82, 85; Eastern, 85; reformist Salafism and, 10–11, 15, 25, 41, 132, 138; Salafist reaction to, 69, 77; technologies of, 77; and Wahhabism, 146; and Western culture, 81. *See also* modernization
modernization, 2, 5, 41; Arab urban life transformed by, 11; Salafi challenge to various manifestations of, 65, 69; and Western hegemony, 41. *See also* modernity; secularism
Mongols, 56, 69; invasions of the, 136; Muslim, 69
monotheism, 68; deistic, 115. *See also* religion
Morocco, 21, 139
muʿāmalāt, 46
Muʿaskar al-Ibāḥiyya, 82, 159
Muʿaskar al-Islāmiyya, 82, 159
Muʿawiya, 48, 98, 159
Mubarak, Hosni, 68
mubtadiʿa, 52, 159
mubtadiʿīn, 159
Muhajir, Abu Abdullah al-, 19; *Points in the Jurisprudence of Jihad*, 53
Muhājirūn, 27
muḥdathāt, 1, 157. See also *bidʿa*
mujtahid/mujtahidūn, 9, 105, 159
Munib Effendi, 128
Muqbili, Salih Ibn Mahdi al-, 65, 154, 180n8
Murjʾism/Murjʾite, 48–49, 152, 159, 176n5; first major text of, 49; popularity with rulers of, 49; rebellion of the, 171n79; theological beliefs of the, 28; three stages of the thought of, 176n2
Muslim Brotherhood, ix, 3, 12, 16, 60–62, 72–83, 108, 111, 152–54; Egyptian, 36, 68; émigrés of the, 37; internal elections in the, 184n35; as a mass political movement, 83; political religiosity of the, 138–*41, 145, 147*; Qutbist current in the, 109, 143, 147; radicalism in the, 80; split in the, 87; Syrian, 21; theorists of the, 79–80, 87–88. *See also* political Islamic movements
musnad, 54, 73, 177n18
mutakallimūn, 42, 46, 159

Mutawakkil, Ja'far Ibn Muhammad al-Mu'tasim Billah al-, 34–36
Mu'tazila/ Mu'tazilite, 3, 30–*31, 34–35, 42, 159, 163n14; Sunni scholars as, 119*. *See also* Mu'tazilism
Mu'tazilism: dogmatic response to, 28; method of, 30–31; preachers of, 34; rationalist theology of the school of, 42, 46, 162n6, 170n71. *See also* Mu'tazila/ Mu'tazilite
myth, 14

Najd, 18, 126–27; eighteenth-century, 47, 102
Najdi, Uthman Ibn Mansur al-: *Manhaj al-Ma'ārij li-Akhbār al-Khawārij*, 19
Najdi Essays, 51, 111. *See also* Wahhabism
Najdi Salafism, 7, 53, 132. *See also* Salafism; Wahhabism
Nakhla, 46
Naqshbandīs, 64, 99, 159. *See also* Sufism
narrator: Ahl al-Hadith scholarly tradition as, 54; credible, 3; Ibn Hanbal as, 51, 136; Salafi, 114; simple, 33; "single narrator" reports, 28
nationalism, 11, 61, 79, 140–*41*; Arab, 107, 183n33; Egyptian, 11, 107; secular, 79–*84, 132, 183n33*
nawāqiḍ, 53, 159
9/11, 1, 62, 89, 106, 179n29; Wahhabism and, 189n28
niẓām ḥukm Islāmī, 140
Nizārī Isma'ilis, 17, 112, 159; leaders of the, 51. *See also* Isma'ilis/Ismailia
nonreformist Salafism, 13, 16, 37–*38*. *See also* Wahhabism

Orientalism, 3–4, 64; classical, 19; critics of, 4; essentialist, 19; Israeli, 69
Ottoman Empire, 12, 17, 69–70, 97; Arab uprising against the, 102; collapse of the, 83, 114; emergence of Wahhabism in the, 132, 188n21; homosexuality in the, 129; modernization of the, 85; officials and landowners of the, 80; pilgrimage routes important in the, 128–29; Salafi reformists in the, 138–39; Wahhabi rebellion against the, 105, 114, 188n22. *See also* Turkey
Ottoman Party for Administrative Decentralization, 12, 165n28

Pact of Umar, 172n87
Pakistan, 36, 107–*8, 154*
Palestine, 2, 56, 61; Hanbali centers in, 162n1; Islamist currents in, 72
Pan-Arabism, 15, 140, 153
patriotism, 61, 140
Platonist tradition, 31
pluralism, 6, 58; and democracy, 58; nonreformist Salafi rejection of, 37; rejection of, 90; religious, 47, 57
poetry, 17; pre-Islamic, 66
political Islamic movements, 2, 25, 138–41, 145, 147; Egyptian jihadi, 50; and Shari'a, 143. *See also* Islamist movements; Muslim Brotherhood

polytheism, 18, 61, 159; Arab, 57; Sufi, 64, 109. *See also* religion
popular culture: imagined culture of ISIL and online, 39; Salafi restrictions on, 65; spurious hadiths drawn from, 53; Western, 39
post-Orientalist, 3–4
prayer: abandonment of, 74; Arab practices of, 121; call to, 45; and fasting, 44; as heresy, 10; Ibn Abd al-Wahhab on, 113; of Ibn Hanbal, 32; the ruler as the legitimate leader of collective, 29; sections of Muslim, 169n66; Sunni, 2, 29. *See also* religion
Prophet, x, 1, 8, 51, 53, 56–57; biographies of the, 45; first generation of friends and disciples of the, 23; imagined companions and descendants of the, 30; intercession of the, 14; ISIL's conception of the, 135; mausoleum of the, 128; personal conduct of the, 8; raiding and plundering legitimized as jihad against the infidels with the blessing of the, 123; return to the teachings and statements of the, 15, 69, 134–35; and righteous successors, 14, 29; scholars of the traditions of the, 17, 66. *See also* companions; Constitution of Medina; Islam; prophetic; successors
prophetic: mission of the, 91, 95–97; model of ISIL of the, 89; tradition of the, 101. *See also* Islam
prophetic Hadith, 8
Prophet Muhammad. *See* Prophet
proponents of democracy, 16. *See also* democracy/democratic
proponents of narration, 8
proponents of opinion, 8, 43, 137, 151
proponents of the traditions, 137
Protestantism, 103–4, 163n8; beginnings of Wahhabism and, 105. *See also* Christianity; Protestant Reformation
Protestant Reformation, viii, 8, 104. *See also* Protestantism
puritanical: heroes and martyrs as, 31; model of religiosity as, 10; parts of the religious establishment that are more independent from the Abbasid state as, 34; persecuted scholars as, 32; Salafism as, viii, 48, 64–65, 104, 107, 111. *See also* Puritanism
Puritanism, 31; Orthodox Sunni, 35; of Yusuf Pasha, 129–30. *See also* puritanical

Qadirīs, 64, 152, 159. *See also* Sufism
qa'im, 171n79
qalānis, 35
qarnī, 169n64
Qasimi, Jamal al-Din al-, 13
Qatlan, Abd al-Fattah, 21–22
qibla, 32
qiyās, 43, 159
Quneitra, 120
Qur'an/Qur'anic, viii, 1, 14–15, 19, 38, 46–49; adherence to the, 8, 12; advocacy of return to the, 26; al-

Qur'an/Qur'anic (*continued*)
legorical interpretation of the, 51; appeal to the, 25, 33, 56; applications of the, 54; classes of memorization of the, 66; as created, 30–31, 34; distribution of copies of the, 64; historical accuracy of the, 66; human reasoning as idolatry against the, 38; interpretation of the, 3, 14, 45–46, 91, 175n112; outward meaning of the, 45; Prophet's wives in the, 110; recitation of the, 32; religious judgments from the, 6; rereading of the, 44; revelation of the, 43; Salafi reliance on the, 59–60; and sword, 76, 102; as uncreated, 30–31; verses of the, 56–60. See also *al-iʿjāz al-ʿilmī;* Barā'a; exegesis; Islam; revelation
Quraysh, 46, 110
Qutb, Sayyid, 33, 69, 74–78, 83–84, 141–42, 154; rejection of Nasserist charismatic control of, 182n25; *Social Justice in Islam*, 79
Qutbi/Qutbites, 68, 182n22. *See also* Qutbism
Qutbism, 36–37, 44, 68, 72–78; in the Muslim Brotherhood, 109, 143, 147. *See also* Qutbi/Qutbites; Qutbist tradition
Qutbist tradition, 62. *See also* Qutbism

Rabia al-Ra'i, 9
rakʿa/rakʿas/rakaʿāt, 29, 169n66
Raqqa, 121
rationalism: of Islamic schools of thought, 42, 49; philosophical, 10
ra'y, 9, 43, 54
Razi, Fakhr al-Din al-, 16, 154; Mafātīh al-Ghayb, 16
recognition: of the authenticity of hadiths, 54; of the four rightly guided caliphs, 28; of the imagined Islamic community, 41; Salafi recognition of credentials, 22; Wahhabi recognition of Muhammad Ibn Saʿud and his heirs as imams, 98, 145
Reformists: classical, 14; detentions of Salafi political, 131; early Salafi, 64–65; intellectual and educational Salafi, 11, 42; and jihadi Salafis, 59; militant Salafi, 11; modernist Salafi, 10–16, 20–25; in the Ottoman state, 138–39; popularizing Salafi, 64–65; reconciliation with modernity of Salafi, 41–42; return to "pure" Islam of Salafi, 41, 139. *See also* Islam; Salafism; Shariʿa
religion: ancestor worship in, 26; compulsion in the outward manifestations of, 56–58; definitions of the term of, 26; duties and outward displays of, 64; popular, 96; pure, 95; restriction of freedom of, 57; and state, 75, 80, 86–87, 93; Wahhabi return to the fundamentals of, 102–11. *See also* Christianity; folk religiosity; God; Islam; Judaism; monotheism; polytheism; prayer; religiopolitical; religious law; superstition; theology

religiopolitical, 5, 138–39. *See also* religion
religious law, 9. *See also* religion
renaissance: in Egypt, 22, 24; in Lebanon, 24; in Syria, 24. *See also* al-Nahda
revelation, 42–47. *See also* Qur'an/Qur'anic
Rida, Rashid, 11–15, 21–23, 68, 73, 154, 182n24; attacks on the scholarly books of Abd al-Raziq by, 66; political activism of, 12; revivalism of, 85; Salafism of, 80–81, 138; *Tārīkh al-Ustādh al-Imam Muhammad Abduh*, 11
Ruwallah, 121

sadd al-dharāʾiʿ, 115, 159, 191n42
Sadiq, Jaʿfar al-. *See* Ibn Abi Talib, Jaʿfar Ibn Muhammad Ibn ʿAli
Safarini, Muhammad al-, 100
Ṣaḥīḥ al-Bukhārī, 110, 143, 152, 163n15, 169n64, 183n26, 191n38
Said, Edward, 4
Saint-Simon, Henri de, 22
Salaf/Salafis: authorities of the, 51; consensus of the, 8, 37–38; creedal unity of, 36; Egyptian, 68; extremist, 19; moderate, 13; nonviolent conservative scholars of the, 60; political and social activism of the, 11, 59–61; puritan, viii, 48, 64–65, 68, 104, 107, 111; radical, 53; return to the, 10–11, 14, 24; revivalist, 95; righteous, 1, 23; scholarly, 60, 66; way of the, 61; Yemeni, 3. *See also* Salafism; Wahhabism
Salafi Bookstore (Al-Maktaba al-Salafiyya), 21–22, 65
Salafism: "apolitical" organizations of, 68; concept of one true Islam of, 24; contemporary, 8, 29, 51; creedal disagreements in, 46–47; declaration of individuals as infidels in, 49; definition of, 1–47; emergence of, 63; Hanbali, 9; history of, 6–16, 63; imagined Islamic community of, 41; institutionalizing, 65; jihadi, viii–x, 19–20, 25, 29–30, 33, 41–42, 47–51, 54–60, 69, 111–16; juristic, 69; modern global, 109; nonreformist, 13, 16, 37–38; official institutionalized, 26; orthodox religious practices of, 11; political, 25, 59–62; puritan, 9, 24, 61–62; quietist, 63–64; regressive, 20–21, 23–25, 46; rejection of the separation of religion and politics in, 37; Shiʿa Imami, 1, 9; sources of law for, 37; and Sufism, 64–65, 84; Sunni Hanbali, 1, 9; as a term, vii, 7–8, 10, 13, 22–23; tradition of, 2; and Wahhabism, 9, 14–15, 57, 62–66, 108. *See also* al-Jāmi Salafism; Hanbalism; Islam; jihadi movements; Najdi Salafism; Reformists; Salaf/Salafis; *Salafiyya*; Sunni; Wahhabism
Salafiyya, vii, 1, 22, 60, 159; as a "blessed" period, 6–7; in creed, 13; Salafiyya message of the Muslim Brotherhood, 196n4. *See also* Salafism
Salazar, Philippe-Joseph, 39–41
Sanusis, 97

Sarriyya, Salih, 52, 59; *Essay on Faith*, 52
Saudi Arabia, ix, 13, 19, 68–69, 113–17, 124–33; Islamic awakening in, 25; Islamists of, 72; liberalization in, 121; Wahhabism in, 63–64, 68, 77–86, 97–133; wars of, 124. *See also* Arabian Peninsula; Al Saʿud (House of Saʿud); Wahhabism
secretary-general, 78
sectarianism, ix, 2, 147–48; political, 81, 89; tribalism and, 76
secularism, 5; Arab, 141; cognitive, 43. *See also* modernization
Seljuks, 17, 70, 163n14
semi-urban, 146
Shafiʿi/Shafiʿis, 9; Ashʿari, 46
Shammar, 121, 123–24
Shariʿa, 6, 15, 29, 43, 73, 80, 92, 111–14, 139; belief in the, 50; as a body of positive law imposed from above that regulates society, 51, 86, 92; classes by al-Muhajir in, 53; implementation in different Arab nations of, 68–69; manuals of, 47; in politics, 12, 57, 143; Reformers and, 13, 20; restrictions of, 17; Saudi Arabia as the worldly embodiment of, 106–7; understanding of jihadi Salafis of the, 58; unity as supported by principles of, 37–38; Wahhabi tradition and, 122–23, 126, 132. *See also* constitution; *maqāṣid; sharʿiyyūn*
Sharʿiyya Society, 65–67
sharʿiyyūn, 47, 51. *See also* Shariʿa
Shatibi, Abu Ishaq Ibrahim Ibn Musa al-, 20
shaykh al-Islām, 77
Shiʿi/Shiʿa/Shiʿite: chroniclers of Saladin of the, 112; combat with the, 96; as infidels according to religious officials of ISIL, 51; proponents of narration of the, 8; rebellion of the, 171n79; "Salafisms" of, 1; Twelver, 49, 51, 59. *See also* Shiʿism
Shiʿism: authorities of the, 8–9, 67; Imami, 7; religiosity of, 26; texts of, 51; traditions of, 19. *See also* Islam; Shiʿi/Shiʿa/Shiʿite
shirk, 12, 38, 55, 96, 98, 159. *See also* idolatry
shūrā, 15–16, 27, 42, 159
Sibaʿi, Mustafa al-, 79–80; Socialism of Islam, 79
Siddiq, Abu Bakr al-, 27–28
sira, 164n18, 175n113
Sivan, Emmanuel, 69
social contract theory, 31
socialism/socialists, 22, 79, 163n8. *See also* Communism/Communists
sociocultural, 2
sociopolitical, 16, 79–*80, 136, 143, 148–49*
Southern California, 5
Soviet Union, 40, 112
Spinoza, Baruch, 22
Subki, Mahmoud Muhammad Khattab al-, 65–66, 154, 180n11; Works: *Fatwas of the Imams Silencing the Innovators*, 66–67; *The Way of the Salaf*, 67
successors, 2, 8, 14–15, 99, 127, 137, 158, 160, 164n15. *See also* Prophet
Suez Canal, 81

Sufism, 11, 109; as a heretical movement, 68; Indian, 64; Salafism and, 64–65, 84. *See also* Chishtis; Naqshbandīs; Qadirīs; Suhrawardīs

Suhrawardīs, 64. *See also* Sufism

sultan/sultanate, 3, 11, 34, 70, 83, 92–94, 98, 120, 140; Ottoman, 96, 114, 128, 130, 188n22; rule of the, 111

sumptuary laws, 36

Sunna, 1–3, 19, 30, 38, 47, 59; adherence to the, 8, 12; advocacy of return to the, 26; appeal to the, 33; applications of the, 54; defense of the, 17; exposition of the, 35; outward meaning of the, 45. *See also* Islam; Sunni

Sunni: appeal to the, 25; authorities of the, 8–9; central tradition of the, 23; moderate, 16; orthodox Sunni puritanism, 35; "Salafisms" of, 1; schools of Islamic jurisprudence of the, 41; swearing allegiance to a caliph by the, 59; traditions of, 19. *See also* Islam; Sunna; Sunnization

Sunnization, 49. *See also* Sunni

superstition, 10, 14, 32; innovation and, 66; religion free of innovations and, 66. *See also* religion

Sura al-Tawba, 19, 89, 122, 176n4

Suri, Abu Mus'ab al-, 78

Suyuti, Jalal al-Din al-, 21

Syria, 13, 64, 81; collapse of the nation-state in, 40; Salafi jihadist groups fighting in, 120

Syrian Civil War, 60

Syrian Congress, 12

Syrian constitution, 80

Ṭabaqāt al-Ḥanābila, 33, 54

Tabari, Muhammad Ibn Jarir al-, 35, 172n87, 190n29

tābiʿūn, 8, 160

Tablīgh/Daʿwa Society, 3

Tablīgh/Tablīghī. *See* Jamāʿat al-Tabligh

ṭāghūt, 112, 160

taḥqīq al-manāṭ, 36, 160

tajdīd, 69

takfīr, ix, 24, 32, 41, 48, 52, 75, 160; Egyptian Islamist, 55; Wahhabi ideology of, 84

takfīr al-muaʿyyan, ix, 30

Taliban, 102

tanqīḥ al-manāṭ, 36, 160

taqiyya, 87, 160

taqlīd, 100, 138, 160

tarbīʿ, 28, 160

Tarikh al-Ustādh al-Imām Muhammad Abduh, 11

taṭbīr, 67

tathlīth, 28, 160

ṭawāghīt, 58

tawḥīd, ix, 36–42, 46, 160

taʾwīl, 67, 160

ṭayālisah, 35

technology, 40; communications, 73, 131, 133; digital, 39; of modernity, 77, 86, 135

theology, 6; debates of, 44; orthodox, 32; Salafi, 22, 36. *See also* Islam; religion

trans-spatial, 73

Tunisia, 139

Turkey, 13, 56, 139. *See also* Ottoman Empire

Turkics, 35
Turner, Bryan, 4

ʿulamāʾ, 32, 35, 160; class of the, 11; dictates of the, 131; Najdi Salafi, 53; open-minded "rationalist," 32; puritanical, 32; Shiʿi, 67
Umar, 3, 14
Umayyads, 124, 152, 173n95; authorities of the, 31; caliphs of the, 35, 37, 98; deviation of the, 176n2
umma, 27, 38, 41, 82, 92, 160
urbanization, 122, 126
usar, 78
uṣūl al-dīn, 6, 9, 160
uṣūl al-fiqh, 6, 9, 20, 160. See also *fiqh*; jurisprudent/jurisprudential
uṣūlī, 6, 8–9, 160. *See also* fundamentalism
Utaybi, Juhayman al-, 60, 154, 180n5
Uthaymin, Muhammad Ibn Salih al-, 68, 109, 135, 152
utopia: of early Muslim community, 24–25; Medinan, 92; of Plato, 89
Uyayna, 18, 117

verse 87, 84
violence, 59–60. *See also* jihad

Wadiʿi, Muqbil Ibn Hadi al-, 3, 16, 180n5
Wahhabis: early writings of the, 47; as infidels, 67; Salafi, 14, 20, 22; Saudi, 30, 68. *See also* Wahhabism
Wahhabism, vii, ix–x, 7, 12–14, 97–133; early, 19, 105, 111–16; hostility toward Sufism of, 64; modern reformism and, 22; premodern, 23; proselytizing by, 63–64; refutation of early, 19; Salafism and, 9, 14–15, 57, 62–66, 108; Saudi political-ideological export of, 107. *See also* Hanbalism; Islam; *Najdi Essays*; Najdi Salafism; nonreformist Salafism; Salafism; Saudi Arabia; Wahhabis
walī al-amr, 65
waqf, 80, 160
West, 1–4, 15, 19–22, 39–41, 71, 76–86, 107
Wiktorowicz, Quintan, 36, 52

Yasa/Yasaq, 56, 70, 160
Yemen, 13, 166n37
Young Men's Muslim Association, 64
yurjiʾ, 49
Yusuf Pasha. *See* Kunj Yusuf Pasha, 129, 195n92

ẓāhir, 50, 56, 160. *See also* Ẓāhirī/Ẓāhirism
Ẓāhirī/Ẓāhirism, 43–45, 153, 160. See also *ẓāhir*
Zakaria, Ahmad Wasfi, 120–21
zakat, 113, 191n39, 192n54
zanādiqa, 110
Zarqawi, Abu Musʿab al-, 51, 53
Zawahiri, Ayman al-, 51, 112
Zaydis, 13; Yemeni, 65, 154
Zionism, 56
Zubaida, Sami, 105–6; *Islam, the People and the State*, 106
zunnār, 35

Stanford Studies in Middle Eastern *and* Islamic Societies *and* Cultures

Joel Beinin and Laleh Khalili, editors

Editorial Board

Asef Bayat, Marilyn Booth, Laurie Brand, Timothy Mitchell, Jillian Schwedler, Rebecca L. Stein, Max Weiss

Max Weiss, *Revolutions Aesthetic: A Cultural History of Ba'thist Syria*

2022

Elise Massicard, *Street-Level Governing: Negotiating the State in Urban Turkey*

2022

Jillian Schwedler, *Protesting Jordan: Geographies of Power and Dissent*

2022

Andrew Simon, *Media of the Masses: Cassette Culture in Modern Egypt*

2022

José Ciro Martínez, *States of Subsistence: The Politics of Bread in Contemporary Jordan*

2022

Andrea Wright, *Between Dreams and Ghosts: Indian Migration and Middle Eastern Oil*

2021

Mona El-Ghobashy, *Bread and Freedom: Egypt's Revolutionary Situation*

2021

Rania Kassab Sweis, *Paradoxes of Care: Children and Global Medical Aid in Egypt*

2021

Hanan Toukan, *The Politics of Art: Dissent and Cultural Diplomacy in Lebanon, Palestine, and Jordan*

2021

Brandon Wolfe-Hunnicutt, *The Paranoid Style in American Diplomacy: Oil and Arab Nationalism in Iraq*
2021

Rebecca L. Stein, *Screen Shots: State Violence on Camera in Israel and Palestine*
2021

Shay Hazkani, *Dear Palestine: A Social History of the 1948 War*
2021

Joel Beinin, Bassam Haddad, and Sherene Seikaly, editors, *A Critical Political Economy of the Middle East and North Africa*
2020

Todd Reisz, *Showpiece City: How Architecture Made Dubai*
2020

Rosie Bsheer, *Archive Wars: The Politics of History in Saudi Arabia*
2020

J. Andrew Bush, *Between Muslims: Religious Difference in Iraqi Kurdistan*
2020

Tamir Sorek, *The Optimist: A Social Biography of Tawfiq Zayyad*
2020

Pascal Menoret, *Graveyard of Clerics: Everyday Activism in Saudi Arabia*
2020

Amr Adly, *Cleft Capitalism: The Social Origins of Failed Market Making in Egypt*
2020

Darryl Li, *The Universal Enemy: Jihad, Empire, and the Challenge of Solidarity*
2019

Sophia Stamatopoulou-Robbins, *Waste Siege: The Life of Infrastructure in Palestine*
2019

Chiara De Cesari, *Heritage and the Cultural Struggle for Palestine*
2019

Narges Bajoghli, *Iran Reframed: Anxieties of Power in the Islamic Republic*
2019

Hicham Safieddine, *Banking on the State: The Financial Foundations of Lebanon*
2019

Sara Pursley, *Familiar Futures: Time, Selfhood, and Sovereignty in Iraq*
2019

Tareq Baconi, *Hamas Contained: The Rise and Pacification of Palestinian Resistance*
2018
Begüm Adalet, *Hotels and Highways: The Construction of Modernization Theory in Cold War Turkey*
2018
Elif M. Babül, *Bureaucratic Intimacies: Translating Human Rights in Turkey*
2017
Orit Bashkin, *Impossible Exodus: Iraqi Jews in Israel*
2017
Maha Nassar, *Brothers Apart: Palestinian Citizens of Israel and the Arab World*
2017
Asef Bayat, *Revolution without Revolutionaries: Making Sense of the Arab Spring*
2017
Nahid Siamdoust, *Soundtrack of the Revolution: The Politics of Music in Iran*
2017
Laure Guirguis, *Copts and the Security State: Violence, Coercion, and Sectarianism in Contemporary Egypt*
2016
Michael Farquhar, *Circuits of Faith: Migration, Education, and the Wahhabi Mission*
2016
Gilbert Achcar, *Morbid Symptoms: Relapse in the Arab Uprising*
2016
Jacob Mundy, *Imaginative Geographies of Algerian Violence: Conflict Science, Conflict Management, Antipolitics*
2015
Ilana Feldman, *Police Encounters: Security and Surveillance in Gaza under Egyptian Rule*
2015
Tamir Sorek, *Palestinian Commemoration in Israel: Calendars, Monuments, and Martyrs*
2015
Adi Kuntsman and Rebecca L. Stein, *Digital Militarism: Israel's Occupation in the Social Media Age*
2015

Laurie A. Brand, *Official Stories: Politics and National Narratives in Egypt and Algeria*
2014
Kabir Tambar, *The Reckonings of Pluralism: Citizenship and the Demands of History in Turkey*
2014
Diana Allan, *Refugees of the Revolution: Experiences of Palestinian Exile*
2013
Shira Robinson, *Citizen Strangers: Palestinians and the Birth of Israel's Liberal Settler State*
2013
Joel Beinin and Frédéric Vairel, editors, *Social Movements, Mobilization, and Contestation in the Middle East and North Africa*
2013 (Second Edition), 2011
Ariella Azoulay and Adi Ophir, *The One-State Condition: Occupation and Democracy in Israel/Palestine*
2012
Steven Heydemann and Reinoud Leenders, editors, *Middle East Authoritarianisms: Governance, Contestation, and Regime Resilience in Syria and Iran*
2012
Jonathan Marshall, *The Lebanese Connection: Corruption, Civil War, and the International Drug Traffic*
2012
Joshua Stacher, *Adaptable Autocrats: Regime Power in Egypt and Syria*
2012
Bassam Haddad, *Business Networks in Syria: The Political Economy of Authoritarian Resilience*
2011
Noah Coburn, *Bazaar Politics: Power and Pottery in an Afghan Market Town*
2011
Laura Bier, *Revolutionary Womanhood: Feminisms, Modernity, and the State in Nasser's Egypt*
2011
Samer Soliman, *The Autumn of Dictatorship: Fiscal Crisis and Political Change in Egypt under Mubarak*
2011

Rochelle A. Davis, *Palestinian Village Histories: Geographies of the Displaced*

2010

Haggai Ram, *Iranophobia: The Logic of an Israeli Obsession*

2009

John Chalcraft, *The Invisible Cage: Syrian Migrant Workers in Lebanon*

2008

Rhoda Kanaaneh, *Surrounded: Palestinian Soldiers in the Israeli Military*

2008

Asef Bayat, *Making Islam Democratic: Social Movements and the Post-Islamist Turn*

2007

Robert Vitalis, *America's Kingdom: Mythmaking on the Saudi Oil Frontier*

2006

Jessica Winegar, *Creative Reckonings: The Politics of Art and Culture in Contemporary Egypt*

2006

Joel Beinin and Rebecca L. Stein, editors, *The Struggle for Sovereignty: Palestine and Israel, 1993–2005*

2006

CPSIA information can be obtained
at www.ICGtesting.com
Printed in the USA
LVHW100749300822
727115LV00002B/18